W9-DGE-095

MY SAX LIFE

MY SAX LIFE

PAQUITO D'RIVERA

A Memoir

Foreword by Ilan Stavans

VIDAS

NORTHWESTERN UNIVERSITY PRESS

EVANSTON, ILLINOIS

Northwestern University Press
www.nupress.northwestern.edu

Copyright © 2005 by Paquito D'Rivera, Havana–New York Music.
Foreword copyright © 2005 by Ilan Stavans. Published 2005 by
Northwestern University Press. All rights reserved.

Printed in the United States of America

10   9   8   7   6   5   4   3   2   1

ISBN 0-8101-2218-9

Library of Congress Cataloging-in-Publication Data

D'Rivera, Paquito, 1948–
    [Mi vida saxual. English]
    My sax life : a memoir / Paquito D'Rivera ; foreword by Ilan
Stavans ; translated by Luis Tamargo.
       p. cm. — (Latino voices)
    Includes index.
    ISBN 0-8101-2218-9 (cloth : alk. paper)
    1. D'Rivera, Paquito, 1948– 2. Saxophonists—Biography.
3. Jazz musicians—Biography. I. Stavans, Ilan. II. Title. III. Series.
ML419.D75A3 2005
788.7′165′092—dc22

                                       2005015234

♾ The paper used in this publication meets the minimum
requirements of the American National Standard for
Information Sciences—Permanence of Paper for Printed
Library Materials, ANSI Z39.48-1992.

All photographs are from the author's collection.

CONTENTS

With Dizzy Gillespie at the Blue Note (1992)

I once asked El Paq-Man, as Paquito D'Rivera calls himself among friends, and whose music I admire profusely, to define the word *jazz* for me. His first reaction was to smile. "*¿Estás loco?*" he wondered. He then answered by invoking a famous Herbie Hancock line. "Jazz," he proudly announced, "is something impossible to define yet always easy to recognize."

With a slight twist, the definition suits El Paq-Man to perfection. Add up his virtuosic cadence, his polyphonic talents, his insatiable knowledge, and his alluring personality, and what do you get? Well, an artist at once indescribable yet utterly unmistakable.

Jazz is *the* music of the United States, first created by blacks, then revitalized by immigrants from all over but especially from the Americas. Today El Paq-Man is *el rey del jazz latino*, an immigrant from Cuba, erudite yet humble, whose career bridges different traditions from the classics to rumba, samba, and tango. Whenever I spend cherished time with him, I'm amazed by his blissfulness. El Paq-Man is *un burlón*, a trickster invariably making jokes not just about language, politics, and the arts but also about himself. In the same night I've heard him improvise from pieces by Bach and Stravinsky, then pay tribute to Duke Ellington, Dizzy Gillespie, and his Afro-Caribbean roots. Every sound is sacred to him. "From Mozart to Machito, there are only twelve notes—the same twelve," he told me after a performance at the Blue Note, in Greenwich Village, some years ago when I wanted him to explain the difference between highbrow and pop. "All I have to do is let myself go. When I compose a piece, the battle is much easier: I simply allow the structures to build upon themselves. If, instead, I'm solely the interpreter of a concerto, my task is to look for new life in the original."

The overall effect puts you literally on your toes. In fact, during that performance a waitress abrasively passed by, forcing a couple of napkins near our martinis to fly onto the floor. When I bent down

Paquito D'Rivera and Ilan Stavans

to pick them up, I discovered, not quite to my surprise, that all the people at our table were tapping their feet. I surreptitiously looked under other tables, only to see the entire audience was doing the same.

Some months later Paquito came to visit me at Amherst and played his sax as well as his clarinet to a packed auditorium. Although he prefers the former instrument, he is a master in both. The audience was mesmerized by his dual loyalty. Is it like bigamy? "The way I approach the two is totally different," he said to me. He said the clarinet is a hard instrument. It's easy for it to make horrible sounds. To play right, you have to concentrate all the time. The saxophone, on the other hand, he depicted as the most beautiful instrument ever invented, "*un instrumento agradecido*," a thankful instrument.

"Leave it for some weeks, then pick it up again, and it will sound fine. But with the clarinet, if you put it down and pick it up, the noise it makes is atrocious: ARAGHHHHH. Maybe this is because the clarinet is a female instrument: you just never know what's wrong with it."

This "bigamy" is proof of El Paq-Man's multifarious capacity. In my personal collection, I have close to thirty CDs by him. But a few years ago he surprised me with a different artifact: a manuscript of short stories. (It eventually became the novel ¡*Oh, La Habana*!) Is he also a writer? Shortly after, he gave me a copy of *Mi Vida Saxual* (*My Sax Life*), published in Puerto Rico in 1998. Jazz players, known for their bohemian existence, are seldom able to describe their own odyssey succinctly. *Mi Vida Saxual* is exactly the opposite: inventive, irreverent, and *muy Paquera*. It is also deliciously polyphonic about everything, a collage of anecdotes, photographs, lexicographic definitions, critical appraisals, political opinions, cartoons—the whole shebang.

No sooner did I finish it than I phoned El Paq-Man to praise him for the hodgepodge and told him the autobiography needed to be translated into English *inmediatamente*. He enthusiastically agreed, then emphasized in Spanglish (his favorite mode of verbal communication), "*Pa'los gringos* I'll concoct a salsa even *más picante!*" So for the Northwestern University Press edition, he updated material and added *sabor*. When he finished, he tried to explain to me the changes but couldn't. "Ilan, *ahora tiene más de todo y menos de nada* [it now has more of everything and less of nothing], but it's just as impossible to define."

¡*Excelente*!

Ilan Stavans

On the road, you can find anything!

FROM ONE SHIPWRECKED SAILOR TO ANOTHER

In one way or another, Paquito has touched all of us, directly or indirectly, making an undeniable impact that will perhaps last an entire lifetime, or as long as a bolero. I've seen this reflected in everyone—Christians and Communists (are they the *moros y cristianos* of Cuban cuisine?), friends, colleagues, and those who know him in person or through his music or patriotic activities. It is an unquestionable truth that after meeting Paco, no one is the same.

Maybe it's due to his music, his art, his personality, his humor, or the well-deserved fame that he has achieved in the world of jazz or classical music (or maybe it's due to the collection of Volkswagens he keeps at home). But one of the things that has impressed me the most about Paco is his human and artistic sensibility, which goes beyond his involvement in this new adventure of writing a book.

Paquito takes refuge in his memories as fiercely as a shipwrecked sailor seizes a log on the high seas. No memory is too trivial to be recalled. A joke increases his value as a human being; a bit of history increases his stature as an artist. He compiles his memories as if they were the treasures on a Spanish galleon. He wields his sharp tongue when explaining the reasons behind everything, and in this way he helps us to relive our Cuban heritage with every step that we take with him.

As I said before, no one is the same after meeting Paquito. And when God eventually has the pleasure to meet him in person, He shouldn't take him too lightly, because as we already know, Paquito has a diabolical sense of humor.

Sergio García-Marruz

Near the Dead Sea (circa 1998–99)

book *n.* a bound set of printed or blank pages; a
literary composition of fact or fiction; the script or
libretto of a play or musical; (*pl.*) written records of
transactions or accounts; a book or record of bets
—*Webster's Universal Dictionary and Thesaurus*

According to the experts, the best way to write a book is by starting to write it. It doesn't matter how, but it's necessary to *echarle bolas*, as they say in Venezuela when one must undertake something with determination. In my particular case, I'd better start once and for all because (among other things) I've been threatening to write this book since way back, from the days when Walter Cronkite was a cub reporter, and I'm embarrassed when friends ask me the same question: "Did you finish writing that damned book or what? . . . You didn't leave me out, did you? . . ." It's either now or never.

The greatest Cuban of all times was José Julián Martí y Pérez, a man of rather small stature but with an immense spirit and talent, as immense as his ingenious wisdom. Compatriots of all stripes blame him for all sorts of behaviors and opinions in order to justify their own bullshit. It's said that Martí once declared that in order for a man to be complete, he must have a child, plant a tree, and write a book. Well, I took care of the reproductive portion years ago, and I'll talk about my son Franco further along. About the vegetation, it's not my fault that New York snow froze the little mango tree I planted with such hopes on the balcony of our apartment on Forty-third Street and Ninth Avenue in Manhattan. And as to the book, I'm finally setting sail on this literary voyage, and if you're reading this page now, it must be because I finished writing it and was lucky to find a publisher crazy enough to put it on the market. And obviously, my dear reader, you bought this book or it was lent to you . . . or maybe you stole it from somebody? I'm just curious. . . .

Well, now that I've begun . . . what next? Even though I've published some newspaper articles expressing my irritation at Commies or talking about the work of my illustrious colleagues (and did a half-decent job), there's a big difference between writing an occasional column and an entire book.

But I can assure you that if I managed to organize my memories and inserted them into the space occupied by this book, then you're going to have fun. Believe me, the things I've seen and the wild characters I've met in all these years of making music all over the globe deserve to be remembered. I promise not to make your life miserable with another one of those idiotic autobiographies written by egotistical bipeds convinced that it's important for everyone to know the full name of their Basque grandmother, the date of her first menstruation, and other biographical bullshit graciously "condensed" in a "pocket-size" volume of 759 pages bound in blue leather and weighing twelve pounds, all for the bargain price of $86.75 (plus tax). . . . Hell, don't they realize that the importance of any person is relative? Unless, after so many years, one of those autobiographical morons can convince me that Einstein's theory of relativity is wrong, I'll consider it absolute dogma.

Case in point. In countries south of the border, it's common and advisable to carry a written recommendation from Colonel So-and-So, who might be an arrogant and ignorant asshole. No one seems to care about the probable abuses committed by this quarrelsome bully, and his orders (and disorders) are carried out instantly by his underlings, who flatter and humor him for a couple of years only to hang him during the next coup d'état. Here in the United States the theory of relativity is applied in a totally different way. Don't even think of arriving at Kennedy Airport with a written recommendation from President George Bush. If by any chance, the assigned customs official happens to be a Democrat, a Communist, a gay activist, a jazz musician, a Puerto Rican nationalist, or a Muslim, you'll most likely be forced to open all of your luggage and hand over your passport because of your suspicious appearance. In short, the customs official will break your balls for a couple of hours while telling you

Salsa-samba-swing show in New York's Beacon Theater with
Flora Purim, Jaco Pastorious, Toots Thielemans, Airto Moreira,
Dave Valentin, and Mario Rivera (1985)

horrible stories about your dear friend the President, who was kind
enough to give you a letter of recommendation.

Another lesson of applied relativity was provided by my good
friend, the great Cuban stand-up comedian Guillermo Álvarez-Guedes,
who is a true star, not only for Cubans but also for millions of other
Latin Americans who fill any theater to capacity whenever he appears,
in addition to buying his books, records, and videos and repeating
his jokes a thousand times. (He even did a very funny recording in
English called *How to Defend Yourself from Cubans.*) Guillermo is
appreciated not only for his humor but also for his cleverness, general culture, intelligence, and philosophy of life. He's also a jazz
lover, so one night we agreed to meet at one of my concerts at the
Blue Note, New York's famous jazz club. It was a very special
evening because my guest artist was none other than the exquisite
Belgian musician Toots Thielemans. The kids in the band were
happy to play with Toots and also to meet the comedian they'd only

been able to admire in recordings. Now they could laugh with him live and in person.

Álvarez-Guedes showed up outside the door on time, as usual, and before even greeting us, suddenly told me, "First of all, this place is expensive. [How the hell did he know if he hadn't even entered yet?] But I don't mind because I know it's gonna be a helluva show, right? So I'll pay my own entrance. . . . Second, I ask you, please don't introduce me to the audience—don't make any reference to my visit here tonight, OK?"

"But Guillermo—" He didn't let me finish.

"Listen, Paco," he continued in a voice halfway between authoritarian and paternalistic, "this is a jazz club, and no matter how successful I am in my profession, the audience that comes to see you doesn't have any fucking idea who I am, and even if they did, tonight at least, they don't even care. These are two entirely different worlds, understand?"

I tried to tell him that I would talk to the audience a little bit about him, but he cut me off again with a curt phrase showing his wisdom and good humor. "Listen to me," he said solemnly, "if you have to explain who you are, you're a nobody." After a well-measured pause, he smiled mischievously at me and added, "You're a real *comemierda!*"

One of the wisest and most helpful men of all time was, without a doubt, Professor Shinichi Suzuki, the violinist, educator, and creator of the revolutionary and incredibly effective Suzuki method of teaching the violin. This method, which begins practically from the cradle, successfully develops the intellectual and musical aptitudes of any child. "One must educate oneself and understand the benefits that come from the greatness of others," teaches Professor Suzuki. "Only if we can understand this concept will we be able to enjoy and take full advantage of being close to worthy people. Never lose your humility, because vanity blurs the ability to perceive truth and greatness, which have so little to do with money, fame, or material wealth."

I truly believe that the human ego, like taxi drivers, politicians, and operatic tenors, is a necessary evil, but it is imperative to learn

First appearance with Dad (La Habana, June 1954)

to control it with periodic doses of humility, mutual respect, and discretion. Otherwise you lose your objectivity and risk turning into an
absolute (not relative) asshole, like that jerk who demanded star
billing at Mario Bauzá's funeral!

Anal-ogous (as in *anal*) cases abound in our profession but I will
try to concentrate on the many positive things that I was lucky to
encounter on my path, and I probably won't dedicate too much time
or attach too much importance to those idle gossips and lying idiots.

*With comedian Guillermo Álvarez-Guedes
and his wife Elsita in Miami (circa 1981)*

Right now I don't have the slightest idea of what I'll be writing about for the following 759 pages of my unauthorized "anti-biography." And the worst of all is that I don't care and I'm even excited, because if you take into consideration that my basic occupation is jazz musician, there's nothing more appropriate than to improvise and see what happens.

Nevertheless, as jazz players, we generally base our improvisations on a basic theme. Therefore, the basic ad libitum theme of this book will be the people I've met over the years in nightclubs, theaters, whorehouses, museums, slum tenements, military bands, hotels, airplanes, trains, sugarcane fields, jazz venues, drunken feasts, airports, symphony orchestras, dance music ensembles, circuses, sugar mills, and embassies. This is, of course, a book first written in colloquial Cuban by a Cuban exile who has spent a lot of years traveling the world to earn his black beans and who now lives in the Big Apple, where he forcibly (and fortunately) has assimilated countless words and mannerisms of Spanglish and other cultural elements that are foreign or similar to his own.

So this book will make reference to bus drivers, tightrope walkers, architects, pianists, singers (almost all of them horrible, of course), grocers, writers, informants, dancers, travelers, military idiots, orchestra conductors (most of them horrible, of course), politicians (most of them shitty ones, of course), cats, dogs, musicians (good and bad), urologists, ventriloquists, and otorhinolaryngologists. (You may not believe it, but *otorhinolaryngologist* was one of the first words that my son Franco learned to say before his first birthday. The other words were *ornithorhynchus*, *puta*, and *saxophone*, to be followed later by a hybrid of his own invention, the *saxoputa*, or "saxowhore.")

Another thing that needs to be clarified—although my friend Sergio García-Marruz is lending me a tremendous hand with the computer and in the preparation of this book, and other very dear mammals are writing something about me for these pages—is that this is not one of those "as told to" biographies. None of that. I wish to declare that, for better or worse, I'm the only guilty party in this literary exploit. The other participants are no more than mere accomplices and shouldn't be given long sentences for this crime.

Finally, I want to apologize in advance to anyone who might feel disturbed by my jokes or any comments that might be a bit out of hand. Unfortunately, what happens is that the truth, like coughing, is impossible to hide, and in some cases, the truth turns out to be as uncomfortable as the cough.

Oh! One very, very important detail. Don't forget that Cubans can switch directly and without notice from a flood of tears to dissolute and licentious laughter. To acquire a better understanding of this phenomenon, I recommend that you read the observations below, made by Dr. Luis Aguilar León about the Cubans in his book entitled *Reflections about Cuba and Its Future:*

Behold! The Prophet Speaks about the Cubans

Sitting on a rock by the seaport, the Prophet contemplated the white sails of the ship, which would take him to his land. A mixture of sadness and happiness inundated his soul. For nine years his wise and loving words had spread through the population. His love tied him to that people, but his sense of duty summoned him to his land. The time to depart was drawing near. Thinking that his ever-lasting advice would fill the vacuum created by his absence diminished his gloominess.

Then a politician from Elmira approached him and said, "Master, talk to us about the Cubans."

The prophet collected in a fist his white tunic and said:

"The Cubans are among you, but they are not yours. Don't intend to get to know them because their souls inhabit the impenetrable world of antagonism. The Cubans drink merriment and sorrow from the same cup. They make music from their tears and they laugh with their music. The Cubans take jokes seriously and make jokes of everything that is serious. And they don't know their own selves.

"Never underestimate the Cubans. Saint Peter's right hand is Cuban, and the devil's best advisor is also Cuban. Cuba has not produced a saint or a heretic. But the Cubans are sanctified among the heretics and commit heresy among the saints. Their spirit is universal and irreverent. The Cubans believe simultaneously in the God of the Catholics, Changó, the charade, and the horoscope. They address their gods with a pronoun used in the familiar style of friendship, and they ridicule religious rituals. They say that they don't believe in anyone, and they believe it. And they neither renounce their illusions nor learn from their disillusions.

"Never argue with them. The Cubans are born with inherent wisdom. They don't need to read, they know everything. They don't need to travel, they have seen everything. The Cubans are the chosen people . . . chosen by themselves. They walk among other people like the spirit walks on the waters.

With Toots Thielemans in Uruguay (2000)

"The Cubans are individually characterized by their congeniality and intelligence, and in groups by their clamor and passion. Each of them carries the spark of genius, and genial characters don't get along with each other. Hence it follows that it is easy to gather the Cubans, and it is impossible to unite them.

"Don't talk to them about logic. Logic implies reasoning and moderation, and the Cubans are hyperbolic and excessive. If they invite you to a restaurant, they don't invite you to the best restaurant in town, but to 'the best restaurant in the world.' When they argue, they don't say, 'I disagree with you.' Instead, they say, 'You are completely and totally wrong.'

"They have a cannibalistic tendency. *Se la comió* [he/she ate it] is an expression of admiration. *Comerse un cable* [to eat a cable] is a sign of a critical situation, and to call someone *comemierda* [excrement eater] is their most usual and lacerating insult. They have a pyromaniac disposition—*ser la candela* [to be the fire] is the greatest compliment. And they love controversy so much that they refer to beautiful women as *monstruos* [monsters] and to erudites as *bárbaros* [barbarians]; and when you ask them to do a favor, they don't say *sí* or *no*, they say, *sí, como no* [yes, why not?].

"The Cubans perceive the solutions even before they know the problems. Therefore, *nunca hay problema* [there is never a problem] for them. And they feel so big that they call everyone *chico* [little lad]. But they are never diminished in the presence of anyone. If taken to the study of a famous painter, they limit themselves to commenting *A mí nunca me dió por pintar* [I never got into painting], and they go to the medical doctors, not to ask them for advice, but to tell the doctors what ails them.

"They use diminutives with tenderness, but also with the intention of reducing others. They ask for *un favorcito* [a little favor], they offer *una tacita de café* [a little cup of coffee], they visit *por un ratico* [for a little while], and they only accept *un pedacito* [a little piece] when you offer dessert to them. If someone buys a mansion, they commend him for purchasing *la casita* [the little house]. Or they praise someone for buying *el carrito* [the little car] when a luxury car has been purchased.

"When I visited their island, I admired their instant collective wisdom. Anyone considers himself capable of destroying communism or capitalism, stabilizing Latin America, eradicating hunger in Africa, and teaching the United States to be a world power. And they are amazed that other people don't understand the simplicity and evidence of their formulas. Thus, they live among you, and cannot begin to understand why you don't talk like them."

The ship had arrived at the dock. Worn out with grief, the multitude gathered around the Prophet. He turned toward the crowd, but his voice was choked by emotion. There was a long minute of moving silence. Then the ship's helmsman shouted, "*Decídase, mi hermano, dese un sabanaso y súbase ya, que ando con el 'schedul' retrasao.*" ("Make up your mind, brother, grab your sheets and climb aboard now, because I'm running behind schedule.")

The Prophet turned to the multitude, made a gesture of resignation, and slowly boarded the ship. Immediately, the Cuban helmsman sailed off into the horizon.

For those of us who went to the world-famous Tropicana not to enjoy its spectacular show but to work, our favorite place inside the huge nightclub wasn't the lounge next to the open-air Bajo las Estrellas cabaret, whose luminous bar had the undulating and melted shape of a Salvador Dalí clock, and where the smoke of black tobacco blended with Cuban rum and the perfume of *mulata* dancers who performed under the tall royal palm trees surrounding the cabaret. Nor did we choose the Arcos de Cristal hall, a glass-enclosed space for rainy-day performances, nor did we head to the smoke-filled Panorámico (the former gambling casino), where the great Peruchín, with that eternal Cuban cigar in his mouth, captivated everyone from the penumbra of the stage by the magic of his piano playing and orchestra.

No, the preferred place to meet in the two hours before showtime for the singers, showgirls, stagehands, choreographers, set designers, animal tamers, rumba dancers, and musicians was the modern cafeteria located to the left of the nightclub's main entrance. Among the many wild and diverse characters found there, the most popular, fun-loving, and happiest of them all was probably Felo Bergaza. Night after night, dressed in multicolored sequined tails, he would make his grand entrance in the middle of the show, playing a white grand piano that rose out of a cloud of bubbles, smoke, and water on a rotating platform covered with lush vegetation. La Fela, as he was lovingly called by his many friends and admirers, was a tropical collage of Carmen Cavallaro and Liberace with a spectacular mastery of the octaves and a theatrical sense of humor. A reddish *mulato*, witty and affectionate, with a big head and full lips always ready for a roguish smile, his mere presence would sweeten the bitterest soul and make the saddest person smile, if not laugh uproariously.

These were the early years of the revolution that had deposed the dictator Fulgencio Batista and raised to power a young Fidel

Castro, who from the very beginning of his long mandate, nationalized every single private enterprise, either foreign or native to the island. The Tropicana was no exception, and that night, among the usual customers in the cafeteria, there was someone who was truly out of tune amid the palm-leaf hats and guayaberas of the *guajiro* ensemble, the tuxedos of the musicians in Armando Romeu's orchestra, the picturesque *guaracheras* (the ruffled, billowing shirts of the *rumberos*), the seminaked, golden-haired tamer of savage beasts, and the scantily clad showgirls in exaggerated, sensual makeup. Sitting at the pink Formica bar studded with glittering stars was none other than Officer Rodobaldo, who was dressed from head to toe in military gear, including a cap, jackboots, and pistol. The brand-new "confiscator" had been sent by the revolutionary government to take over this "paradise under the stars," the Tropicana Club.

Upon his arrival, the normal bustle of the crowd, the typical jokes of the performers, and even the clatter of dishes suddenly evaporated. Many whispered cautiously about the appearance of the new boss who had so little in common with this world of fantasy and dreams. The atmosphere grew tense. The festive spirits that always characterized this spot seemed to have escaped through the entrance, fleeing from this disturbing character in a discordant military green.

Self-censorship is one of the first lessons to be learned by those subject to the mass control of totalitarian regimes. That night, no one dared to laugh out loud: the crowd behaved in a timid and disciplined way, as in a military camp. Then, all of a sudden, a familiar howling voice, known by that jungle's entire artistic fauna, erupted and shattered the awkward silence, restoring joy to the inhabitants of the forest:

"Yessirrrreeeee . . . here is La Felaaaaaa!!!!!"

It was (who else could it be?!) Felo Bergaza, who threw open the cafeteria's glass door and made his triumphant entrance, dressed completely in white, dancing ballet-style steps and mimicking Tchaikovsky's "Waltz of the Flowers."

After he glided through the entire room, turning pirouettes and dancing on tiptoe from table to table, La Fela landed spectacularly on the only vacant stool at the bar, right next to the man dressed in an inharmonious olive green uniform.

"Ta-raaaaaaa!" Felo sang as a form of coda and grand finale to his choreography, dramatically closing the fermata on the final chord by magnificently clashing an imaginary pair of cymbals while bowing to the astonished audience.

The excited crowd roared their approval in unison, clapping their hands deliriously over the extravagant and bright performance of the improvised ballet dancer. Everyone, that is, except the shocked confiscating agent. When he recovered from his initial surprise, he stood up indignantly and energetically pointed his finger in the air, demanding immediate silence.

"COMRADE!" he shouted into the pianist's face. Felo adopted one of his typical theatrical poses, placing one hand on his chest and the other on his hip, and while feigning profound surprise, looked at the silent crowd around him, and then, raising his eyebrows, finally addressed the irritated new boss.

"Did you call me COMRADE?" said La Fela, dropping his jaw and opening his eyes so wide that they seemed to pop out of their sockets. "Shit, you mean to tell me you're a *maricón* too?!"

This time around, the loud, unanimous laughter achieved thunderous dimensions.

More than thirty years later, a similar effect was created when I told this story to a group of participants at the Miami Film Festival that included the sax player Chombo Silva; actor Andy Garcia; singer Willy Chirino; writer Guillermo Cabrera Infante and his wife, actress Miriam Gómez; bassist Cachao; journalist Norma Niurka; film director Jorge Ulla; and the festival's artistic director, Nat Chediak, who told me when he finally managed to control his laughter, "Hey Paco, you should compile all of those stories in a book. I guarantee you, quite a few people would like to read about that 'sax life' of yours, you dig?!"

MY SAX LIFE

To my parents, who inculcated a love of music in my life, and to the group of Cubans who have done more for Cuba, after our patriots and martyrs—our musicians.

—Dr. Cristóbal Díaz Ayala

MUSIC AND MUSICIANS

The word *music* is derived from the name of the nine daughters of Zeus, the Muses. In Greek mythology the Muses were the patronesses of the arts. The arts reflected, then and now, political ideals, in their quest for freedom and artistic beauty.

As I said before, anytime Cubans want to give weight and credibility to an idea, we attribute it to José Martí. Among the many brilliant sayings we have credited to him is that music is the soul of the people and the highest form of beauty (while Napoleon defined music as the least distressful of all noises . . . what an asshole!). I thank God and my father for the blessings which this marvelous profession has given me throughout my life, providing me with nourishment for both body and soul.

Tito, my father, who used to practice his tenor sax twenty-six hours a day, told me that I usually sat next to him, trying to imitate him with a little plastic sax. There's even a photo of me somewhere, taken when I was a few months old, in which I'm crying in my crib with a paciphone (a hybrid of a pacifier and a saxophone).

In other words, at home we were exposed to all kinds of sax-related activities, which explains my early homosaxual tendencies.

As I was growing up, it was necessary to perform a change of sax, to acquire a bigger sax. My first sax became rather small, so I switched from that curved soprano to a brand-new alto sax, though I kept the small one in case of emergency.

At a very young age, I was taught how to read music by my father (a man endowed with a healthy pedagogical talent) through clever educational games that he had invented.

"Solfeggio is the basis of any musical education," was a wise phrase he repeated many times, like the Gospel. Lalo Schifrin's father, who was concertmaster of the Colón Theater in Buenos Aires, went even further. "If you can't read it or write it, it's not music, my son." That's why I refuse to pay attention when very talented artists declare, almost as if it were a virtue, that they never learned how to read music. Some musically illiterate musicians have stated that it would interfere with their creativity, but I suspect that the real reason is because it's much more fun to look in the mirror while playing "Straight No Chaser" by ear with a Thelonious Monk record than to dedicate half an hour daily to solfeggio lessons following the Slava Method.

Charlie Parker made the following comment to a group of young musicians: "First, let me see your craftsmanship, and then your creativity, and not the other way around."

I always had a certain gift for improvisation, to feel by ear whatever section of the music I wasn't able to read with precision in the technical exercises. My old man knew all of those books by heart, so he would laugh when I tried to fake it and would say, "With your talent, it's easy to play spontaneously whatever you come up with, but first you've got to be able to play well what others have invented. That's what being a professional musician is all about. Otherwise, you'll be an extraordinary individual who will only be in demand for what you know or for what you can learn by ear."

In March of 1996, my wife, the soprano Brenda Feliciano, managed to convince the bassoonist Bill Scribner, the artistic director of the Bronx Arts Ensemble, to make the complicated arrangements required to bring the maestro Félix Guerrero from Cuba to participate in a musical tribute to the legendary Cuban composer Ernesto Lecuona during the centennial year of his birth.

An exceptional musician and educator, Guerrero played banjo

and guitar as a young man with the Palau Brothers, the Martínez Brothers, and other popular Cuban orchestras of the thirties and forties before enrolling at the Fontaine Bleau Conservatory in Paris, where he won first prize in composition and orchestration and then a scholarship to study with Nadia Boulanger at the American Conservatory of Music in Fontainebleau. Later on, he worked closely with Maestro Lecuona, orchestrating and recording in Madrid several Cuban and Spanish zarzuelas (Spanish operettas) that were composed by the distinguished pianist.

Guerrerito (as he was called in Havana with affection and admiration by his musical contemporaries) is a phenomenal guy. Just by conversing casually, you can learn as much from him as if he were an open book.

"Music is an art when you play it at home for entertainment," commented the venerable maestro, sitting in the living room of our New Jersey residence, while trombonist Pucho Escalante, guitar players David Oquendo and Sergio García-Marruz, and my wife and I listened in fascination. "But when music is your livelihood, then it's your trade, and you must learn as much as possible about whatever relates to it.

"The first time I went to see my orchestration teacher, I wanted to write a symphony, and he sent me home to orchestrate a paso doble. When I finished that assignment, he allowed me to work on a danzón.

"The teacher must have noticed the look of disappointment on my face because he immediately told me something I'd never forget: 'You didn't like that, right? . . . Remember that you're poor and you're a musician, which is like being poor twice, so learn your trade well if you don't want to starve to death.'"

"Listen, Dizzy, is it true that Charlie Parker never studied music and played by ear?"

"That's not true," the great trumpeter replied.

I continued to probe Gillespie by saying: "But there are some people who play phenomenally without knowing anything about music. Isn't that true, Birks?"

At home in New Jersey with Maestro Félix Guerrero

"No," the old maestro categorically denied. "Not the way that Bird played. To do that you have to know exactly what you're doing."

Yet some musicians reject learning how to read music because they claim it's not sufficiently artistic. I reply that plastic surgeons who specialize in noses and breasts are not allowed as medical students to reject the study of the intestines, the anus, the urinary tract, and other less "creative and artistic areas" of medical science that happen to be mandatory. Unless they have this background, these dangerously creative aesthetes would artistically fuck up patients on the operating table.

Carlos Emilio Morales, the first electric guitarist to acquire a certain fame in Cuba, learned to play by ear, and that's how he made a living at the beginning of his career, but as soon as he began to encounter problems and limitations due to what I regard as "transitory musical blindness," he found a solfeggio teacher and very soon doubled his number of gigs. "Man, I got tired of being Andrés Ciegovia," said the witty and well-fed guitarist (alluding to the fact that *ciego* means "blind" in Spanish).

It's said that the great bassist Anthony Jackson, frustrated over his inability to read music, locked himself up in his Manhattan apartment for an entire year, refusing all engagements until he learned to read correctly (exactly as God had ordered!).

Personally, I think it's completely inconsiderate that while the rest of us read our parts, saving money and hours of tedious rehearsals, we have to send a cassette beforehand to the one who doesn't read so he can learn his part, or otherwise we'll spend the entire rehearsal working with the "creatively blind": TU-TU-RU-TUTU-TU. . . .

"Listen, maestro, the deal is, I don't read," a young drummer told me once. But what's really fucked up is that ten years later, in another session, I was approached by the same guy, who stated, with a punk-ass smile, "Look, maestro, err . . . remember, I don't read, OK?" Shit, I could understand if he was Stevie Wonder or if we were talking about AIDS or another incurable illness, but that damned problem can be resolved with a little book that costs eight dollars or ten dollars at the most, a couple of weeks, and a small-time instructor.

But since they learn the repertoire as they go along, and even on the road, by the second weekend they have everything under control, so those audience members who attended their first gigs and told horrible stories afterward will never understand how someone who went to the last concert of the tour was delighted at how well the band played. I frankly don't believe that such uneven performances should be tolerated, especially since people are paying to see a quality show and don't give a damn about whether it's the twenty-seventh concert or the third disconcerting concert of the tour.

I refuse to put up with that shit, having played in zillions of debut performances with people like Andy Narell, Alon Yavnai, Mark Walker, Claudio Roditi, Fareed Haque, David Finck, Antonio Sánchez, Jon

With Yo-Yo Ma (New York, 2003)

Faddis, Yo-Yo Ma, Jordi Rosi, Pernell Saturnino, Pablo Zinger (and Ziegler too!), Nicky and Mike Orta, Michel Camilo, Oscar Stagnaro, Edmar Castañeda, Mario Rivera, Horacio "El Negro" Hernández, Diego Urcola, Slide Hampton, John Lee, Paul Van Wageningen, Manuel Valera, Andy González, Lew Soloff, Juan Pablo Torres, and Dave Samuels, with little or no rehearsal, the whole stage filled with music stands, and everything sounding as if we'd been rehearsing for two weeks, without any visible damage to the creativity of these illustrious professionals.

In any occupation (maybe with the exception of organized crime), the more one knows, the better. Attorneys don't attend Harvard to unlearn or forget their legal expertise, and architecture students do not learn to build skyscrapers by divine inspiration. In the same way, I've never heard of anyone who played the very difficult clarinet part of Stravinsky's *L'Histoire du Soldat* or Alban Berg's Violin Concerto by ear, have you?

"Talent without education is as useless as an unpolished diamond," the Argentine philosopher José Ingenieros once wrote. I'd add that no one can be considered superior for having less knowledge, and so-called popular musicians are no exception. My advice to younger musicians (particularly those who intend to work with me someday) is to get hip to sight-reading. It doesn't have anything to do with creativity. It makes your musical work easier and it feeds your wallet.

Yo-Yo Mammoth

L'Historie du Soldat *(Spain, 2002)*

It was in 1953 when that beautiful curved soprano sax arrived at our home. My old man, Tito—an agent of the French Selmer Company in Cuba—ordered it especially for me. That little instrument was (after my mother) the most beautiful and useful present he ever gave me. I remember that the first melody I learned to play was a jingle for Camay soap, which went like this:

Camay

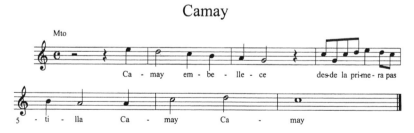

(Ca-may will beau-ti-fy you from the first bar to the last, Ca-may! Ca-may!)

And by the following year, I had already made my debut at a party celebrating the end of the academic year at the Emilia Azcararte School, playing the habanera entitled "Tú," written by the Cuban composer Eduardo Sánchez de Fuentes. He was a racist asshole, but it can't be denied that he wrote some beautiful songs, like the very lovely romanza entitled "Corazón," to cite another example.

Gilberto Valdés and Dr. Fernando Ortiz were always irritated by Sánchez de Fuentes, whose eagerness to take merit away from Afro-Cubans and to deny their leading roles in musical history led him to dwell upon "the Taino Indian roots of our music," apparently based on a certain cassette discovered in the tomb of an Indian character by the name of Guarina many centuries after Pánfilo de Narváez, in his noble crusade to evangelize the indigenous population, proceeded to devoutly slice the windpipe of every native found on his godly mission.

More than four centuries had passed since the cruel massacre of Cuba's indigenous population. And forty-two years went by after that school party before I finally recorded "Tú," in a Chesky Records release entitled *Portraits of Cuba*. It was recorded in New York with masterful arrangements by that monster of orchestration, the Argentinean Carlos Franzetti.

Over the years I have worked considerably with Franzetti in his multiple facets as pianist, conductor, arranger, and composer of diverse genres. His musical talents, which appear to be boundless, also include composing the *Gemini* Concerto, a concerto for clarinet and orchestra, especially for me. The concept behind the CD was also Carlos's original idea. He was inspired by Miles Davis's famous *Sketches of Spain* with Gil Evans's arrangements, but instead he used melodies and elements of Cuban music strictly from a jazz perspective.

Franzetti has a very peculiar sense of humor, and when he found out that I was writing this book, he called me to recommend that, besides the obligatory chapter about the women in my life, I should also include one about the Argentineans in my life due to the large number of compatriots of Evita Perón who have crossed my stages: pianists Jorge Dalto, Aldo Antognazzi, Billy Reuter, Dario Eskenazi, Pablo Ziegler, Daniel Freiberg, Baby López-Furs, and Jorge Navarro;

bassists Alfredo Lemus, Pablo Aslán, and Kike Alvarado; flutists Rubén "Mono" Izarrualde and Jorge de la Vega; bassoonists Albero and Andrea Merenzon; trumpeters Fats Fernández, Diego Urcola, Juan Cruz Urquiza, Américo Bellotto, and Gustavo Bergalli; singer Julia Zenko; saxophonists Andrés Boiarsky and Oscar Feldman; guitarists Horacio Blank, Ricardo Lew, Francisco Rivero, Claudio Ragazzi, and Luis Salinas; the very funny comedian Jorge "El Gordo" Porcel; and conductors and composers Jorge Calandrelli, Gabriel Senanes, and Lalo Schifrin, with whom (together with his adorable wife Donna) I share a close friendship that is, in a certain way, a result of our mutual relationship with Dizzy.

Although we had talked many times by telephone and made a thousand plans to work together on a project, I met Lalo personally on the sad occasion of Gillespie's funeral.

"Hello, Paquito, I'm Lalo Schifrin," said the illustrious author of *Gillespiana* when we embraced in tears next to the coffin of our beloved teacher and boss, our dear friend. In a world where there is a prolific production of discordant apples, John Birks "Dizzy" Gillespie was a unifying element, even at the time of his death.

This was the beginning of a beautiful personal and musical relationship that enabled us to record several albums with the London Symphonic Orchestra, along with Jon Faddis, James Morrison, Ray Brown, and Grady Tate (*Jazz Meets the Symphony*), in addition to many live performances around the world.

Some mischievous fuckers define *ego* as the little Argentinean that we all have inside and say that Argentineans look at the sky and smile when there's lightning because they think that God is taking their picture. But I've visited their beautiful nation several times and have had very good relationships with those from the land of Jorge Luis Borges. When talking about Argentineans, I can only sing their praises, maybe with the sole exception of that character who wore a beret and went to my country to mess everything up, and who later tried unsuccessfully to repeat the same joke in Bolivia with an unfortunate outcome for him but a good one for Bolivians. Shit, if the Commies had taken over that country and had appointed Che

Guevara as minister of hydraulic works, they would have run out of water, even in Lake Titicaca.

Since I was a toddler in a crib, my life has been surrounded by sounds and people connected directly or indirectly to things that produce (good or bad) sounds, but in most cases art has nothing to do with it. And I say this precisely because the sound-making part of our profession is nothing but a small piece of the gigantic and complex pie that forms the absurd and fascinating world known as show business (or what we call *farándula* in Spanish).

> *farándula*—professional deceivers; in olden times, a troupe of traveling comedians
>
> *farandulear*—to show off ostentatiously, to claim an excessive level of importance
>
> *farandulero*—an imposter, a quack, a cheating and boastful person

These definitions, translated from the Larousse Spanish dictionary, explain why as a child I hated the way my grandparents would greet me when I arrived at their home, "Here comes the *farándula!*"

Although I feel an almost mystical love for artistic expressions, I have always detested the idiotic *faranduleros* who are attached like a curse to our profession. My hatred of hollow *farandulerismo* was inherited from my father, who, a few days after my first performance, motivated my early musical vocation by making me an honorary member of the *Sindicato de Músicos de Cuba* (Cuban Musicians' Union). I didn't seek a membership in the parallel union for singers, actors, dancers, and other performers because, as my old man used to joke, "You'll find nothing there except whores and vain people."

I'd say that my opinionated father's assessment is somewhat exaggerated, but no one can deny that on the whole there's an alarming number of mediocre people with a certain degree of power and influence who contaminate the music business, where artistic quality has become almost irrelevant.

Throughout the years, *faranduleros* have grown in number, dumbing down and destroying the music world, where the innovations of Astor Piazzolla, the exuberant talent of Paco de Lucía, the graceful lyrics of José Antonio Méndez, or the ingeniously transparent harmonic and melodic beauty of Tom Jobim's music are totally eclipsed by Julio Iglesias's (or Madonna's) most recent girlfriend, Diego Armando Maradona's chronic imbecility, and Michael Jackson's alleged pedophiliac adventures.

During the seventies, Cuba was visited by a famous Spanish dancer (I think it was Antonio Gades) who had just returned to the stage after several years of retirement dedicated to the breeding of pigs.

"And didn't you miss the artistic scene while you were in retirement?" the interviewer Eva Rodríguez asked the famous artist.

"No, not at all," the dancer immediately replied. "Since I was surrounded by pigs, everything reminded me of the theater."

On one occasion, I was given an award by a certain *farandulesca* organization at the Waldorf Astoria Hotel in New York. I had to share the award with a new and very young pop singer who was soon forgotten. When a journalist expressed his surprise on encountering such a mismatched couple, I had to respond, "Well, I hope that next year, if the tenor saxophone award is given to Branford Marsalis, he'll be forced to share it with Bill Clinton, to see if Marsalis will take it with the same good sportsmanship as I did." Honestly, I don't believe that there was any malice behind the organization's intentions, but, folks, there's a time and place for everything and everything should be according to its place and time. Don't you agree?

In 1996 I was touring Europe with the Caribbean Jazz Project, and while reading a magazine in the hotel discovered that the three tenors (Domingo, Carreras, and Pavarotti), conducted by Zubin Mehta, were scheduled to perform in Budapest, but for some reason Luciano Pavarotti had to be replaced—by nothing more, nothing less, than Diana Ross. Such a decision is, in my judgment, like announcing a

The Caribbean Jazz Project at the Heineken Jazz Festival in Puerto Rico (1997)

performance by Sarah Vaughan, Carmen McRae, and Ella Fitzgerald with the Count Basie orchestra under Frank Foster and then replacing any of the three legendary jazz vocalists with Boy George. Incidents like this make me understand why clarinet great Artie Shaw retired prematurely from the business just at the pinnacle of his career.

But you also have to recognize that even though there are negative things in our profession, not everything is bad, and when you're away from the artistic environment, you begin to miss it a lot. So now, when I retire, I'm going to buy myself a hog farm like the flamenco dancer. That way the change won't be so abrupt.

My old man opened a modest importing business that sold instruments, books, and musical accessories. It was located on Virtudes 57, between Consulado and Prado, in the heart of Havana, that marvelous city immortalized by Guillermo Cabrera Infante in his novel *Tres Tristes Tigres* and destroyed shortly after by Dr. Castro, inch by inch.

Among the many friends and clients who visited this small enterprise were musicians such as Cachao, Arturo "Chico" O'Farrill, Bebo Valdés, Chocolate Armenteros, Mario Bauzá, René Touzet, Peruchín (who also played the alto sax and used to come to buy reeds), Gilberto Valdés, Jorge Bolet, José "Chombo" Silva, and Ernesto Lecuona.

My father had a young friend called Jesús Caunedo who played the clarinet and tenor sax very well, but for some reason he decided to switch to the alto and immediately developed a very personal style blowing that E-flat horn. Caunedo (also known as La Grulla, "Crane," because his tall, slim body made him look like one of those birds) became one of my early influences as an altoist, to the point where many years later, when I was playing a record of his called *Portorican Jazz*, my wife Brenda said "Hey, Morris [she calls me Morris because my mother's name is Maura], that guy in the recording plays just like you!"

I didn't even realize at the time how much those musicians were contributing to my artistic formation. My father had in his tiny office within the store one of those really big RCA phonographs, and that's how I heard for the first time the *Caprice en Forme de Valse* for saxophone by the French composer Paul Bonneau and other heavy stuff recorded by Marcel Mule, who revolutionized the technique of the contemporary sax. From that same office, my father imported textbooks from the Conservatory of Paris that changed the direction of various generations of Cuban saxophonists. He predicted correctly that I would base my future style on elements of the French school created by Mule.

In the early fifties, the old phonograph was replaced by our first record player, which enabled us to listen to new LPs in addition to the old records. For the debut of this appliance, Tito brought a marvelous album by the orchestra led by Benny Goodman, the king of swing, recorded at New York's Carnegie Hall in 1938, with Lionel Hampton,

With Guillermo Cabrera Infante in his London home (1981)

Gene Krupa, Harry James, Teddy Wilson, and other heavyweights of those times. Even today it is one of my favorite recordings. When I listened to that album for the first time, my childish mind already began to dream of coming to New York someday to play *swing*.

The collection kept growing, with recordings by Duke Ellington, Al Gallodoro, Count Basie, Dave Brubeck, Artie Shaw, the French flutist Marcel Moïse, Lester Young, Jimmy Dorsey, Charlie Parker, and a modern clarinetist named Buddy DeFranco, who impressed us with his technical command and peculiar style. Many years later, during a jazz festival in Florida, I asked Buddy to allow me to perform with him the first piece of his that I had ever heard, "Out of Nowhere," as a dedication to the memory of my father, who admired

With Tito Puente and Cachao in New York

With Buddy DeFranco and Nick Brignola (Clearwater Jazz Festival, 1985)

Buddy so much. On that occasion, another great woodwind player, Nick Brignola, sat in with us on the bandstand.

In 1955, after twenty-two years of service, my father put in for retirement from the army band, outraged by all the murders and other abuses of power perpetuated by Fulgencio Batista's regime. In that band, he also worked with one of the most distinguished Cuban instrumentalists, the flutist and bandleader Roberto Ondina (also known as Juan Pablo), who figures prominently in the memoirs of Erich Kleiber, who was the principal conductor of Havana's Philharmonic Orchestra for several years.

The maestro Ondina, a typically witty Cuban *mulato*, was an absolute virtuoso and played the piccolo like no one else that I've ever heard, up to today. Loved and admired by all, Ondina died at the beginning of the seventies *con las botas puestas* (with his boots on), as they say in my native land when death grabs you while you're at work. He died of a heart attack during a television program of the

National Symphonic Orchestra, transmitted from the studios of Havana's Focsa Building. Perhaps as a result of his humble and bohemian character, devoid of great ambitious desires, his extraordinary art never crossed the boundaries of his native country. The only evidence of his talent can be found in Kleiber's book and in the memories of those of us who had the immense good fortune of listening to his magic flute.

Tito's departure from the army gave him more time to be attentive to (and argue with) my mother. It also gave him more time to devote to my music lessons and to my brother Enrique, who was born in 1950. And it liberated my mother from washing and ironing those damned sergeant major uniforms that she hated so much. My old man detested militarism, and he only enlisted in the navy in order to make a living. From his life in the military, he preserved only his discipline, his seriousness, and his strength of character. I'm grateful today because these qualities contributed to the success of my career—the former sergeant major was uncompromising about my musical studies. In his book, there were only two ways of doing things: to do things well or not to do them at all. When someone praised my work, he taught me to answer, "Thanks, but I still have a lot to learn." Arrogance and conceit were obviously not part of Professor Rivera's educational diet, as he truly believed that having certain abilities does not give anyone the right to mistreat or look down on others. As a result, I have never understood the relationship between being a successful artist or a famous athlete and becoming a notorious asshole.

Although he loved jazz, my father never had a talent for improvisation. Instead, he could play a furious staccato on tenor and adapted concertos and pieces written for flute, clarinet, or violin. There was, among others, his adaptation of the very difficult "Hora Staccato," recorded by Jascha Heifetz and later by the great Al Gallodoro in an alto sax version. Although I tried very hard, I confess that I was never able to command the double and triple staccato in the masterful manner shown by Tito, and, in fact, on the album entitled *Contrasts* (where Gallodoro recorded his double staccato

Playing duets with reed virtuoso Al Gallodoro

version of "Dark Eyes"), I was forced to wave the white flag and try my luck with something else.

For some reason I never understood, my old man gave up his solo performances at an early age and became totally devoted to my musical career. He prepared me to perform a varied popular reper- toire which included Cuban and Spanish music and a bit of swing (which is how he liked to refer to North American jazz). He booked me on various radio and television programs and in theaters and nightclubs, where I appeared dressed in really cool suits designed by my mother, a true star of the school of custom sewing. Tito and his adorable wife created a new musical character: "Paquito D'Rivera, the smallest saxophonist in the world."

I immediately began to enjoy my "artiste" status very much. One vivid memory in particular dates from when we were booked to play for a few nights at the Pennsylvania cabaret in the beach area in Marianao. The show featured an international dance couple, a tango singer who I believe was Berta Pernas, the magician Mandrake, and the one who impressed me the most: a rumba dancer named Normita X (I know her last name, but I don't want to get into any controversy), known for dancing to the rhythm of Cuban drums in a bikini with silver fringes while somehow circumgyrating, at variable and independent speeds, each of her enormous tits (or at least they appeared to be enormous at the time), in order to finally, as if simulating the departing flight of a human airplane, furiously shake in unison her powerful meat propellers.

In one of my first television performances, I appeared with a trio of clowns and with the eccentric Spanish musicians known as Gaby, Fofó, and Miliki. I had a great time performing with such hilarious musician-comedians. Miliki played the accordion and Fofó played the concertina, a small and intriguing instrument that is like a miniature accordion. Since Gaby had a curved soprano similar to my own, sometimes we played together, backed by the orchestra under the direction of pianist Obdulio Morales, a frog-faced friend of my father.

People used to say that Obdulio's eyes were exaggeratedly protruding from his head, but as the bassist Yoyi Soler pointed out many years later in Miami, it's not really that his eyes popped out too much but that his face was too far back.

Soon the witty young Spaniards became so successful that, in addition to the popular television program, they were able to set up their own circus tent next to the roller coaster at Marianao Beach's Coney Island amusement park.

Like so many artists from different parts of the world, Gaby, Fofó, and Miliki decided to reside permanently in Cuba, which always welcomed anyone who tried to get ahead in a land where the term *foreigner* didn't seem to have much practical use. Miliki writes in his beautiful book of memoirs:

> Our connection with the Island of Cuba and its people was deep and full of absolute affection. There I found my life companion, and in that eternally captivating and unforgettable land, three of my children were born.

Professionally, in 1949 we were pioneers in the medium of television in Spanish with Mr. Gaspar Pumarejo on channel 4 in Havana, and later as exclusive artists of CMQ Television, with promoter, genius, and friend Goar Mestre.

Another lifetime would not suffice to express my intense love for that island and its people. Those memories are an inseparable and important part of my existence.

"I went there to do a week or so of work with a Venezuelan singer, when Adolfo Guzmán offered me a job playing, arranging, and conducting. Then I stayed for almost a whole year and nobody bothered to ask where the hell I came from and when I was planning to leave or anything," said the multitalented Venezuelan musician Aldemaro Romero.

The endless list of similar cases included Libertad Lamarque, Lucho Gatica, Alfonso Arau, El Indio Araucano, Dick and Biondi, Sonia and Miriam, Los Chavales de España, Luis Aguilé, Pedro Vargas, and, of course, the man who composed "Romance de la Habana," the most beautiful song dedicated to our city of Havana, the Costa Rican troubadour Ray Tico.

Cuba permeated the soul of these artists so deeply that during the exodus after Fidel Castro's takeover in 1959, many of them didn't return to their native countries but instead moved to the Cuban communities of Miami, New York, New Jersey, and Puerto Rico, where even today they continue to perform for their people—the Cubans!

Everything was going well in my early musical career until 1956, when a certain minister of communications by the name of Ramón Vasconcelos introduced a controversial law that prohibited those under the age of eighteen from working on television and radio. After that, my old man managed to get a contract with La Voz Dominicana, a Dominican television and radio enterprise. In the summer of 1957, we left Cuba on a Delta Airlines flight that transported us to Santo Domingo, then known as Ciudad Trujillo. That son of a bitch Rafael Leónidas Trujillo (aka Chapitas) had bestowed his name on the capital of a country that suffered so much under his long dictatorship.

It's said that Trujillo, notorious for his ferocity and cruelty, bravely decided to shoot it out to the end on the night when he was ambushed and killed. But once again I quote José Martí, who said, "Bravery has no merit when it is not accompanied by a noble cause." That's why I'm not impressed by the presumptuous and bullying behavior of that coward who had previously murdered so many defenseless Dominicans as well as many Haitians.

However, in the midst of the worst misfortunes, the Caribbean people have always kept their traditional sense of humor. The Cuban singer Rolando Laserie related how the paranoid dictator used to make his own phone calls in the middle of the night to military posts all over the country to make sure that all the officers were at their assigned places. On one occasion, very late at night, Lieutenant Joselín Taveras decided to get away from his post temporarily to go to the nearby home of his mistress and assigned Sergeant Peña to take his place, disregarding established orders.

RRRIIIINNGG!! . . . "Post Number Four, hello!" answered Sergeant Peña.

"Do me a favor, tell Joselín to get on the phone," said the caller.

"Lieutenant Taveras is not available at this moment, and besides, this is not the proper time to be making crank calls, so go to sleep and call back tomorrow morning," arrogantly replied the sergeant before hanging up the telephone.

RRRIIIINNGG!! . . . "Shit! What do you want now? Didn't I ask you to call tomorrow or don't you understand what I said?"

"You don't know who you're talking to, right?" the voice on the other end softly asked.

"No. And I don't care. Why?"

"Well, because you happen to be talking to Generalíssimo Rafael Leónidas Trujillo Molina." After an almost funereal moment of silence, Sergeant Peña became short of breath. Courageously, he asked the cruel dictator, "And do you know who you're talking to, General?"

"No, I don't," coldly responded the tyrant.

"Thank God!" said the sergeant, greatly relieved, as he hung up the phone.

Trujillo was so amused with the frightened soldier's clever reaction that he traveled in person to Post Number Four. Laserie recalls that after stripping the lieutenant's stripes from Taveras's shoulders and placing them on Sergeant Peña's uniform, Trujillo exclaimed, "Shit, don't tremble; today you made me laugh and that deserves a promotion!"

The tyrant and his cronies owned almost the entire country (whatever they didn't own belonged to the gringos).

The television-radio station was not an exception. It was controlled by Chapitas's brother, Petán, who liked the music business, particularly the showgirls (well, you can't blame him for that). It's well known that the political repression at that time was terrible, but we had an unforgettable stay in Santo Domingo, surrounded by loving and hospitable people whose speech and customs were similar to those in Santiago de Cuba, my mother's hometown.

In the Dominican Republic, I was backed by several high-quality orchestras, among them one called Angelita, led by Tavito Vásquez, who taught me how to play merengue with the sax. I shared the stage with famous Latin American artists such as Nelson Pinedo, María Luisa Landín, and the Dominican singer Lope Balaguer, who was related to Joaquín Balaguer (aka La Gallinita Ciega, or "Blind Hen"), a high official in Trujillo's government who years later would be elected Constitutional President of the Dominican Republic several times.

As the old saying goes, since happiness doesn't last long in a poor man's home, we signed a contract with the Matum Hotel of Santiago de los Caballeros, the country's number-two city ("What do you mean by 'number two,' señor?" the inhabitants of that city would protest), where we had no choice but to play with the worst orchestra on the entire planet after being accustomed to the good bands in the capital. Musically speaking, as we say in Spanish, *pasamos las de Caín* (we suffered Cain's divine punishment) in Santiago, but in terms of the human quality of the people, they were as nice and pleasant as the rest of the population of that enchanting Antillean country.

On the whole, our experiences on that beautiful sister island were so inspiring that we left with tears in our eyes, promising to return someday.

My return was not possible until thirty years later, when the Dominican pianist Michel Camilo, so appreciated in Santo Domingo, invited me to visit his native land, where I was received with the same love I'd found years before. During my visit, I was surprised by a gift of a book that recounted the history of La Voz Dominicana, the national radio and television station, in which I appear in a photograph playing with Tavito Vásquez and the Angelita Orchestra. I took this chance to look up Tavito, who was the most representative of Dominican saxophonists, and I located him at work with a Latin jazz group at the Jaragua Hotel.

Some years later, I received the sad news that Tavito had passed away. My friend, the Dominican percussionist Guarionex Aquino (who worked with Tavito on the night of his death), told me that Tavito ate excessively and that the members of the band were always worried about his health. But on that sad night, the bandleader, making a determined effort, followed his sidemen's advice and didn't eat dinner before he climbed on the stage of La Bricciola restaurant to play his last piece. "The truth is that my solo came out well, don't you think?" the saxophonist commented to Guarionex when he finished soloing over a Charlie Parker piece that he loved playing. These were the final words that the beloved musician said before collapsing on that small stage as the result of a massive heart attack that took him away from us forever.

By the mideighties, now in New York, Michel Camilo played the piano in my Havana–New York ensemble. The other members of this extraordinary group were Claudio Roditi (trumpet), Lincoln Goines or Sergio Brandão (bass), and the dynamic Portinho (trap drums).

Around that time, when we were involved in the Brazilian

sound, Michel and I learned a lot from the band's Brazilians and their friends, especially from the extraordinary trumpeter Claudio Roditi— a formidable composer, teacher, and soloist who combines bebop with Brazilian musical elements like no one else.

Claudio began his tenure with my quintet playing valve trombone, an instrument I adore and that he used on my album *Live at the Keystone Corner*, also featuring Carlos Franzetti on piano, Steve Bailey (aka Peluo, which in Cuba means "Hairy One") on bass, and the percussive support of Daniel Ponce and Ignacio Berroa. Later on, Claudio used the trombone again on the album *Explosion*, featuring Steve Gadd, Rufus Reid, Michel Camilo, and Howard Levy on the diatonic harmonica (which he makes sound more chromatic than Richard Wagner himself).

After that, that Carioca meathead sold his trombone to devote himself again to his rotary valve trumpet, but I had already fallen in love with his style, so it didn't make any difference to me if he played the *berimbau*, the contrabassoon, or the ocarina.

With Brenda's mom, Carmen, Leny Andrade, and my mother in Caracas in the late eighties

Through Claudio and Portinho we met Leny Andrade, the petite "Grand Dame of Brazilian Jazz," with whom I later had the pleasure of working. Happily, she has remained very close to my family, which has adored her since the first day we met.

It is generally true that instruments that produce sound relatively easily (such as the piano, the guitar, the flute, or the bass) are extremely difficult to master. And although practically all of us are capable of singing, there are very few professional singers who do it with sufficient mastery and good taste to impress their accompanists, the musicians. Their poor quality generally does not prevent those singers (with the assistance of a good publicity machine) from acquiring fame and fortune in a short time and with even shorter talent. However, this phenomenon is precisely the source of their insecurity, and in many (too many) cases, their level of arrogance and despotism increases as the level of their vocal skills decreases. There's an old musician's joke that the only difference between a singer and a gangster is that we can at least negotiate with the one carrying the machine gun.

Due to those (and many other) reasons, those of us who belong to my profession have a very exclusive and small group of singers whom we admire, among them Ella, Tony Bennett, Sarah Vaughan, Beny Moré, Nat "King" Cole, Celia Cruz, Elis Regina, and a few others. It is not a coincidence that the diminutive Carioca diva with the sensual voice and rhythmic style occupies a place of honor in such a distinguished and selective league.

Leny possess a very humble and charming personality. She enjoys cooking very much and on occasion has displayed her culinary talents in our kitchen. Once we invited her to a little party at home to honor the Argentinean guitarist Luis Salinas. The guest of honor arrived early and told me, "Listen, *che* [that's what Argentineans call each other—and everyone else, for that matter], your cook looks exactly like Leny Andrade!"

I played dumb and changed the subject. When we were in the middle of a jam session, Leny didn't hold her tongue any longer and began to sing. Upon hearing her, the confused guitarist exclaimed with surprise, "Holy shit! . . . She even sings like Leny Andrade!"

Neither Leny nor Luis understood what was going on, but the rest of us, aware of the situation, had a great laugh, even more so when Luis's countryman, trumpeter Dieguito Urcola, jokingly asked, "Look, *che* Salinas, don't you think that the gardener sitting at the piano looks like Cesar Camargo Mariano?" What happened was that the legendary Brazilian pianist was also on the guest list of the welcoming reception and Salinas didn't know it!

Although I come from a country with good brass sections, Roditi was the first trumpeter I worked with who was more concerned with the music than with his lips. Besides spending all of their time imitating fire sirens and playing high-pitched notes that only dogs can hear, the trumpeters from my country were always talking about lips as if they were about to be filmed for a Revlon lipstick commercial or something like that. If a student wanted to be told he had good potential for the trumpet, all he needed to do was blast a very loud, whistlelike scream as high as possible on the final chord, even if the note had nothing to do with that (or with any other) chord.

"*Tremenda bemba!*" some members of the Orquesta Cubana de Música Moderna would exclaim in admiration (using Cuban slang for *fat lips*). I was leading this band when a character we shall refer to as Panchito—a young kid who came to practice sometimes with us—spent the entire night waiting for the chance to blow his impressive whistles above Varona, Trompetica, El Guajiro, and Arturo and Andrés Castro, our current trumpet section. In all fairness, I should say that Panchito had some musical talent and certainly had good chops but had bad influences. I never heard him trying to play a little phrase by Kenny Dorham or Chet Baker, but instead it seemed that he had studied all of the recordings made by Yma Sumac.

Unfortunately, at least during those days, Panchito was not an exception but part of a true plague of gymnastic, trapezoidal trumpeters who were intent on creating a very strange fusion of Rafael Méndez and Maynard Ferguson with an extremely exaggerated Harry

James vibrato thrown in. Add to that a light Chapotínesque caricature (as in Félix Chapotín) plus a few drops of machismo and bad taste, and the result was as lethal as crossing Alicia Alonso with Popeye the Sailorman.

Coño! . . . The best cure would be to prescribe a heavy dose of Claudioroditillin (a Brazilian penicillin) to the trumpeters of my native land, *caramba!*

Caricature of Claudio Roditi by Jean-Louis Rassinfosse

During one of the numerous trips that I made to Europe as a trumpeter in Paquito's group, we took an airplane from New York to Madrid, and I was "thrilled" to discover that my suitcase didn't reach its destination. These tours, of course, always result in some type of challenge for everyone. We were transported by bus during the next part of our trip, and it took us approximately five hours to reach our destination. Meanwhile I was only thinking about the things I had to purchase: toothbrush, toothpaste, pajamas, underwear, etc. (In reality, the underwear was my main concern.)

Finally, despite our fatigue and everything else, the show had to go on. And that night, after the opening number of the concert, Paquito began to introduce the members of the band. I remember that he said something like this:

"Ladies and gentlemen, it is a pleasure to be here in Spain, our motherland, and it's so great to be able to speak in my native tongue."

At that moment, I approached Paquito and said to him, "Paquito, that's all very nice, but you're speaking in English! OK?"

—Claudio Roditi

Camilo, the young and talented Dominican pianist, not only composed and recorded many of his pieces with me but also arranged works by other composers and assisted me with my research of Venezuelan music, since he had worked before with Aldemaro Romero y su Onda Nueva. Around that time, the guitarist Fareed Haque reacquainted me with the Venezuelan *valses* for guitar composed by Antonio Lauro. I arranged and recorded many of those *valses* in versions for clarinet solo or for a jazz group. I say that he reacquainted me because years earlier I had listened to those marvelous *valses* in Cuba played by guitarists such as Jesús Ortega, Carlos Molina, Flores Chaviano, and even by the great Venezuelan soloist Freddy Reina, who played them with the *cuatro*, a typical four-stringed instrument in Colombia and Venezuela.

First as guest artist with Camilo, then with my quintet, and finally with Dave Samuels and Andy Narell in our Caribbean Jazz Project, I appeared in the jazz festival celebrated in the Dominican Republic every year in the awe-inspiring Altos de Chavón Amphitheater, in the very beautiful small town of La Romana, so named because it is a replica of an ancient town of the Roman Empire.

Through the years I have maintained a very special relationship with Dominicans. I have visited their country many times, and one of my favorite friends is a passionate madman named Mario Rivera. Besides playing all the saxophones and the flute very well, Mario is a sort of guru among Latin musicians in New York, especially those active on the jazz scene.

A musician who has not visited Mario's home in Manhattan has not truly visited this city. He lives in a three-bedroom apartment on Ninety-sixth and Amsterdam, and you can find every type of instrument and audio equipment (turned on) in every room, playing the most diverse music, going from Stan Kenton to Tito Rodríguez, and from Ornette Coleman, Juan Luis Guerra, Piazzolla, and Jacques Ibert to La Patrulla 15, Irakere, and Antonio Carlos Jobim.

Mario not only enjoys playing tenor, alto, soprano, and baritone saxes (he's got a very active sax life of his own!); *melodica;* vibes; *bongó;* bassoon; flute; piano; piccolo; alto flute; cornet; and *tambora* but also enjoys performing on those instruments along with whatever is playing on the stereo. The bad part is that he gets most inspired after midnight, which does not exactly thrill his neighbors. And since he travels with a good portion of his arsenal, he is known to have the same after-midnight sessions in his hotel room in any spot on the planet. His neighbors' lack of understanding does not make Mario any less valuable in my eyes. I'm reminded of what Slide Hampton told me once, after one of those evenings that always seem to stretch into dawn, "I never knew anyone with so much love and dedication to music as your Dominican friend Mario Rivera."

I also have a very special connection to this beautiful island: my grandfather Hilario married a beautiful Dominican lady who kidnapped him (with his approval, of course) and took him to San Francisco de Macorís, where he lived the final and happiest years of his life. I shall be eternally grateful to Grandma Andrea for all the love and care that she gave him.

In August of 1957, we flew from Santo Domingo directly to Puerto Rico to work at the Normandy, a hotel shaped like a ship. (I was told that a famous Puerto Rican architect related to the composer Sylvia Rexach had designed it.) We were also scheduled to do some television shows.

Next to the Normandy, there was a motel-cabaret called El Escambrón, which had one of those stages that goes up and down. There I was backed by Machito's Orchestra, directed by the legendary Mario Bauzá. Also playing in the show were the very fine Irizarri de Córdoba Duo and the Facundo Rivero Quartet. On the Isla del Encanto (Island of Enchantment, as Puerto Ricans call their wonderful country), I was struck by the respect and admiration among Puerto Rican musicians toward Cuban music. We Cubans are enormously grateful to the Puerto Rican people not only for their special links to our music but also for the generosity shown to us throughout our politically troubled history.

One cannot write a complete history of Cuban music without mentioning the Puerto Rican musicians Rafael Hernández, Pedro Flores, and Ruth Fernández. There are still many Cubans who have not realized that "Cachita," "El Cumbanchero," "Bajo un Palmar," and other ultra-Cuban melodies were not born in the largest of the Antillean islands but in Puerto Rico.

"Cubans turned me into a real human being," said the Puerto Rican singer Daniel Santos. In 1980, when I had recently arrived in the Big Apple, that unforgettable character named Frank Grillo (aka Machito) commented, "Cuban music was kept alive all of these years in New York thanks to the Puerto Ricans. Otherwise, forget it!" I found plenty of proof of the love and respect of the *Portorros* (a term used by Cubans to refer to the people of Puerto Rico) toward our music in people like Jerry and Andy González; Bobby Capó; Tito Puente; Bob Sancho (a true addict to the *son montuno*); Bobby Sanabria; Frankie Malabé; Milton Cardona; Dave Valentin; Néstor González; Nestor Torres and his father, Manny Oquendo; Giovanni Hidalgo; Ray Barretto; and so many others! I personally have learned many things about my own culture through them, and especially through the musicologist René López, who knows more about it than most *Cubiches* (Cubans) I know.

Back in the fifties, who among us would have guessed that before long the Puerto Ricans in New York and on the island itself would provide the greatest help to us when we fled from the Communist dictatorship that made our lives miserable? There is not even one Cuban exile who isn't (or whose family isn't) indebted to a Puerto Rican brother or sister for some favor during these long years of banishment from our country. Those from the land of José Martí have not known a home as warm, a wife as sweet, or a friend as loyal and unselfish as the ones we have found among the compatriots of Eugenio María de Hostos. Someday, after we return to our native soil, I hope that we will be able to return the same hospitality and sincere affection to those good people.

In my case, I had the immense fortune of crossing paths with one of those marvelous Puerto Rican women at an especially bitter moment in my life. This happened in 1981, when I was walking on the streets of New York with a broken spirit, sunk in a deep depression. My son was far away and my marriage was breaking up. Cuban

At home with Eddie Palmieri, Bobby Carcassés, Bob Sancho, Mario Bauzá, and Patato Valdés

The soprano and her sopranist at the Grammys ceremony in Los Angeles, California (2000)

authorities were making threats against my wife and refused to allow her and my son to leave the country. At the same time, my wife, a victim of her Communist formation, showed an absolute lack of character and quickly lost hope that we would be reunited. Certain factors not worth remembering here, combined with the efficient work conducted by the agents of the tenebrous DSE (the Cuban KGB), rapidly managed to achieve the objective of destroying our marriage.

Fortunately, in her place, God sent me the Puerto Rican soprano Brenda Feliciano, an exceptional human being with whom I have been united professionally and affectionately since those sad days. Among other heroic deeds, she personally took care of the very difficult arrangements required to get Franco and his mother, Eneida, off the island. She even risked traveling to Cuba under the pretext of going to a jazz festival that she never attended. Finally, the efforts of this tenacious soprano, combined with the goodwill of others and a few dollars of mine (which ended up in the pockets of some Castroite military goon . . . Laguardia? Ochoa? Abrahantes?) succeeded in getting both mother and son off the island. And not long after that, Eneida's parents followed.

When she was already in the United States, doña Ofelia (Eneida's mother) became ill, and she was hospitalized without any cost, thanks to the friendship between Brenda and Bob Sancho, the administrator of a prestigious New York hospital, who made those noble arrangements in a very kind and humanitarian manner.

The complicated business of getting Franco, Eneida, and her parents out of Cuba was conducted through a Cuban woman who lives in Miami and is married to an old fart from Sweden. They operate a fully computerized human supermarket that sells relatives, university graduates, public figures, political prisoners, and so forth.

"The prices have come down a lot lately, Señor D'Rivera," said the woman, while turning the pages of a small book that could have been a menu or a list of prices. "But take it easy and stop writing all of those things in the newspapers. Otherwise the people over there will get pissed off and things will become more difficult. Do you understand?. . . So no more stories in the press, OK?"

To make a long story short, I gave that woman the money she had asked for, without, of course, receiving any signature or contract, since the agreement was obviously as illegal as purchasing slaves. Despite my reservations, I thought that if I didn't do it, I probably would never see Franco again.

When the agreed-upon date arrived, with the bucks already on the other side of the Straits of Florida, Brenda convinced me not to murder the Swedish-Cuban couple, or to set their house on fire, as they had in fact been successful in getting others off the island before. However, when I found out that the passports of Eneida and Franco had been revoked by the authorities shortly before the date of their scheduled flight, I canceled an entire European tour with my quintet, bought a fax machine, and devoted myself to writing letters to newspapers throughout five continents, denouncing the case. It was exactly the opposite of what Eneida suggested during those years (and what was suggested by the human trafficker in Miami, who wished to avoid any bad publicity).

To help me in my efforts, I retained the professional services of my friend Peter Levinson, the president of Levinson Communications—one of the best public relations companies in the United States—with whom I had previously worked at the beginning of my jazz career in New York. Pedrito (a term of endearment we have for him in our home) and his highly efficient work team played a vital role in calling the public's attention to the violation of my family's human rights.

At the same time, I wrote letters to, or in some way or another advised, Mercedes Sosa, Fito Páez, Joan Manuel Serrat, Miriam Makeba, Lucecita Benítez, Charlie Haden, Sonia Silvestre, Chico Buarque, and other "tourists of foreign revolutions," as my fellow compatriot writer Carlos Alberto Montaner would say. "Socialism is a sport that, like bullfighting, is best played off the field." As expected, I never received a reply from any of them.

Singer-songwriter and Harvard Law School graduate Rubén Blades was the only one who offered, free of charge, his services as an attorney in international law to fight for the rights of Franco and Eneida. I first met Rubén Blades in Cuba during the gigantic concert known as Havana Jam, which was organized by CBS Records in 1978 in the enormous (and horrible) Karl Marx Theater. At that time, he was able to visit his grandmother, who still resided in a neighborhood of Havana. Although his father is Panamanian, he is the son of the Cuban actress and vocalist Anolan Díaz. Some say that she swore not to return to Cuba or see her mother as long as Castro was in power, but because of the delicate nature of this matter, I never asked Rubén about it.

In the Big Apple, Blades became a regular—along with my wife Brenda, Daniel Ponce, Victor Paz, Lenny Hambro, Cándido Camero, Tom Malone, Marvin Stamm, Jorge Dalto, Jon Faddis, and me—at those morning recording sessions doing jingles for radio and TV commercials, led by the legendary Arturo "Chico" O'Farrill.

"Because I admire you professionally and I hold you and Brenda in high esteem, I'm offering to go to Cuba as your lawyer to protest against the injustice that they are arbitrarily committing against your son and his mother. You would only have to pay the cost of my travel expenses and my stay in Havana," Rubén generously offered when he heard about my problem.

Despite our lamentable arrogance and our other better or less known blemishes, it is undeniable that the island of Cuba and its creative, enterprising, and prosperous people have always generated a tremendous fascination throughout the world.

As evidenced by the discovery of the yellow fever mosquito by Carlos J. Finlay in the late nineteenth century; the incendiary speeches by José Martí in New York, Philadelphia, and Tampa before the Cuban Revolution of 1895; the Soviet missile crisis in 1961; and the massive exodus of the people who jump into the sea, running away from the "achievements of socialism"; Cubans have always managed to make headlines. Whether it's the craze for the latest mambo by Pérez Prado, the latest gossip about Los Van Van Orchestra in Miami, the sharp humor of comedian Álvarez-Guedes, the Hollywood triumphs of Desi Arnaz and Andy Garcia, the huge musical hits of Gloria Estefan, the fast ball of "El Duque" Hernández, the novels of Zoé Valdés and Guillermo Cabrera Infante, or the knockouts of Teófilo Stevenson, Cubans have never been out of the spotlight for long.

The best explanation for the public's fascination with Cuba can perhaps be found in the pages of *Cuba, la Isla Fascinante*, a majestic book by the noted Dominican intellectual Dr. Juan Bosch, who was, unfortunately, a well-known Castro sympathizer. Written between 1951 and 1952 but only recently published in a joint edition financed by the Cuban and Dominican foreign ministries, the book makes it very clear that the island that fascinated Dr. Bosch with its virtues and defects was from the era B.C. (before Castro). During his stay in Cuba he married a Cuban woman and had a child born in Santiago de Cuba, perhaps the region on the island that most resembled his country.

COPYRIGHT © JAY GOOD

With Rosarío Kennedy, Rolando Laserie, and Andy Garcia

"To be Cuban is a prize," wrote the Dominican; but this insightful book could not be published in its day in the country that bewitched him because of a stupid and counterproductive coup d'état by Fulgencio Batista a few months before elections, forcing the writer to go into exile in Chile. However, as the saying goes, "After the dust clouds comes the mud," and so after the yellow dust of the strongman Batista, came the red mud of the bearded Castro. The rest is ancient history, and I say *ancient* because Cubans, who for once are not exaggerating, have the longest-lasting dictatorship on the planet.

A few years ago, Cuba was again in the headlines over the case of Elián González, the boat boy whose mother drowned in the waters near Florida and whose father shortly afterward demanded his immediate return to Cuba. "President" Castro, who tenderly called the boy Eliancito, was the first to join the father's protest, seconded by loud gangs wearing matching T-shirts with the image of Elián. This in a country where supposedly, due to the imperialist embargo that is responsible for all the bad things in Cuba, the people have no clothes to wear. The protesters also used oceans of ink to print thousands of posters—in a place where not even octopuses have ink. And paper? Not even to wipe your ass!

On this side of the Straits, among those who were preoccupied with paternal rights and the mental health of the boy, were sports personalities, calypso singers, international terrorists, gossip columnists, New York politicians, salsa stars, flamenco dancers, Latin American *militarotes*, Puerto Rican painters, the Pastors for Peace, and Marxist priests (what a mess!), besides the countless number of characters belonging to a diverse international zoological club whose members are fascinated at a distance by that green Jurassic figure, the *Comediante en Jefe*.

As we all know, for more than forty years, you could leave or enter Cuba only by permit, and not exactly when and how you want. Such was the case of Celia Cruz, who years ago asked for and was denied permission to visit her mother on her deathbed, surely for reasons of national security, I guess.

I myself had better luck, and after emptying my pockets on the tablecloth to the "Interconsul" authorities, I had to wait only a little more than eight years for Cuban authorities to allow my son Franco and his mother to be reunited with me in the United States. I must ask (and I'll refrain from using stronger language): where the hell were those tourists of foreign revolutions who were so preoccupied with Eliancito and his dad when so many abuses were being committed in Cuba? And how is it that not one of them wrote a single letter to protest or raised a voice in defense of Celia Cruz and her dying mother, or supported my paternal rights, or were concerned about my son and his mother's mental health during almost a decade in captivity in my country or, better said, what is left of my barren country, Cuba, *la Isla Fascinante*?

I will always be grateful to Rubén Blades for his solidarity with my family, but happily, it wasn't necessary to employ his legal services, thanks to the huge international commotion that Brenda and I created. At last, while in Tokyo in January 1989, I was notified that the Cuban emigration authorities had returned Eneida's and Franco's passports, and a quickly approaching date of departure had been authorized. So upon completing my appearances at the Blue Note–Tokyo, I flew directly from Japan to Miami in order to welcome Eneida and Franco, along with Brenda and my friends Marcos Miranda, Normita Rojas, and Alberto Romeu, early on the morning of January 11, 1989.

It was a great triumph after a long struggle, one that could not have been won without Brenda's huge moral, affective, physical, and logistical support. After almost a decade of tears and frustrations, my Puerto Rican companion was the only one who didn't seem to lose hope, with her sole reward the return of my previously missing smile and the unconditional love of my entire family.

But this was not the first or last migratory miracle performed by Brenda or her family, who became so concerned with the suffering of the Cuban people that on innumerable occasions they participated in decisive—and sometimes hazardous—actions to benefit many of my compatriots, inside and outside the island.

One of the most exciting cases involved bassist Rafael Almazán, his wife, and his children. The plot seems to have been taken from a Hollywood movie, as Almazán himself tells us in his amazing story:

> I remember how my grandfather Pepe and I shared beautiful noon-time conversations that resulted in the best classes of Cuban history that an adolescent could have ever received. But what I remember with most affection is how he blushed while telling me what an old-fashioned gentleman would regard as a vulgar remark, "Isn't it true that General Maceo had balls?"
>
> Fourteen years later, if I could send him an e-mail in heaven, this would be the text: "Grandfather, there's a Puerto Rican lady

who turned out to be the current version of your general." Well, to make a long story short, here's what happened:

For years my wife and I had traveled outside of Cuba—she traveled as an English interpreter and I as a musician, mostly to capitalist countries. We traveled on dozens of occasions, always separately and for work-related objectives. On a 1982 tour to New York, I met Brenda Feliciano. Paquito called his wife from Japan and told her, "During my absence, be attentive to my friend Almazán, who's going to be on tour in New York." Such magic words resulted in the best visit with the best hostess.

Although this trip was followed by others, I never requested political asylum. "When you travel abroad, you don't leave relatives behind, you leave hostages." I learned this phrase from a friend, and it echoed in our ears every time we thought about our ardent desire for freedom. We didn't dare try to flee because we were aware of the consequences.

In January of 1991, I received an offer to join a group led by a certain singer who was going to Mexico on a permanent basis in exchange for sending large sums of dollars to Cuba. However, this project—like all of the projects concocted in Cuba—suffered from an incurable and endemic ailment. Those projects of "fame and fortune" outside of Cuba were nothing but lies. Thus, our two weeks of work ended and we found ourselves on the street, penniless. From his mansion, the "singer" decided that January 4 would be the date of definite return. Of course, that created an internal revolution.

After much difficulty, through the Cuban state recording company EGREM, I ensured my stay in Mexico as an independent musician, with the condition of sending dollars to Cuba. A month later, when Paquito and Brenda went to Mexico to work, we met at a hotel and talked about the subject of political asylum in general, and they hinted that they had occasionally helped friends in need.

I obtained an official (but fictitious) work offer for my wife Grisell, with a good salary, plus housing and school for the children. Obviously I encountered intentional obstacles imposed by the Cuban government, and on top of everything, I was driven to the wall and surrounded by danger when EGREM forced me to sign their "collaboration" agreement. Ten months later, taking every conceivable risk in the world, I returned to Havana with a third work offer for Grisell and to discuss the "extortion" terms with EGREM.

This collaboration agreement is the shakedown mechanism by which the Cuban government extorts dollars from its own citizens. I was obliged to pay for my airplane tickets, lodging, basic needs of life, work-related expenses, wardrobe, the services of an artistic representative, etc., etc., etc. In turn, EGREM would receive my entire monthly salary (in dollars) in Cuba (whether I was employed or not).

Grisell belonged to the UJC (Union of Communist Youth) and later to the PCC (Cuban Communist Party). She believed in Fidel and thought that she was fighting for noble ideals, but the dirty deeds that she began to witness through the years combined with the ongoing deceptions plus the ophthalmologic/ideological treatment that I gave her (in order to open her eyes and enable her to take a look at the political shit that she defended) made her change her opinion. One night she told me, "We must definitely get away from all of these things; we live among monsters, and my children are not going to carry this cross." It so happened that the "main monster" had just dictated the death penalty against Ochoa and his friends, and such Dantean theater was worthy of the most abominable repugnance. This is why when we had the opportunity to go to Mexico, it appeared to us that the gates of heaven had been opened.

After completing the "slave trade" arrangements, we faced a new problem because, by remaining in Mexico illegally, we risked being deported. So the decision to go to the United States became irreversible. We decided to call New York.

And what a great decision that was! After the telephone rang two or three times, a voice answered, "Hello." After I identified myself, the voice said, "*Mulato*, how is it going?" (This is one of Paquito's typical turns of speech, which he applies to Chinese, Blacks, Bosnians, or Swedes, without regard to color.) Then as if sensing something wrong, he asked, "What are you up to? . . . What's happening to you?" I quickly told him what we had decided to do. His answer was firm: "This will be resolved, don't worry." When I called Paquito later that evening, he told me, joyfully and calmly, "Everything has been resolved; imagine that you're already on the other side of the border. Brenda is leaving tomorrow to work for three or four days in El Paso, Texas, and her mother will accompany her there. Doña Carmen says she will get you across. And believe me, if doña Carmen says that, you're practically on this side of the river, pal."

Months later, in the home of Alberto Romeu, here in Miami, Paquito told me that after I called the first time, upon hanging up the telephone, he informed doña Carmen Barrow of what was happening. Without hesitating and while taking care of other things that she was doing at that moment, Ms. Barrow told him, "When they call again, tell them that there's no problem, I'll take them across." She said it with as much nonchalance as if he had asked her for the bathroom soap and she had replied, "Yes, my dear, I'll take it to you right away." With that same amazing naturalness.

Brenda and Carmen flew to El Paso, and we went to a travel agency in Mexico City owned by a friend, who got our airplane tickets for a Saturday afternoon, when there were hardly any tickets left. But imagine the horrible surprise we experienced when we arrived at the airport and discovered that the place was filled with diplomatic vehicles and the typical *guayabera*-wearing goons. Those Cuban state security agents were heading toward the same location as we were due to the fact that Aeroméxico had inaugurated its first flights from Mexico City to Havana! The Cuban ambassador was there with his retinue of paid assassins. This forced us, afraid of being recognized, to hide from them for twenty-five minutes. Since my family left first, I went to the restroom on the other side of the building to avoid running into the Cubans but had such bad luck that two of them saw me and asked what I was doing there. I responded that I was sending a letter with my friend to my family in Camagüey.

Finally, at 12:30 P.M., I was sitting in the airplane headed for Ciudad Juárez, thinking and trying to place in order what we had agreed to with Brenda's mother by telephone. We landed at 3:00 P.M. and got into a taxi, which took us to the Artisans Center, near the border, where doña Carmen would be waiting for us.

To avoid arousing suspicion, we hid our bags and my Fender bass in the shrubs around the museum, and the children were left to guard them in case doña Carmen arrived while we were looking for her on the other side of the museum. At 5:20 P.M., she at last showed up, drained of much of her strength and energy because she had taken off running after Brenda's matinee performance. At 6:00 P.M., we picked up our luggage and went to a hotel. Without letting us say a word, Ms. Barrow paid for our room and said, "Be calm and take this [an envelope with a hundred dollars], eat, rest, and relax. Tonight I'll pick you up to go across the border." She turned around and left in her car. The following hours were long and agonizing. We ate and bathed, but we were too nervous to rest. Instead we watched vampire flicks on the television. When doña Carmen knocked on the door at 11:20 P.M., we jumped with terror, thinking that perhaps Dracula, holding a stake in his hand, was coming to destroy us.

Carmen made me trim my beard and change my hairstyle. She made sure that I was wearing Dockers pants and a Gap shirt because she thought that my Lee overalls and tennis shoes made me look like a Cuban *balsero*. At 11:30 P.M., we initiated our expedition across the border. Carmen was driving, with Grisell sitting next to her. That way they could engage in any required conversations with the border authorities, while I—sitting in the back seat with the children—would pretend to be sleeping to avoid being obligated to talk. The car was decorated with souvenirs, and we would pass as members of a New York performance company that had traveled to El Paso. Grisell was supposed to be the wardrobe mistress, I was a musician, and Ms. Barrow was, of course, the vocalist of the show.

In case the authorities asked, doña Carmen made sure that Grisell knew the name of the play in which she had recently performed, the name of the wardrobe mistress in the company, and so forth. When there were only three cars ahead of us to cross the border, she reviewed with Grisell what she had learned, but Grisell only replied nervously, "What play? What wardrobe mistress?" The children, with their eyes closed, said, "Papi, let us know when we get to La Yuma"—a Cuban colloquial term, used to refer to the United States, probably resulting from the mispronunciation of the word *United*.

It was midnight when Grisell lowered the passenger side of the window to talk to the border guard. Appearing to be only concerned about the travelers in the back seat, he asked, "And those in the back?" The zero hour had arrived. Guided by the hand of God, Grisell answered in impeccable English, "These are my children and this is my husband." Satisfied with her reply, the border guard raised the barrier while saying, "Well . . . go ahead."

I could not get over my amazement, realizing how easily we accomplished our objective, considering the thousands of imaginable situations that could have taken place in which I would have had to commit a suicidal act to gain my freedom or pull off a James Bond–style adventure. Thousands of scenarios crossed my mind. My trance was broken by the voice of my son, repeating over and over, "Papi, let me know when we get to La Yuma." With all the joy in the world, I lifted both of their heads up and told them, "My children, what you see in front of you is La Yuma." "Cool!" exclaimed Fabián and Claudia in unison, while contemplating the "spaghetti" (a complex of interweaving superhighways) in front of them. Doña Carmen had to tell us to be quiet because she feared that our collective shouting could be heard from the distance.

Later, while staying at a Travelodge, Brenda, who was anxiously waiting for the results of our adventure, called Paquito, who asked immediately, "Did SuperCarmen make it?" Paquito showed again that sense of humor, which never abandons him for a second.

Doña Carmen showered us with sweetness and kindness and made us feel comfortable from the first moment we met her. She chatted briefly but wisely with all of us and made me feel as if I were in a Western movie, sitting in front of the Indian tribe's grandmother, who had gathered all of the members of the tribe to share her wisdom.

That is how this story ends and a new one begins. A new story for us with a future of peace and liberty.

P.S. Doña Carmen, may you enjoy the splendor of God's glory!

"Doña Carmen, I should've chosen you instead of your daughter Brenda," I lovingly teased that enchanting woman who made any mother-in-law joke incomprehensible. A loving, cultured, and highly amusing woman, she possessed every human virtue.

The only times I've ever seen her lose her temper were when I allowed Brenda to make a dangerous trip to Cuba to help Franco and Eneida, and when I teed her off by indulging in too many jokes about Puerto Ricans—by asking how many Puerto Ricans you need to hang a lightbulb from the ceiling and by saying that Superman must be a native of Bayamón or Santurce because he wears his underwear over his pants. And I kept going with all this crap until she had had enough and told me, "Look, do you know the difference between a Cuban and a can of shit?"

"Err . . . well, not really. I don't know, doña Carmen," I answered, a bit frustrated and surprised since doña Carmen T. Barrow (who had a doctorate in education, among other university degrees) never expressed herself in such terms.

"The can—OK?" she said while looking directly into my eyes.

I was about to shit my pants, but the rest of the people in the living room, beginning with my mother, were thrown into fits of laughter at the bright thought expressed by the distinguished lady, who became one of my mother's favorite friends.

That is how my mother-in-law was—a woman who was born to help others and whose noble and generous spirit will forever live in our hearts.

In 2003, Fabián Almazán, that amazed little boy who years before had illegally crossed the border from Mexico to the United States in the company of his no-less-amazed parents and older sister, shared the stage with my quintet during an open-air festival in Miami. Fabián was the pianist in a jazz group representing the prestigious Dave Brubeck music school in San Francisco, where on his own merits he had won a full scholarship.

After the gigs at San Juan's Normandy in the summer of 1957, I was not able to return to Puerto Rico until 1982, when I played in one of Olga Guillot's farewell performances. I had not seen Olga since I appeared as a child in a television show on Havana's channel 2 (Tele-Mundo) with Pumarejo, a brilliant guy from Santander, Spain, who, among other things, brought color television to Cuba. That was around the time when the Commander-in-Chief arrived and changed the course of Cuban history. No more color television (except red). Olga left, Pumarejo left, and everyone and his mother left!

When I returned home in September of 1957, it seemed that the bizarre Vasconcelos Law banning young performers from television had been swallowed by the earth, so I immediately performed at Santa Clara's Cabaret Venecia, at the National Theater, along with Pedrito Rico, Armando Roblán, the Valdivia Sisters, and a very beautiful Cuban woman named Marta Picanes, who danced to Spanish music. Many years later, I saw Marta at a radio station in Miami dressed in street clothes, as beautiful as ever, but I was yearning to see her with her concave back comb on her head, wearing one of her showy Spanish flamenco outfits.

Although we kept performing on the most popular television shows, by 1958 Tito began to direct me toward the classical genre with works by Mozart, Weber, and other composers—pieces written originally for clarinet and adapted by my father to be played on my curved soprano. As I said before, he had already rearranged classical compositions in his earlier recitals as a classical soloist on the tenor saxophone, so he could draw on that experience to prepare new material. He then presented me at various recitals and concerts conducted by the most renowned Cuban maestros, such as Rodrigo Prats, Julio Gutierrez, and Adolfo Guzmán, in addition to the venerable Gonzalo Roig, who directed the Banda Municipal de la Habana (later to be known as the Banda Nacional de Conciertos).

By availing myself of the many good friends that my old man had in this field, starting from a very young age I was able to observe very closely and learn directly from the best in each musical genre because—despite the social and political problems created by Batista's dictatorship—Havana's musical environment was truly magnificent in its range and diversity.

In the areas of opera, ballet, and symphonic and chamber music, the ladies of the Pro-Arte Musical Society presented, in their wonderful theater auditorium, great national and international artists of the stature of Jorge Bolet, Vladimir Horowitz, Eugene Ormandy and the Philadelphia Symphony, Alicia Alonso, Jascha Heifetz, Andrés Segovia, Victoria de los Angeles, and Ernesto Lecuona. The Saturday night gala performances of this society were repeated on Sunday afternoon at a more reasonable price (or free) for students or low-income people.

In addition, a group of fans and musicians founded the Club Cubano de Jazz, which brought to the Havana 1900 and other venues high-caliber musicians from the United States, such as Zoot Sims, Philly Joe Jones, Bill Barron, Eddy Shew, Stan Getz, and Sarah Vaughan, who alternated with local musicians in their jam sessions.

Since my father was a musician and an instrument salesman, I remember attending many rehearsals and even witnessing some of those breathtaking shows choreographed by the legendary Rodney (Roderico Neyra) in the incredible Tropicana cabaret, that paradise under the stars, where I sat on the remarkable stage of the orchestra led for twenty-five years by the maestro Armando Romeu. From that orchestral platform, which was magically suspended eight feet above the floor, I listened to the incomparable singing of Nat "King" Cole with a very good guitarist named John Collins. Surely it was in this enchanted place that the idea was born to record his famous album sung in Spanish that included arrangements written by Romeu: "El Bodeguero," "Acércate Más," "Bésame Mucho." Do any of you remember that album?

"The Most Beautiful Cabaret in the World," as it was also called, was located a few blocks from our house in Marianao, which explains why I spent a good part of my childhood in that exotic place, surrounded by beautiful people wearing extravagant attire, dancers, magicians, and, above all, good music. The truth is that Armando Romeu always had the best musicians in the city: Mario Romeu or Bebo Valdés on piano, Chico O'Farrill and Luis and Pucho Escalante on trumpets and trombone, Gustavo Mas on tenor, Cachao or Kike Hernández on bass, and the great Guillermo Barreto on drums—I don't know if I'm making myself clear, but in Cuba that was a hell of a crew—plus the musical arrangements that Romeu wrote or transcribed from records from the States. . . . Listen, my friend, what can I tell you, it was like being in heaven.

When the priests in a rectory located behind the cabaret complained that the orchestra was too loud, things got a bit ugly. Then that old lion Armando Romeu had the clever idea of forming a softer-sounding saxophone orchestra. With six or seven saxes and a rhythm section, he accompanied Rodney's monumental Tropicana show for several months, making it sound like a real big band without all the volume. With this imaginative solution, the priests didn't complain anymore.

The best person to document and describe the fabulous fifties in the fabulous city of Havana is Dr. Cristóbal Díaz Ayala, the author of the book *Música Cubana: Del Areyto a la Nueva Trova.* Despite the friendship that binds us (and the good Jewish attorney who represents me in legal emergencies), I quote part of his valuable study without permission:

> When Paquito used the dedication of my book as a quotation in one of his chapters, I felt very honored and told him to use whatever he wanted, and that as soon as the book was published, I would sue him for ten million dollars (of course, as long as he would lend me

"El Trio," circa 1970, with Carlos del Puerto on bass and Emiliano Salvador on piano and drums

his Jewish lawyer). This would guarantee that the entire world would become aware of the publication of his book because the importance of news is measured by the dollars involved, so when someone files a lawsuit for ten million Yuma (Cuban slang for "U.S.") dollars, he becomes the news. Naturally, afterward we will settle the case with a nice reconciliation banquet, like in the good old days, with cigars, coffee, toothpicks, and the complimentary photo at the end. . . .

The humor of Tito's son is a very serious matter. He has the wit of Mark Twain, but with four-letter words thrown in as condiments.

Besides, while being funny, Paquito mixes important ideas and concepts about music and musicians, sometimes stepping on other people's toes, as in his passionate crusade for musicians to have perfect mastery of technique and sight-reading. Arguments against his beliefs can be found among popular musicians, but it cannot be denied that musicians have to read music in order to interpret it.

His perceptive observation of the crucial role played by the Puerto Rican public and musicians in keeping our music alive outside of Cuba after 1960 is unquestionably true. In fact, Puerto Ricans' devoted admiration for our music was an important factor in my decision to investigate and write about Cuban music. And this truth, by the way, is frequently repeated by Paquito in his personal engagements.

Without editorializing but describing true situations, Paquito takes us backstage and behind bureaucratic walls, among artists and musicians, and he tells us who's who. He is an honest and brave man, endowed with a natural ability to observe, analyze, and narrate. I don't know how long the book of this brilliant musician will be, but however long it is, I'm afraid it will seem too short, and you and other readers will also feel the same way. As a humorist, perhaps Paquito is not as well known as Woody Allen, but there is no doubt that he is a better clarinet player and even has better looks (which should not be too difficult, after all).

I must clarify to my colleague Woody Allen that this business about the clarinet and his physical attributes are solely the opinions of Cristóbal, who surely wants to provoke discord and quarrels between us and later get a good laugh at our expense.

Woody, I don't have anything to do with that crap, OK?

Se acabó la diversión
Llegó el comandante y mandó a parar.

The fun's over
The commander arrived and put an end to it.

—Carlos Puebla, Cuban troubadour

1959

What happened on the first day of January of that fateful year to the inhabitants of the Pearl of the Antilles is a sad and well-known story. For that reason, I'll cover this matter in the least possible space.

In my family, as in the vast majority of Cuban families, we were all (or almost all) anti-Batista. That's why it seemed so odd when, standing in front of the television set immediately after Fidel Castro's inaugural speech at the Columbia military base, my mother made this categorical judgment:

"This guy is worse than that other son of a bitch they got rid of, so we're going to have to get the hell out of here really fast!" (No one understood what she was saying.)

A similar scene was taking place at the home of the popular actor-comedian Guillermo Álvarez-Guedes when his friend Alfredo Cataneo—the famous comical character and member of the Trío Taicuba—went out to the balcony and, after taking a very deep breath, solemnly declared:

"Only those who can swim will be saved!!!"

Years later, in New York, the commander Eloy Gutiérrez Menoyo (who was born in Spain but risked his life for the Cuban Revolution and later spent twenty-two years in Castro's prisons) told me how a banquet was held at the Columbia base during the first days of January

Fidel Castro's first speech illustrated by my mother, Maura D'Rivera

1959 to celebrate the victory over Batista and he had to sit next to Castro's mother (you may not believe this, but the guy had a mother!). When Menoyo congratulated her for her son's successful accomplishments, the lady answered:

"Listen, kid, I hope he behaves this time because, between you and me, ever since Fidel was very little, everything he did with his hands, he fucked up later with his feet."

Unfortunately, that young and charismatic man with a beard kindled a light of hope in a great number of Cubans who were fed up with all the repression and abuse of power. But the immense pile of shit that he produced cannot be cleaned up, not even with all the toilet paper in the world. Toilet paper that, by the way, quickly disappeared from Cuban bathrooms.

When Castro took over, I was only eleven years old. In the beginning, the pressure exerted by the new agencies of the revolutionary government over the artists was more or less tolerable. I believe that in those early days the maestro Ernesto Lecuona had not yet been removed from his well-deserved position as president of the association of Cuban composers.

Born in Guanabacoa on August 6, 1895, Lecuona passed away in the Canary Islands on November 29, 1963. He was, without any doubt, the most representative of all Cuban composers and one of the very few non-Iberian musicians who occupies an important position in the anthologies of zarzuela and Spanish music in general.

A disciple of his sister Ernestina and other notable pianists of that era (such as Hubert de Blank, Joaquín Nin, and Alfredo Peyrellade), Lecuona showed, from a very early age, his natural gift as an exceptional pianist, but a brilliant career as an international concert pianist was eclipsed by the huge popularity of his own works.

Lecuona possessed a prodigious left hand, applied in a very peculiar style to danzas and other compositions for keyboard that became part of the repertoire of many great piano soloists around the world, such as Kathryn Stott from Great Britain and Thomas Tirino from the United States, who have recorded most of Lecuona's vast catalog.

Yet his work is almost totally ignored in Cuba. Once, while visiting Zaragoza, Spain, in the 1990s, the Cuban guitarist and composer Leo Brouwer, the grandson of Ernestina Lecuona, commented that young Cuban pianists had heard Lecuona's name but had almost no idea of the legacy of this musical colossus who made extraordinary contributions to the contemporary music world while creating and inspiring orchestras that still exist today. He composed music for the theater, cinema, radio, and television in addition to cultivating under his positive aura illustrious figures such as Esther Borja, Rita Montaner, Ignacio Villa (aka Bola de Nieve), Sarita Escarpenter, Félix Guerrero, Luis Carbonell, and Bebo Valdés.

Fed up with the many arbitrary actions of the government, like millions of his compatriots, Lecuona went into exile in Spain in 1961, where he died shortly thereafter, close to the land that inspired his beautiful suite *Andalucia* but far away from the native soil that gave birth to "Siboney," "Rosa La China," "María La O," "Niña Rita," and other immortal pages of our music. Ironically, during the centennial of his birthday, a group of the maestro's admirers and some of those *Ñángaras* (feverish Commies) who made his life miserable thirty-five years earlier organized in Havana an international competition in homage to the distinguished artist, perhaps to prove that one cannot obstruct the sun with one finger. And Ernesto Lecuona is like an immense sun that shines in our memories, like an infinite melody that can be found in the heart of every Cuban, here and there, today and forever.

The winner of the competition was a young Cuban pianist who "voluntarily" donated the prize of two thousand U.S. dollars to the revolution. (No comment!)

The composer of "Malagueña" was the most renowned, but there were many other Cuban artists who, like Lecuona, were devoted to Spanish music. I don't know if it was "Jueves de Partagas" or "El Cabaret Regalías" (both of which I regard as nicotinic shows because they were sponsored by cigarette brands), but in one of those television programs I personally met a curious character named Aquilino, a Cuban *mulato* saxophonist who lived in Madrid and made a living playing *paso dobles* and other Iberian musical genres, usually in bullfighting rings all over Spain, where he was publicized as Aquilino and his Cuadrilla. There was another Cuban-born *mulato* saxophonist named Roberto Romero, also known as El Negro Flamenco, who lived in Mexico almost all of his life. My father felt a tremendous admiration for Romero, and when he spoke of great Cuban saxophonists, he always mentioned El Negro Flamenco and his intimate friend Vicente Viana, who died in a premature and tragic way.

According to Tito, Vicente (who was a member of the police concert band as well as the musical director of the Cosmopolita Orchestra) had a girlfriend that he repeatedly mistreated. The unhappy woman warned Vicente that one day she would not let him come into her home anymore. Although she loved him, she was not willing to endure such abuse indefinitely. Well, it seems that the lady followed through on her word, and after several months of entreaties failed to convince her to open the door for him, the young virtuoso, tormented by the loss of his loved one, shot himself in the heart with his regimental revolver. On various occasions, I heard this sad story told by my father, who painfully remembered the sad loss of his beloved and admired colleague.

He always added a delicate but firm piece of advice at the end of the story:

"My son, never mistreat a lady. Don't forget that each of us was brought into this world by a woman."

Along with Vicente Viana, Lito Rivero, Joaquín Benítez, an oboist named Abelardo Cuevas, and other enthusiastic young musicians, in 1943 my father formed the Conjunto Sinfónico de Saxofones, surely inspired by the famous Saxophone Quartet of Paris, founded and directed by Marcel Mule.

Carlos Averhoff, his disciple Miguel Villafruela, and a few other cultivators of the classical genre on the island followed this tradition years later. I personally composed music and performed on various occasions with Carlos Averhoff's sax quartet. My pieces *Wapango* and *Elegy to Eric Dolphy*, recorded by Gerald Danovitch's Canadian sax quartet and by other groups, were originally conceived for Carlos's quartet. Later on, Cuban composers such as Andrés Alén, Jorge López Marín, and Leo Brouwer ("Ludus Metalicus") began to write music for the instrument, inspired by the work of Averhoff and his students, who revitalized the school of classical saxophone playing that had been initiated by Tito and Vicente. Struggling against wind and tide, Carlos Averhoff is the only party responsible for keeping alive that tradition of the classical saxophone in our country.

During the days when I was first writing these pages, Julio Martí and Javier Estrella—two Spanish producers of all kinds of musical events—called me to talk about the idea of organizing in Galicia,

Spain, a gigantic festival covering the entire range of styles found in the musical art of Cuba, from *son* and rumba to symphonic, jazz, and chamber music.

In 1994, I had met in La Coruña various young Cuban classical saxophonists, and right away I came up with the idea of offering, within the framework of the planned event, an homage to my father. I immediately contacted Carlos Averhoff, who was practically without work in Havana, to invite him to participate and to ask him to assist me in getting in touch with his disciple Miguelito Villafruela, who was working as a saxophone instructor in a school in Santiago, Chile.

I also intended to bring Javier Zalba on the baritone (joined by yours truly on the soprano) to form an entirely Cuban saxophone quartet and to include in the repertoire many of don Tito's favorite pieces, such as Bonneau's *Valse Caprice*, Lecuona's danza "Al fin te ví," and other works of diverse styles that my old man liked to play.

Villafruela was very enthusiastic about the idea of such an homage, and a few days later I received a parcel from him containing programs, his résumé, a couple of posters, and a CD that he had recorded that interpreted the music of the composers of the Americas.

Years before, I had accidentally found in a Tokyo store an LP recorded by Villafruela, and I was impressed by how much he had advanced in his technical and stylistic command. What I didn't like were the liner notes by the annotator Jorge López Marín because the statement "A graduate of the National School of Art, Miguel Villafruela is already the first Cuban virtuoso of classical saxophone" ignores the legacy of Vicente Viana and others before him.

On his new CD, Villafruela included only composers from the American continents, such as Ernesto Lecuona, the most representative of the Cuban authors, but the liner notes failed to mention Lecuona's abhorrence of those who abused their political power by making his life miserable and forcing him into exile and death in Spain.

The liner notes also failed to clarify that the saxophonist Sigurd Rascher, when making his debut in Havana in 1941, didn't arrive on his own but was engaged by the ladies of the Pro-Arte Musical Society.

Among other things, those ladies founded the National Cuban Ballet, built their two-thousand-seat Auditorium Theater, and placed it at the disposal of all the social classes. (You didn't even have to pay with dollars to get in!)

"It would be impossible to omit Lecuona in a repertoire of Cuban music," the notes correctly pointed out, and I would add that it is impossible to talk about the classical saxophone in our country without first mentioning the name of don Tito Rivera, who offered the first classical saxophone recital at Havana's Escudero Hall, accompanied by pianist Rafael Ortega, performing the works of Mozart, Gilberto Valdés, Gottschalk, Cervantes, Gershwin, and Lecuona, on June 7, 1945. (This was ten years before the birth of Villafruela.)

And before this recital, tenor-man Tito Rivera founded the Conjunto Sinfónico de Saxofones in 1943, along with Joaquín Benítez on soprano, Cachichanga on the baritone, Lito Rivero on second tenor, and on the alto the great Vicente Viana, another very important pioneer of the Cuban classical saxophone who has been ignored more than once by Villafruela. Coincidentally, the Conjunto was formed just one year after *le patron* of the classical saxophone, Marcel Mule, was honored with a prestigious professor's chair at the Conservatoire National Supérieur de Musique de Paris, the first saxophonist so honored since the legendary Adolphe Sax died in 1894.

Everyone is well aware of how little interest the Marxist hierarchs have in admitting any positive development that took place before 1959 while at the same time minimizing the contributions of Cuban artists currently in exile. This has been made possible thanks to the systematic and often self-imposed terror endured for almost four decades by individuals such as the one who wrote the incomplete and factually incorrect liner notes accompanying the musically accomplished recordings of Miguel Villafruela.

Let's not forget the time an almost totally unknown Cuban writer, Nancy Morejón, during a visit to New York, told her interviewer that there was no Cuban writer by the name of Guillermo Cabrera Infante. It is not surprising, then, that the writer of the Villafruela liner notes would arrogantly proclaim in a section entitled "Maestros and Their

Conjunto Sinfónico de Saxofones (La Habana, 1943)

Successors": "Since 1941, when the saxophonist Sigurd Rascher performed Debussy's Rhapsody and Ibert's Concertino at the Auditorium Theater, no other saxophonist had appeared in classical concert programs in the capital or the interior of the country until Villafruela performed."

If that were true, then in June 1962 I must have been playing the national anthem of Vietnam, "La Cucaracha," or some pop song by commander Juan Almeida on the television program called *Música de Camara*, directed by the violinist Carlos Agostini (who died in Miami a few years ago) and accompanied by two pianists—Pura Ortiz and Rafaelito Ortega. Although I would swear that I was really playing Darius Milhaud's *Scaramouche*, Eugene Bozza's Improvisation, and, coincidentally, Jacques Ibert's famous Concertino da Camera. (My mother keeps a photo of that performance as a memento.)

And many years before that, when my childish hands were still too small to hold an alto, I played on repeated occasions the very difficult Concerto no. 2 by Carl Maria von Weber adapted to the soprano saxophone, first with Enrique González Manticci and the CMQ Radio Orchestra and later with the National Concert Band under the baton of the venerable maestro Gonzalo Roig.

By that time, after adapting the Weber concerto and so many other classical, romantic, and contemporary works, my father's fingernails were aching from performing this, that, and so many other concerti. What happened is that my family and I never kissed the dictator's ass (or those of the culturally deprived members of the dictator's coterie). We were not card-carrying members or any of that shit.

I wrote respectfully but firmly in my letter to the talented and confused Villafruela:

> The time has come, my dear Miguelito, to put the cards on the table. And precisely because I have admired you since you were very young, I must tell you that times change, and they change in a very fast manner.
>
> As José Martí correctly declared, "The word was made to tell the truth and not to conceal it," and considering your musical virtues, you don't need to be allied to the mob that has created so much division and damage with their lies and half-truths.
>
> To summarize, I will repeat the same words that I directed to Gonzalo Rubalcaba from the pages of various New York dailies when he dared to say that life in Cuba is not that bad (although he doesn't live there): "You cannot grow Nordic apples in a tropical plantation of mangrove trees. You cannot derive benefits from two

sources at the same time, you cannot serve God and the devil at once." And you and I know the latter one very well, Miguelito!

Santiago, Chile, Monday, March 18, 1996
Maestro Paquito D'Rivera
P.O. Box 777
Union City, New Jersey 07087
U.S.A.

Dear Paquito:

Last Saturday, I sent you a letter to thank you for the material about the Evansville jazz competition, and I explained to you that I had not received your comments about my CD.

They have just arrived.

The respect and admiration that you professionally deserve prevents me from responding to your diatribe, and I only regret that the magnificence of your musical art is not the bond that unites two artists, as I thought when you surprisingly called.

It is not a question of apples or mangoes. There are many apples. But there is nothing musical about an apple; it is not an important factor when playing an instrument.

If you value music above all, I'm open to talk about music. If not, you have the wrong person.

I reiterate my professional appreciation.

Miguel Villafruela

For some reason I can't remember now, my ex-manager, Helen Keane, gave me this pearl of wisdom: "No one has to apologize for sins he didn't commit, or feel bad for demanding credit where credit is due." I would add that if it were the other way around, I would never think twice before apologizing and publicly recognizing my mistakes. Rectification is a quality of wise men.

Thus, I hope that someday the great soloist Miguelito Villafruela will have the wisdom to apologize for the numerous acts of injustice

Playing Weber's Clarinet Concerto no. 2 with legendary composer Gonzalo Roig and the National Concert Band (La Habana Amphitheater, 1960)

that were committed, with his complicity, against his noble musical forerunners, and that the real and truthful history of the classical saxophone in our country will one day be told.

I've tried to throw some light on this matter and I must state that, regardless of the wrong interpretations and sensationalism of some journalists, I have nothing at all against and indeed am very much in favor of Villafruela, Rubalcaba, and all those young talents who feed the pride of all Cubans and who have been victims of a system in which they were raised that is full of misinformation and terror. And if by any chance they don't want to (or can't) speak the truth, I will, and I will with no hesitation constantly denounce the cruel and arbitrary Communist system that has done nothing but separate artists and people wherever it has been put into effect.

In April 1960, it was still possible to come and go from the island with a certain degree of freedom. In that year we were able to fulfill our strong desire to travel to New York in order to perform at the Teatro Puerto Rico along with Rolando Laserie, Celia Cruz, and Lola Beltrán, accompanied by a magnificent orchestra led by the Puerto Rican trumpeter César Concepción.

By that time, a friend of my dad, the trumpeter Alfredo "Chocolate" Armenteros, was already in New York. I not only looked up to him as a musician but also admired his elegant attire and very special character. Among the many good things that I inherited from my father, I treasure my friendship with Chocolate, who to me is a symbol of Cuban music and musicians. Chocolate was with us for almost the entire time that we toured the city of amazing skyscrapers.

Noticing that I was overwhelmed, he asked me with his typical charm:

"Well, my man, tell me what you think about the Big Apple!"

But I was frankly in such a state of shock that I shrugged my shoulders and didn't know what to say. I was finally walking around that marvelous asphalt jungle that I'd been dreaming of ever since that long-ago afternoon when Tito brought that Benny Goodman record home. After that first visit to New York, when I heard the solos of Krupa, Hampton, and Teddy Wilson, they seemed to blend with the noises of that gigantic city, and Benny's clarinet sounded as if it had a life of its own. Even today, after so many years of living here, I think sometimes that everything is a dream because it's only in dreams that you see the things that normally occur here on a daily basis.

*   *   *

With Alfredo "Chocolate" Armenteros on my first visit to the Big Apple (1960)

Once, my good friend the Finnish pianist and big-band conductor Esko Linnavalli was looking through the pages of the *Village Voice* and made the following comment: "What happens culturally in this city in one day is equivalent to what happens in any other large city of the world in an entire year."

Here you can have the best Japanese food for lunch in one of the many sushi bars throughout the city, have a nice cup of espresso at Starbucks on the way to the Museum of Modern Art to enjoy an exhibition of contemporary paintings from Mongolia, and then attend a matinee show at the American Ballet Theater, where it is possible to find, as their invited guest, Alicia Alonso or Fernando Bujones or even the two of them at the same time. (You never know, pal, this is New York!)

After viewing the ballet, you can choose between the Metropolitan Opera (with Pavarotti or Plácido Domingo singing or conducting the orchestra) or the New York Philharmonic under Loren Maazel. Or you can check out the Mostly Mozart Festival that takes place annually at Lincoln Center. Or you can attend a zarzuela at the Repertorio Español Theater. Later on, you can devour a delicious Brazilian dinner at Cabana Carioca before going to the Village to listen to good jazz in any of the numerous clubs in that bohemian neighborhood, where in one night you can choose between Herbie Hancock and Joe Henderson, not to mention Oscar Peterson, Pat Metheny, Elvin Jones, Maynard Ferguson, Count Basie's Orchestra, or Chick Corea. Of course, a night of good music is not complete without dancing, so you can dance the night away, for example, at the Copacabana salsa club, where it's likely you'll find Eddie Palmieri, Rubén Blades, or even both of them. (You never know, my friend, this is New York!)

The impresario who contracted us in April of 1960 for the show at the Teatro Puerto Rico, located on 138th Street in the Bronx, was a very picturesque Puerto Rican named Catalino Rolón, who provided lodging for us at the One-Two-Three Hotel on Forty-fourth Street, a few steps away from Times Square. My dad told me that once a week Catalino came to pay us. He would stop his gorgeous two-door Cadillac in front of the hotel, open his trunk, and take out a bag of money and a .45 revolver. Our salary was never as secure!

The shows were very entertaining, and I felt I was in my own element, surrounded by great musicians, stagehands, curtains, lights, costumes, makeup, and dancing girls. I even memorized the lyrics to all Rolando Laserie's songs, including vocal improvisations and everything. So it was strange to find out from Tito Puente years later that Rolando sometimes forgot his lyrics, which is why he came up with his characteristic vocal trademark—"De peliiiiculaaaa!"

My father used to relate the story of the night when I arrived at the theater feeling so ill and weak that I almost couldn't blow my instrument. Then Tita, a female angel who was Rolando Laserie's wife, took me to her dressing room and said some prayers for me while tenderly reclining my head on her bosom for a few minutes. Well, to make a long story short, when I came out of her dressing room, I felt as good as new and ready to do my show!

After that I understood why Laserie was always in a good mood.

Feeling a bit homesick and ignoring the wise warning issued by my mother after Castro's rise to power, old Tito decided to return to Cuba so that I could perform with the CMQ Radio Orchestra, playing an adaptation of Carl Maria von Weber's Concerto no. 2. That orchestra was led by Enrique González Manticci, an old Communist who had visited the Soviet Union several times. As a result of believing in such a shitty ideology, he even ended up resembling the helmsman in *The Battleship Potemkin*. But I have to admit that he was a very enthusiastic pioneer of classical music in Cuba as well as the founding member of the Riverside Orchestra and the National Symphony.

I also appeared on Alfonso Arau's television show. Arau was a versatile Mexican comedian who, in love with the revolution, decided to separate from his partner Corona to remain in Cuba. A little later, supported by the revolutionary government, he founded Havana's Teatro Musical, housed in the remodeled Alkazar Cinema (formerly the Alhambra Theater) on the corner of Consulado and Virtudes, while he rehearsed with his new experimental company of actors, dancers, singers, and orchestra at the former Santa Clara Convent, seized by the government from the Catholic Church.

Upon our return from El Norte (the North—another colloquial way to refer to the United States), my dad, who was a natural teacher, learned to play the clarinet for the sole purpose of teaching me how to command that complicated instrument. (According to Frank Wess, the clarinet was invented by five guys who had never met each other.)

He must have taught me well because Tony Taño (who led the orchestra of the theatrical company founded by Arau) asked my father if he could hire me as first sax and clarinet in Havana's Teatro Musical, where I would have the opportunity to establish connections with key characters in my future career, such as Chucho Valdés, Carlos Emilio Morales, and Leo Brouwer, the composer-in-residence for the project.

My old man accepted the offer upon the condition that I not abandon my classes at Marianao's Caturla Conservatory with Enrique Pardo (clarinet), Lolita Torres (choir), Juan Elósegui (solfeggio), José María Bidot (theory), Juan Blanco (history), Alfredo Diez Nieto (orchestral practice), Harold Gramatges (chamber music), and Félix Guerrero (harmony). And that I take advantage of this opportunity to express my deepest and most sincere gratitude to those distinguished professors for sharing with me their knowledge, which has been so valuable in my career.

That season at the Teatro Musical was one of the happiest and most musically formative periods of my life. At the age of fifteen, I occupied one of the top positions in the most original and creative theaters of the day, receiving a relatively high salary while dressing elegantly and rubbing elbows with the best performing artists in Havana.

During my stint at the theater, I participated in the recording of Chucho Valdés's first albums (Jesús Valdés y su combo was the name of his first recording ensemble). He wrote an arrangement for me of the José Antonio Méndez composition "Mi mejor canción," a bolero that I adored. Many years later I rerecorded that wonderful song, using the same intro that Chucho wrote for that occasion, in a project called "Forty Years of Cuban Jam Sessions."

Through Chucho, I met and participated in the only known recording of Amado "Guapachá" Borcelá, a very creative artist who sang a mixture of bebop and Cuban music. Guapachá died prematurely while taking a siesta at his mother's home. It was said that his younger brother, a *tumbador* (conga drum) player named Pedro, mysteriously died under the exact same circumstances years later.

In those early recordings, Chucho always used the Matanzas-born flutist Julio Vento, a character out of an adventure tale who could adapt to any style of music in addition to being a very good sketch artist. One night, when Julio sat next to me in the orchestra, I observed as he drew a perfect self-portrait on his wooden music stand and then, a while later, added a rope around his neck. That is how wacky the guy was. He had been in the navy band with the Romeu family and always had a special love for the sea. Almost on a daily basis he took long walks along the shore while smoking his pipe, as is customary among old sea dogs.

One day he came over and told me, "Look, kid, keep this pipe you like so much because I can't deal with this fucked-up system anymore. I'm getting the hell out of here no later than tomorrow." The following day Julio didn't show up for rehearsal, so the bandleader, Tony Taño, asked me if I knew anything about the flutist. Although it is a serious crime there to know and not inform, I decided to play dumb and didn't say anything.

A little later, we found out that the Cuban coast guard had caught him on the high seas, floating on a tractor tire in search of freedom, as he was nearing the *Oxford*, a U.S. ship.

Somebody told me that his father, an old Communist militant and member of the so-called Partido Socialista Popular (People's Socialist Party), had named him Julio Antonio in homage to Julio Antonio Mella, a leftist student leader who was assassinated in Mexico in the thirties as ordered by the Cuban dictator Gerardo Machado.

Ironically, Julio ended up serving a minimum of three years of hard labor for trying to escape from a system that his father considered ideal. And it wasn't the last case—years later, Vladimiro Roca, the son of Blas Roca, one of the founding members of the Cuban Communist Party, was sentenced to a long prison term for opposing the same regime.

All told, Julio and several of his children spent many years in jail for the sole crime of publicly expressing their disagreement with the regime. It wasn't until the mideighties that he was suddenly transported from his isolation cell to the airport and then flown to Miami. He wasn't even given the chance to stop by his home to say good-bye to his family, which hadn't had any contact with him all the years that he had spent in one of the infamous *tapiadas*—a bricked-up cell without windows or a door.

Everyone in the orchestra missed Julio because he was a very good musician as well as a mischievous devil who was notorious for his many practical jokes. Once he was able to get a twenty-four-hour pass from the prison farm where he was sent the first time he was jailed, and as a present he brought me a *majá Santa María*, a harmless snake found in the Cuban countryside. After that, my favorite joke was to place the snake in women's purses while they were not paying attention. All I had to do later was to ask them for matches or a pen. I had a good laugh at their horrified screams when my little pet jumped out.

On one occasion, I dropped a *majá* inside the bell of the baritone saxophone played by an old-timer named Virgilio. During a low note, the *majá* violently jumped out and landed on the bandleader's music stand. I don't need to tell you the kind of chaos that erupted. And to top it off, this happened during a performance. After that incident, I was forbidden to bring my pet inside the theater. It was a cruel and unfair punishment because that little reptile truly enjoyed music.

The atmosphere in the Teatro Musical was so pleasant that whenever I didn't have to attend classes at the conservatory, I went there early to sit in on the acting and dancing classes or to plan some joke with my favorite accomplice, the trombonist Tony Leal (aka Culito de Mono, or "Monkey's Little Ass"). Culito de Mono enjoyed taking bassist Kike Hernández to eat heavy foods, such as boiled cabbage, avocados, and beans, in order to fill the bassist's enormous belly with gas and later have a good laugh when he laid nonstop farts. Once during a general rehearsal, Kike discharged such a loud fart from the orchestral pit that the dancers came down from the stage to see what was the matter.

The conservatory had its own charm and picturesque characters, such as a violin student with certain mental problems. A devoted student, Ramos adored the waltzes by Strauss and Tchaikovsky and hated contemporary music. Each time he found us rehearsing or listening to something a bit too heterodox for his taste, he would frequently write messages on the school blackboards: LONG LIVE STRAUSS! DEATH TO STRAVINSKY!

Since Ramos attended all of the chamber music practices with us, one day I prepared a practical joke especially for him. I wrote a little piece for brass instruments, a cello, and a pair of percussionists (bass drum, snare, and cymbal included), which began with a violin solo (Ramos's solo, of course) in a "super-classical" style, and little by little, as we kept gaining ground, things became stranger and stranger.

"Do we have the same music? . . . Are we reading correctly? . . . Are there any copying errors?" asked the serious but slovenly student while this fat guy named Miguelito Reína had to hide behind his cello to laugh.

By the final rehearsal, after a few initial measures of the violin solo, I made the agreed-upon signal to the percussionists, who began to beat their instruments loudly, aided by us all, provoking a deafening cacophony that attracted the attention of everyone in the school. Everyone came running to our classroom to see what the hell was happening, while Ramos bolted from the room, red in the face with indignation, holding his violin in one hand and his violin case in the other.

That was the last time that I saw the nervous youngster up close. From then on, whenever he saw me coming, he turned around and went the other way.

In that conservatory I met a young and very talented pianist, a student of Zenaida Manfugás, named Tania León, who was my accompanist during my graduate recital at the Bellas Artes concert hall. Shortly thereafter, I had to complete my obligatory military service, and the future became dark and unpredictable for young artists in our country. However, this courageous woman, who was then still in her teens, managed to emigrate to the United States, where, totally on her own, she became a founding member and musical director of the Dance Theatre of Harlem and established a successful career as a pianist, conductor, and composer.

After graduating with a major in piano, theory, and solfeggio from the Carlos Alfredo Peyrellade Conservatory in the heart of La Habana I enrolled in the Alejandro García Caturla Conservatory in Marianao, on the outskirts of the city, to study with renowned pianist Zenaida Manfugás. Student life at the conservatory was vibrant, orchestrated by the energy of passionate professors who cherished each of our accomplishments like personal trophies, preparing us for a world of music that extended beyond the waters that surrounded our beloved island.

Most of us students were eager to be the best that we could be at our craft. Although we had fun, we were so serious in our studies and so devoted to our playing that at the end of the day, when classes were over, we would hang around and the jam sessions would begin. We would create pieces out of our spontaneous improvisations and marvel at our inventions.

I met Paquito while we were enmeshed in that tapestry.

One day, Professor Manfugás greeted me with the news that I had been assigned to play the piano at a recital. This recital gave me the chance not only to play the Brahms Clarinet and Piano Sonata opus 120 in E-flat as the concert centerpiece but also to be the accompanist for a variety of modern works. Paquito and I were the featured performers and this recital would fulfill the requirements of my postgraduate studies.

Paquito and I rehearsed not only at the *conservatorio* but sometimes at home, serenading Mamota, my grandma, and the building where I lived with works not normally heard in my little Havana neighborhood.

As our rehearsal period and preparations for the concert progressed, we found out that we had many common interests, such as our fondness for jazz and the avant-garde, and an immense curiosity about the music of other cultures. It was during one of those rehearsals that we plotted a surprise encore for the audience at the end of our formal program. In those days I used to create tunes for my brother, also a musician, and I would sing at home accompanied by assorted ensembles of fellow students who would gather at our home on weekends. One of my songs, "Ciego Reto," a melodically ascending bossa nova, was the one that Paquito and I selected.

Our concert, held at the Palacio de Bellas Artes recital hall, was a triumph. The audience, which included our classmates, families, and friends, responded joyfully. Indeed, our professors were very proud of our performance. To this day, however, we are not too sure that they approved of our Latin jazz rendition of "Ciego Reto." Perhaps they thought our improvisations shouldn't have been mixed with the traditional classics, or the modernists. They applauded our skills, but they were a bit shocked and not too happy with the way we concluded our quasi-debut program.

I arrived in the United States on May 29, 1967. Three days after my arrival in Miami, I decided to continue onward to

New York. Within a year of my arrival, while accompanying ballet classes at the Harlem School of the Arts, the legendary ballet dancer Arthur Mitchell heard me play. Arthur invited me to become his pianist and a charter member for a project that he had in mind. I had no idea that my fate would drastically change my pianistic ambitions and that I was to become within the span of two years the founding musical director, composer-in-residence, and conductor for the Dance Theatre of Harlem.

We traveled all over the United States, America Latina, and Europe. The years flew by and news of the success of the Dance Theatre of Harlem traveled home in my letters, pictures, reviews, and telephone calls. Those were hard years that I could hardly endure because I could not go home to deliver the news in person. I was not permitted to return home until February 1979. The biggest loss in my family during those years was the death of Mamota. She was my father's mother—the one who took me to the conservatory when I was four years old and who asked them to take me and teach me music because she thought I had an affinity for that art form.

I spent the first week of my return in La Habana walking the streets of the city with my parents, my brother, my brand-new nephews, and my niece. They loved my accent, and Alain, the youngest of them at four years old, told me that I talked so funny. . . .

We arranged a last dinner before my departure on February 16, 1979, at the cabaret Tropicana. All my family was there. It was then that my father told me that he had a surprise for me. My family had always loved surprises. My father didn't want to tell me what it was. All of a sudden . . . there, incredibly, among so many people, was Paquito!

Paquito came as *alegre* as I always remembered him. When I left Cuba I had lost contact with all my classmates, my neighbors, and my friends. It was so hard to stay in touch with each other. It was so hard to get a letter home, it was so hard to get a connection for a call. My mother didn't even have a phone. . . .

There was Paquito, and we started to tell each other of our travel experiences, his with Irakere and mine with Dance Theatre of Harlem, trying to catch up on twelve years in a couple of hours. In a matter of hours, I was leaving again.

Paquito had brought me a present: a shell from our Caribbean sea. It was painted with a scenic Cuban landscape and he had inscribed a dedication in the back of the shell, which was mounted on a wooden frame. I brought his present with me along with the presents my family had gathered for me.

There are no pictures of that moment, no pictures of our dancing together that night, no pictures of me dancing with my father, my mother, and my brother. When my bag went into the machine that x-rayed each bag, the film was erased. I learned about the blank negatives from the camera shop where I had sent the film to be developed.

Many friends in our New York Cuban community were in touch with each other, especially those involved in the performing arts. The day the announcement of the Irakere's performance at the Beacon Theater appeared, the news traveled at the speed of light. I happened to be in New York at the time. I knew that Paquito would be playing with the ensemble. There were people at the entrance of the theater protesting the appearance of Irakere in New York. I bought a ticket, went in, and there was Paquito. I had at home the present that Paquito had brought me at the Tropicana upon my first return to Cuba. Paquito was in New York for the first time since my arrival in 1967, and I was at the Beacon Theater the evening of that performance to support him the same way he had supported me just months before in La Habana.

After the performance, we saw each other and hugged and celebrated at his parents' apartment in New Jersey.

We said good-bye not knowing when we would see each other again.

In the late seventies through early eighties I began directing Latin American musicals at different Spanish-speaking venues in New York: Teatreo Duo, Puerto Rican Traveling Theater, and Intar, among others. One of the singer-actresses with whom I collaborated most of the time was Brenda Feliciano.

Brenda was one of the most sought-after talents in our Latin American theater scene. She played the lead role in *Carmencita,* a Latin version of the opera Carmen that I arranged, directed by Manuel Martin Jr., a well-respected Cuban writer and director.

We were mainly based at the Intar Theater in Theater Row on Forty-second Street. I was serving as music director and conductor for the musicals then.

It was a memorable day when I heard on the news about Paquito leaving Irakere while the group was on tour in Europe. We heard that Paquito was in Spain. By keeping in touch with his parents, I found out when he would be arriving in the States.

My father died a year after my first return to Cuba. I continued to visit my family every time I was allowed to do so. In one of my visits to La Habana, shortly after Paquito's arrival in New York to live, I brought him pictures of Franco, his son. Paquito was desperately trying to bring him to the States.

When I heard that Brenda and Paquito had gotten together, I was surprised and delighted at the same time. I knew Brenda's family and was very fond of Brenda's mother and her sister. For me, it was a sensational coincidence that Brenda and Paquito had decided to form a union.

During the 1980s, I was music director and conductor for the Brooklyn Philharmonic Community Concerts. We offered concerts at Prospect Park at the Celebrate Brooklyn Series every summer. Paquito was already immersed in the New York music scene. We planned a concert to celebrate our onstage reunion after twenty or so years of not performing together. The concert featured him as a soloist as well as Betty Carter. The concert was sold out. The highlight of the performance for both of us was an arrangement of "Ciego Reto," our encore for our first recital so many years ago in La Habana.

Last year, while reminiscing together at my home, I showed Paquito the shell he gave me that night prior to my departure, after my return to La Habana in 1979. He was very surprised that I cherish that gift as a moment frozen in time that still carries the spirit of my entire family under the Cuban sky. We both have copies of the printed program of our first concert together at Palacio de Bellas Artes in 1964. Our heartfelt personal links date back almost two generations now. We never imagined then that we would continue our musical path so far away from our original roots and, to top it off, we now live only fifteen minutes from each other.

—Tania León

▼▼▼

Jazz:
Malignant breed, product of
the decadent western society

—Mao Tse-tung

A music created mainly by black
Americans in the early twentieth century
through an amalgamation of elements
drawn from European-American and tribal
African musics. A unique type, it cannot
safely be categorized as folk, popular or
"art music," though it shares aspects of
all three. It has had a profound effect on
international culture, not only through its
considerable popularity, but through the
important role it has played in shaping
the many forms of popular music that
developed around and out of it.

—*New Grove Dictionary of Jazz*

JAZZ

That's basically the introductory paragraph in the prestigious *New Grove Dictionary of Jazz* about the exciting type of music that pianist Herbie Hancock once described as "something very hard to define and so easy to recognize." Although many writers consider jazz to be the most significant and influential music of the twentieth century, the etymology of the word *jazz* is very obscure. The term came into general use around 1913 to 1915 to identify a type of music that developed in the southern states of the American union by the late 1800s. Coming to prominence at the turn of the century in New Orleans and played mostly by black musicians, the genre was at first called ragtime. It featured a very syncopated, rather instrumental style and had among its leading practitioners the likes of pianists Scott Joplin, Jelly Roll Morton, and James P. Johnson; cornetists Buddy Bolden and King Oliver; and later trombonemen Kid Ory and Jack Teagarden, saxophonist-clarinetist Sidney Bechet, pianist Earl "Fatha" Hines, and the ineffable Louis Armstrong, who became the indisputable symbol of jazz music around the world.

The basic concept that shapes this genre is the very epitome of what a true democracy should be: a soloist expands on his ideas as the rest keep their mouths shut and listen with respect while the rhythm section (like it or not) helps him to end his solo in the best way, instead of making his life impossible through opposition, as is usually the case in politics.

Nevertheless, misunderstood and discriminated against from birth, jazz was accepted and respected in its native country only after much time and work. Yet even today many students at all levels still think that Louis Armstrong was the first man to walk on the moon! And outside the United States, this controversial art form has caused serious political problems to its practitioners and their fans in many parts of the world.

Mainly a vocal form and a direct descendent of Negro spirituals, the blues came out around 1900 and soon became an important element of jazz interpretation. A key figure of the Blues Era was the composer J. C. Handy, whose "Saint Louis Blues" has become something like the national anthem for jazz people. Some of the most outstanding interpreters of the blues were vocalists Bessie Smith, Jimmy Rushing, and Billie Holiday. After the 1920s, jazz became more and more sophisticated as it spread to New York, Chicago, and even to the Old World, where it became all the rage. The jazz arranger appeared, and with him bigger bands. Paul Whiteman popularized "symphonic jazz," even adding a string section to his "society" orchestra, while Catalonian violinist Xavier Cugat did a kind of light Latinized version of Whiteman's formation.

At the other extreme was the passionate "jungle style" of Edward Kennedy "Duke" Ellington, the first great jazz composer. The 1930s coincided with the style known as swing, and the rumbling Big Band Era took off with leaders like clarinetists Benny Goodman, Woody Herman, and Artie Shaw; pianists William "Count" Basie and Fletcher Henderson; trombonists Jimmy Dorsey and Glenn Miller; percussionists Lionel Hampton, Gene Krupa, Chick Webb, and Buddy Rich; saxmen Jimmy Dorsey, Illinois Jacquet, and Benny Carter; and singers Cab Calloway and Billy Eckstine. Around 1941 pianist-arranger-composer Stan Kenton created his Artistry in Rhythm Orchestra, and later in that decade, the Progressive Jazz Orchestra, which gave its name to the movement it inspired. Kenton's most ambitious project was his forty-three-piece Innovations in Modern Music Orchestra, with strings and an extended wind section. Due to stylistic problems (the music moved better with smaller ensembles) and especially to economic factors, big bands became scarce, but old-time cultivators of that exuberant genre have survived through the years, among them Bill Russo, Thad Jones, Arturo "Chico" O'Farrill, Gil Evans, Jon Faddis, Bill Holman, Machito and his Afro-Cubans, Jimmy Heath, Maynard Ferguson, Tito Puente, Slide Hampton, Bob Mintzer, Frank Foster, Wynton Marsalis, Rob McConnell, and Maria Schneider in America, plus ensembles like the UMO Orchestra in Finland, the Francy Boland–Kenny Clarke Big Band in Paris, the BBC Orchestra in London, the WDR and NDR Big Bands in Germany, and the Metropol Orchestra in Denmark, which has a format similar to Kenton's Innovations in Modern Music Orchestra. Personally, I always say that every time I want to have some fun and lose some money, I organize a big band!

With Bobby McFerrin, Daniel Ponce, and Wynton Marsalis (New York, 1981)

One of the main offshoots of jazz, bebop, was developed in the forties by such luminaries as Dizzy Gillespie, Charlie Parker, Bud Powell, Max Roach, Kenny Clarke, and Thelonious Monk. Although solidly rooted in earlier jazz styles, bebop was considered revolutionary in its day due to the angular phrases used in its themes and improvised solos, its fancier and more adventurous harmonies, and its uneven, rather unpredictable use of tempo by the rhythm sections, which differed from the insistent four-beat approach taken by swing musicians in the past. After the fifties, the word *bop* (a shortened form of the vocables *bebop* and *rebop* that were commonly used in scat singing) generally encompassed the various subgenres that grew out of the original genre: cool West Coast jazz, hard bop, and even the premodal period of Miles Davis and John Coltrane, the most influential and widely imitated saxophonist since Charlie Parker.

Free jazz, often associated with the civil rights and black power movements, was a name first applied to the avant-garde jazz of the sixties, particularly the work of Ornette Coleman, Charlie Haden, Cecil Taylor, Sun Ra, Albert Ayler, and the late work of Coltrane. Surrounded by an aura of seriousness and social commitment, the music is best defined by its absence of tonality or predetermined chord progressions. Collective improvisations on totally free structures replaced the characteristic bebop harmonies.

Emerging almost at the same time as the avant-garde jazz movement in the sixties and seventies, jazz-rock combines the techniques of modern jazz improvisation with the instrumentation, inflections, and rhythmic approach of soul and rock and roll music. The range of tone colors was widely expanded by adding the electric Fender piano as well as plenty of other electronic effects and synthesizers. Also known as fusion, this style became the most common and popular jazz style of the seventies and eighties, having among its most representative practitioners players like Chick Corea, John McLaughlin, Jaco Pastorious, and the Brecker Brothers. Styles such as smooth and pop jazz, funk, and acid jazz are closely related to jazz-rock.

As a natural consequence of the multinational and multicultural society of the United States, the jazz idiom has expanded enormously and includes extensive contributions by people of so-called Latin origins. Eminently improvisational, jazz shares common roots with most musical genres of the New World: the only difference is that while the African slaves destined to work on the cotton fields of the Protestant United States had their instruments and culture torn away from them, those who arrived in Brazil, the Caribbean islands, and certain parts of the mostly Catholic South American continent were permitted to play their drums on Sundays and holidays. That's perhaps why those non–U.S. styles are rhythmically much richer. The legendary pianist Jelly Roll Morton spoke very early in the twentieth century about what he called the Spanish tinge to American music. Manuel Pérez, Alberto Socarrás, Mario Bauzá, Juan Tizol, Tito Puente, Arturo "Chico" O'Farrill, Emiliano Salvador, Luis Bonfá, Fats Navarro, Machito, Lalo Schifrin, Ray Barretto, Cachao, Antonio Carlos Jobim, Chano Pozo, Bebo and Chucho Valdés, Astor Piazzolla, Michel Camilo, Dave Valentin, and many other musicians from south of the border have been crucially important to every single period in the history of jazz music.

Although Cubans share musical affinities with Puerto Ricans, Mexicans, and Venezuelans, a very different historical relationship is found between *Cubanos* and *Brasileiros*—two communities sharing common musical and religious origins that regard themselves as totally distinct cultures. This separatist attitude is also obvious in the groups of Latin American immigrants in countries such as Germany, France, and the United States, where it is common to speak of Latin America and Brazil as if they were mutually exclusive entities. (As far as I'm concerned, this is as absurd as excluding Portugal from Europe, but that's the way it is!)

In New York City, for example, the division between *salseros*, or Latin jazz musicians, and their Brazilian counterparts is so accentuated that artists who practice both types of music—such as Dave Valentin, Danilo Pérez, Mark Walker, and Michel Camilo—are comparable to exotic birds. (And that's without even mentioning other kinds of Latin music that have enriched the jazz language, such as the almost totally unknown Peruvian *valses*, the Venezuelan *joropo*, the Mexican *huapango*, and the refined, elegant Argentinian tango.) It all seems to prove that only what's Afro-Cuban is important. It's as if the rest of Latin jazz has been suspended in time and space between Cuba, Puerto Rico, and the Palladium in New York, and Latin jazz was something only made back in the forties and fifties (with unquestionable brilliance) by Machito, Mario Bauzá, Tito Puente, and Chano Pozo.

"Neither the Cubans play samba, nor the *cariocas* know a damned thing about the *clavé*," an extremely charming Cuban showman known as Boniato (Sweet Potato) once said in Spain, and he wasn't wrong at all! I can't count the number of times I've seen a "Latin" percussionist show up at a samba gig with a *güiro*, an enormous cow bell, and a pair of timbales, or an American jazz pianist sneaking a rather disturbing *montuno* pattern into a bossa nova, or a Brazilian drummer stubbornly trying to play his *batucada* on top of a *montuno!* Among the thousands of fans devoted to Celia Cruz, Johnny Ventura, Tito Puente, or Eddie Palmieri, few would recall the names of Elis Regina, Gilberto Gil, Gal Costa, or Pixinguinha. And in the multitudinous salsa shows organized by Dominican impresario Ralphy Mercado at Madison Square Garden, it would be very difficult to find a single compatriot of Pelé, the king of soccer.

The Brazilians for their part are entrenched in their colossal musical arsenal between the Atlantic and the Matto Grosso, totally ignoring the very beautiful dances written by Lecuona, Mario Ruiz Armengol, and Noro Morales, and the immortal boleros written by Maria Grever, Fernando Mulens, and Sylvia Rexach. In my modest opinion, Brazilian music contains the most balanced formula of rhythm-melody-harmony in the world. Delicately rhythmic, Brazilian musicians use the most sophisticated harmonies, even in their most popular street music, without sacrificing a bit *el sabor criollo* of their *escolas do samba*. The melodies and lyrics of their songs are very inspired and romantic without being tacky, and I sincerely believe that it's a pity that the language barrier has deprived Spanish-speaking Latin

Americans of the pleasure of Brazilian music and prevented its diffusion among us.

A lot of water has passed under the bridge since Jelly Roll Morton played his ragtime at the Storyville bordellos. A century later, we should look back and mention some Latino pioneers who made their everlasting mark in the jazz field.

Born in Manzanillo, Cuba, on September 18, 1908, and dying in New York on August 26, 1987, Alberto Socarrás is credited with the first recording of a jazz flute solo on February 5, 1929, in a piece called "Have You Ever Felt That Way?" as a member of the Clarence Williams Orchestra.

Meanwhile, Puerto Rican valve trombonist Juan Tizol contributed substantially to Duke Ellington's repertoire, and Cuban saxophonist-clarinetist-trumpeter Mario Bauzá was instrumental in launching Ella Fitzgerald's career by introducing her to Chick Webb in the 1930s, as well as in getting Dizzy Gillespie in touch with Chano Pozo, Machito, and Chico O'Farrill, an association that subsequently led to the development of "Cubop," a precursor of what we today call Latin jazz.

Radiocentro (Radio Center), Havana, 1962 to 1963.

"Psssst, hey comrade. . . . Yes, you, who else could it be? . . . You're here with that little 'yas' group, right?"

"Well, yes, we're here to record a radio show. . . . Why?" I replied, somewhat frightened.

"OK. . . . There's an order to stop the recording, so tell your people to grab their bags and get going. . . . And look, kid, don't ask too many questions because this order comes from high up. Maestro Arnau said that Armandito Zequeira and Tito Rivera's son are walking around with an arsenal of imperialist instruments, and we can't allow that here, you understand? We can't allow that!"

Evidently that spokesman for the "higher authority" didn't have the slightest idea that the "kid" he was talking to was the very son of Professor Tito Rivera. I gathered that the "imperialist instruments" that he was referring to were my saxophone, a few cymbals belonging to Alberto Romeu, and Kiki Villalta's electric guitar.

The man who ordered the cancellation of our jazz (imperialistic music!) recording, the maestro Roberto Valdés Arnau, was in reality a cultured and intelligent guy. What happened was that he had been a Communist from way back, and after years and years of reading jokes by Marx (Karl, not Groucho), speeches by Mao, and little pornographic novels that he used to hide secretly between the pages of *Das Kapital*, he was not surprisingly beset by certain maladjustments, problematic ulcers, and uncontrollable (cerebral) diarrhea.

His arbitrary order was nothing new. It happened before, during the time of Stalin, when Russian musicians were forced to exchange their "decadent" western saxophones for bassoons, oboes, and other instruments more in tune with "the historic moment."

"I don't like jazz," publicly declared Soviet premier Nikita Khrushchev around 1962. "I used to think it was static when I heard it on the radio. All music and art are ideological, and peaceful coexistence in the field of ideology is treason to Marxism-Leninism." This story and much more are recounted by Fred Starr in his passionate *Red and Hot: The Fate of Jazz in the Soviet Union*, a book about musicians and jazz aficionados in the Soviet Union.

And I make reference again to Starr's book for his description of Khrushchev's denunciation of modern dance, dodecaphony, and above all, what the premier called that jazz obsession. As a result, in the autumn of 1964, the Moscow Jazz Club was closed down, the Dream Café in Kiev ceased to hire jazz bands, and the manager of the Aelita in Moscow was fired for "disseminating Western influences." On October 14 of that same year, the official musicologist in the Kremlin was removed from office, replaced by no one more, no one less, than Leonid Brezhnev himself!

A similarly sad incident was related by the musicologist Helio Orovio (author of the *Diccionario de la Música Cubana*) during an interview with the music journalist Luis Tamargo. Criticizing the bureaucratization of art, Orovio cited the hair-raising story of how a Chinese pianist, during the time of the Cultural Revolution, had his hand cut off in public for refusing to stop playing that "decadent western music" (meaning jazz).

When Mao captured Shanghai in 1948, the city's nightlife shut down simply because the Communists considered those "decadent" nightclubs totally incompatible with socialism. A similar argument was made by José Llanuza, the man chosen by the Cuban government to close those "polluted dens of vice and corruption."

"In 1970 jazz music not only disappeared completely from the face of our homeland, but it became the symbol of the Occidental capitalism and its rottenness," the Czech writer Milán Kundera wrote in his harrowing novel *The Joke*. Published in Prague in 1967, with 120,000 copies sold in a few days, Kundera's book was prohibited and removed from book stores and public libraries two years later.

In other words, after visiting China and the Soviet Bloc countries on numerous occasions, the apparatchik Valdés Arnau was simply carrying out what he considered his duty in closing down our recording session, "tropicalizing" with typical Marxist arbitrariness the lessons he had learned during his stays in the ideological heart of the system. His actions give you an idea of what was in store for Cuban jazz lovers in the years following 1959.

Returning to Helio Orovio's *Diccionario de la Música Cubana* (translated into English as *Cuban Music from A to Z*), I believe that it's important to emphasize the difficulties the musicologist must have faced before the first edition of his book was published inside Cuba in 1981. For example, it wasn't until the second edition of this standard reference book was published in 1992 that he was allowed by the island's cultural authorities to include none other than Celia Cruz. This is comparable to omitting Frédéric Chopin from Polish music books only because he lived in France almost all of his life. Or eliminating Sidney Bechet from the history of jazz in the United States because he went off to Paris with Josephine Baker and there spoke boldly against the prevailing racism in his native country. These three artists had distinct and easily understandable reasons to leave their native countries and establish their professional careers someplace else, and this is precisely what they did. Yet, unlike Celia Cruz, neither Chopin nor Bechet was omitted from the musical reference books of their countries. But since everything that the revolution builds with its hands it consequently screws up with its feet, the revised and "expanded" edition of Orovio's dictionary contains a full-page picture of political singer-songwriter Silvio Rodríguez and only wallet-size pictures of Maestro Lecuona and Celia. . . . Shit, these people have bigger timbales than Tito Puente! . . . Am I right?

The interview with Helio Orovio was the highlight of my career as a journalist. Along with Paquito, Mario Rivera, Leonardo Acosta, comedian Álvarez-Guedes, and Dr. Kevorkian, Orovio is one of my idols. The interview was published by *Latin Beat,* a magazine that has featured Paquito's mischievous face on its cover more times than that of any other musician, dead or alive.

On the other hand, translating Paquito's anti-biography from Spanish to English (and at times from Marianao Beach slang to U.S. colloquial language) has been a difficult but pleasurable experience. I don't know what's more amusing— Paquito's escape from the Barajas Airport in Madrid (à la *Moscow on the Hudson,* via a Commie taxi driver), the memorable Bulgarian diarrhea epidemic, or the cruel affair (as perpetrated by Comrade Enrique Plá) involving Carlos Averhoff's violated doggie bag, which you will read about further on.

Although it was immediately obvious that *es un jamón* (it's a ham) had to be interpreted as "it's a piece of cake," I had a hell of a time translating words like *otorrinolaringólogos* (otorhinolaryngologists) and *ornitorrinco* (ornithorhynchus), those exotic terms that Paquito's precocious child Franco learned before his first birthday.

Coincidentally, I have always wondered if Paquito named his son after a Falangist *generalissimo* from El Ferrol, the Galician town where incense was popularized during the Middle Ages in order to lessen the environmental effect of the detrimental armpit aroma emanating from thousands of sweaty pilgrims who came to worship their anti-Islamic patron saint.

Last but not least, this translating ordeal has changed my plans for the future. Stimulated by Antonio Gades's example and Paquito's inspiring retirement planning, I also hope to be able, upon permanently abandoning my present enterprises, to purchase a hog farm. After all, health-conscious North Americans are eating more of the "other white meat"— annual pork consumption in the United States has increased from forty-nine pounds to fifty-three pounds per capita during the past nine years. Seventh-Day Adventists and Orthodox Jews are probably not too thrilled about these nutritional developments, but it looks like Paquito and I have a bright future ahead of us as hog farmers!

—Luis Tamargo

Although I was exposed since early childhood to every type of music, my formal encounter with that marvelous genre called jazz, along with its technical and aesthetic aspects, took place with the help of the members of Felipe Dulzaides's group Los Armónicos, particularly through the guitarist Pablo Cano and the pianist Paquito Hechavarría.

Hechavarría was the first person whom I saw playing the vibraphone, an instrument that had fascinated me since I listened to the recordings of Lionel Hampton with Benny Goodman's orchestra. Two other Cuban musicians, Armandito Romeu and Remberto Egües, were able to play the vibraphone very well. Like the banjo, the washboard, the electric guitar, and the drum set, the vibraphone is an instrument native to the United States.

When I finally settled in New York in the early eighties, I had the opportunity to work with such great vibraphonists as Tito Puente, Milt Jackson, Hendrik Meurkens, Severii Pissalo, Bobby Hutcherson, Victor Mendoza, Gary Burton, Jay Hoggard, and Lionel Hampton. Then I formed the Caribbean Jazz Project, along with two of my favorite musicians, the spectacular Andy Narell (on steel drums) and Dave Samuels (on marimba and vibraphone).

▲▲▲

Although I had listened to many of his recordings, I personally met Paquito D'Rivera for the first time at the airport in Charlotte, North Carolina. I didn't have any difficulty in recognizing him—the alto sax case, black leather pants, very white Panama hat, and mischievous kid's smile.

But it wasn't until a few years later that we were able to play together—in September of 1993, for a New York concert at the Central Park Zoo, when the radio station CD-101 asked me to form an all-star band, which was led by Paquito, Andy Narell, and me, backed by Dario Eskenazi, Richie Morales, and Mark Eagan.

Almost instantly during our first rehearsal we became aware of the unique timbre that resulted from blending the sounds of our three frontline instruments. I had played and recorded with Andy previously and was familiar with our instrumental combination, but by adding alto and clarinet, a whole new dimension was created. This was the beginning of the Caribbean Jazz Project.

Paquito's musical personality is a very special combination of jazz, classical training, and Afro-Cuban traditions, mixed with an incredible sense of humor. If you have to look for the humorous angle of any situation, let Paquito find it. Just give him the microphone, and you'll see what I'm talking about.

He is *buena gente*—a really good guy. He looks like Pete Fountain after eating too much rice and beans, and has the humor of Spike Jones and the flatulence of Shamu the killer whale.

Wherever Paquito is, you can always count on his honesty, sincerity, and musicality.

—Dave Samuels

(Should I say thanks . . . or fuck you, dear Samuels?)

With the Caribbean Jazz Project (CJP), we recorded and traveled throughout the world and soon achieved great popularity, not only due to the quality and prestige of the soloists but also as a result of the versatile and powerful rhythm section composed by the Argentinean pianist Dario Eskenazi, heir to the elegance of his compatriot Jorge Dalto; the extraordinarily solid and competent Peruvian bassist Oscar Stagnaro; and Mark Walker, one of the most professional drummers I have met, with the best reading ability and the highest degree of adaptability and subtlety that I have known in my extensive career.

I was so dazzled by Samuels's elegant, firm, and expressive style that I immediately asked him to appear as guest artist on my record *A Night in Englewood* with the United Nations Orchestra. The other soloists were Slide Hampton and Claudio Roditi.

I have played and recorded considerably with the King of the Timbal, and although I know that some readers will be surprised to find Tito Puente's name among the vibraphonists mentioned earlier, I must tell you that despite the fact that he's better known for his timbal skills, he had a very personal style of playing the vibraphone. If you need further evidence, listen to his version of Noro Morales's extremely beautiful *contradanza* entitled "María Cervantes." I believe you can find it on the album *On Broadway*, recorded by Tito in the mideighties with Jorge Dalto on piano.

Another great vibraphonist I worked with was the incomparable Milt Jackson when Dizzy organized that Dream Big Band for a television special recorded at New York's Lincoln Center in 1981. Gerry Mulligan, Bags, and I were the soloists in Dizzy's "Groovin' High." Among the members of that superband were Jon Faddis, Pepper Adams, George Duvivier, Melba Liston, Curtis Fuller, Victor Paz, Frank Foster, Max Roach, Marvin Stamm, Paul West, Candido, and Grady Tate.

During the beginning of my association with CBS, McCoy Tyner recorded the album *La leyenda de la hora*, on which I was able to include a very good *tumbador* (conga player) that we met at Verna Gillis's Soundscape nightclub—Daniel Ponce. I recommended that he play in a couple of pieces McCoy had written for the project that had a certain Latin flavor, but when McCoy heard how this Cuban monster played, he used him on the entire album. Years later, McCoy went on to use yet another Cuban drummer, Horacio "El Negro" Hernandez, the son of the shining character and jazzophile of the same name. El Negro became very popular among American musicians because of his original style and his always joyful, youthful, and optimistic personality, which is so well reflected in his style and stage presence.

The recording took place in the legendary New Jersey studios of Rudy Van Gelder, in a beautiful architectural structure designed by the famed architect Frank Lloyd Wright. Among the members of that band, organized by CBS, were Chico Freeman, Hubert Laws, Marcus Belgrave, and Avery Sharpe (who had been Tyner's bassist for many years). Speaking of vibraphonists, we had one of the top cats—Bobby Hutcherson.

I worked with vibist Jay Hoggard in a production of Bruce Landvall for Elektra called *The Young Lions*, along with Wynton Marsalis, James Newton, Hammiett Bluiett, and John Blake. We spent much more time talking about lawyers and royalties (and asking each

With McCoy Tyner

other why Mike Gibbs, a white musician from Zimbabwe, was directing a group of black musicians from the United States) than about
music itself. Only in America!

I deeply respect mallet player Victor Mendoza for his brilliant
educational efforts in favor of Latino jazz students at the Berklee
College of Music and have had the delightful experience of recording
with his group on various occasions. Since the Mexican professor is
a good composer and an indefatigable scout as well, he recommended
the young Panamanian pianist Danilo Pérez and the formidable Mexican drummer Antonio Sánchez to work with my band.

During a jam session with Sarah Vaughan at the Pori Festival in
Finland, I met a very young and excellent vibraphonist named Severii
Pissalo, who deeply admired Dave Samuels. I invited him to work
with me at the Village Vanguard back in the eighties.

Four-mallet pioneer Gary Burton is a musician whom I've admired ever since my Finnish friend Esko Linnavalli sent me the CD
Country Road and Other Places (with guitarist Larry Coryell), but I

never had the opportunity of sharing the stage with him until pianist Pablo Ziegler and producers Pat Philips and Ettore Stratta invited me to perform at a wonderful Tango concert in Carnegie Hall in 2000. Besides a fantastic group of dancers, other artists featured that unforgettable evening were saxophonist Joe Lovano and singer-actress Julia Zenko. This event proved that an evening of Latin music can be more than an endless series of multipercussion solos on top of a forte and fortissimo single-chord *montuno* pattern.

In my list of distinguished vibraphonists, I also want to mention Hendrik Meurkens, "the German Hope," as he calls himself, a harmonica player, a vibist, and a very inspired composer, who like me is enamored of Brazilian music and has written a few tunes for my different musical groups.

But I experienced one of the most emotional moments of my career when I played for the first time with Lionel Hampton, before a crowd of thousands, at Idaho's Moscow International Festival, where Lionel was one of the featured artists. We played Eubie Blake's "Memories of You," one of the first jazz melodies that I learned from the Benny Goodman record that my father brought home almost fifty years ago.

My dad worked for one or two weeks every year with the orchestra that accompanied the cabaret show at the Capri Hotel. In another large hall in the hotel (the site of the former gambling casino) Los Armónicos performed. These musicians and singers interpreted Cuban and international music and also devoted a large part of their show to jazz, which always had a growing number of fans and followers in Havana. Back in 1960 and 1961, Felipe Dulzaides, the leader of Los Armónicos, was allegedly involved in a conspiracy to assassinate Fidel Castro. What actually happened was never clear, and after his release from jail, the pianist never mentioned that dangerous episode. He was said to be related to a person named

Miguel or Manuel García, who was the national director of prisons at that time. This relative was able, in a miraculous way, to remove his cousin from the trial and had his thirty-year prison sentence commuted to "only two years" with a pledge of "good behavior" for the following twenty-eight years.

In my opinion, this story is highly dubious, since I never heard, before or after Dulzaides's imprisonment, of anyone who was involved in the slightest imaginable action against the dictator whose sentence was commuted. If the poor guy had any luck, he was locked up in a dungeon and the key was thrown into the Gulf of Guacanayabo— and it was only on rare occasions like this that the guy's skin would be saved. What is more likely is that Dulzaides's participation in the botched job could not be proven, so they resorted to the very common practice on the island of applying the "minimum" sentence of two years. During those two years of "rehabilitation," Paquito Hechavarría temporarily occupied Felipe's position. He didn't have the extraordinary leadership talent that Felipe had in spades, but he played the vibraphone and the piano a lot better. The remaining members of the band were José Franca (bass), Nelson "El Flaco" Padrón (drums), Margarita Royeros (vocalist), and Pablo Cano (electric guitar).

Tito noticed that I was getting hooked on American music, so he introduced me to the jazz cats at the Capri Hotel, and right away Hechavarría the pianist and Franca the bassist helped me to learn and improvise upon some numbers from their repertoire. That was when I "collided" with my first blues, which happened to be Barney Kessel's "Barney's Blues." Pablito Cano, with his ever gentle and polite character, taught me how to read the symbol chords. "Look, kid, don't be frightened. This is a piece of cake," he said on the first day of classes in the musicians' dressing room, while scribbling the following data on a napkin: "A = la, B = si, C = do, D = re, E = mi, F = fa, G = sol." He added, "It's like a little poem, don't you think?"

Before long, they would all go into exile in Miami, where several decades later, they still live and take part in the musical world of that city. After learning all of those useful little things from Cano,

Hechavarría, and the rest of the musicians in that band, I was able to apply what I'd heard in recordings by Benny, Dizzy, Bird, Paul Desmond, and Buddy DeFranco much more easily to my own playing.

After Felipe was released from political prison, he organized a new band because all of his former musicians were already in Miami. His sound was inspired by the British pianist George Shearing, and his group played many of Shearing's tunes in addition to the hit parade. Working with this group was hip. It was impossible to be bored because of the range of the repertoire and the quality of the musicians around him.

"The best way to live through a socialist regime is the same way you live through a tornado: drunk or sleeping!" Felipe would murmur, half joking, half serious. Although Felipe was a rather technically limited pianist, he had the special ability to extract the best from each member of the band. He never learned to read music too well, but he accumulated by ear an immense and eclectic musical archive. He was a very fine accompanist and engaged in very few solos, and because he was well aware of his own limitations, he learned to apply the eleventh commandment: "Don't fuck around."

No one remembers exactly who gave Felipe the nickname Burro Triste (Sad Donkey), but the truth is that after taking a good look at him, you realized that his face could have been taken from the Spanish poet Juan Ramón Jiménez's book *Platero and I*, in which the main character is a Spanish donkey. The musicians engaged in wordplay by calling him "Burripe" or Felipe "Burraides." For some reason that I don't understand even today, neither Burr—pardon me, Dulzaides— nor his family ever learned to accept this common and harmless joke. He was aware of those nicknames, but since everyone loved and respected him, no one dared to use them to his face.

In his group, there was a guitarist named Lafont who was casually called Burro Loco (Crazy Burro) all the time, although he didn't like it either. On a certain occasion, I happened to be sitting in that set when Dulzaides was ready to count down the first tune, and without realizing the implications, I said, "Hold it right there; the Burro is not here!"

Everyone, including Dulzaides, looked at me without believing what I had just said. After an embarrassing silence, I tried to mend the difficult situation by adding respectfully, "Not you, maestro, the other Burro!"

Well, at least no blood was spilled that time, and the musicians—as well as Felipe—had a good laugh over my burrolike behavior.

In 1960, during the last visit of the dean of Cuban arrangers, Arturo "Chico" O'Farrill, to the beautiful city of Havana, the members of the Club Cubano de Jazz arranged his appearance with a big band at the theater of the labor union CTC (Confederacíon de Trabajadores de Cuba). In addition, they brought the Mexican lead trumpet César Molina and a pianist from the land of the Aztecs by the name of Raúl Stallworth.

In a conversation I had with O'Farrill in 1995 at Victor's Café in Manhattan, after one of his performances at Lincoln Center, he told me that in the repertoire he took to Cuba for that last performance was a piece called "The Bass Family," and the soloists were the brothers Papito, Felo, and Kike Hernández, all of whom were bassists.

Years later, in Miami, I recorded an album entitled *Forty Years of Cuban Jam Sessions*, and the piece "Tres Tristes Tigres" (in honor of Cabrera Infante's novel translated into English as *Three Trapped Tigers*) was specially written for three generations of Cuban bassists: Cachao, Nicky Orta, and, again, Kike Hernández.

Around the very early sixties, on one warm afternoon in Havana, a very charming, bug-eyed pianist named Samuel Téllez took me to play a couple of numbers with his group at one of the jam sessions that were still being held at the Havana 1900, the venue where the Club Cubano de Jazz had presented Zoot Sims, Stan Getz, and other jazzmen from the North back in the fifties and early sixties. That afternoon, I admiringly saw Chucho Valdés playing for the first time. I was only thirteen years old, but his way of playing the piano sounded to me like something you could only hear on American records.

"Hey, Samuel, who is that guy?" I asked my friend.

"Oh, that's Bebo Valdés's son. Helluva player, huh? Seems like his old man taught him well."

Playing with Lionel Hampton at his jazz festival in Moscow, Idaho, in the early eighties

"Helluva player? He's a monster pianist," I added, trying to use the special lingo used by Havana musicians at that time.

At the Hotel Nacional's Cabaret Parisienne, Amadito Valdés—a great friend of my father—played lead alto with the orchestra of Leonardo Timor, a trumpeter who not only accompanied the featured show but also played swing numbers with orchestral arrangements by Harry James, Woody Herman, Duke Ellington, Stan Kenton, and Count Basie. I went there every night to get together with Amadito Jr., Valdés's son, and other young friends who were newcomers on the musical nightlife scene. My other accomplices were Rembert Eüges, Sergio Vitier, Fabián García Caturla, and a percussionist named Carlitos Godines. From there our first combo, Los Chicos del Jazz (meaning "the Jazz Kids"), was born. Our repertoire included "Lullaby of Birdland," "Barney's Blues," "Perdido," and a few other pieces that I can't remember. We used to hang out, hoping to get an opportunity to jam, at the Capri, La Gruta, La Zorra y el Cuervo, and other small clubs.

It was at the Cabaret Parisienne where Timor the Toad—as he was affectionately called by his friends—began to organize the popular Jazz Tuesdays with his big band, Pucho Escalante's nine-piece band, and the Free American Jazz, an interesting quartet that featured two American musicians, Mario Lagarde and Eddy Torriente, who arrived in Cuba as members of the Black Panthers, or something like that, and remained permanently on the island. The rest of the group was formed by Pepe El Loco (Madman) on drums and Gonzalo Romeu on bass (years later Romeu received a scholarship to study in Moscow and became a good symphonic conductor and pianist). Other bassists who worked with the American musicians were Julio César, author—among other things—of the comical "Danzón que se traba" ("The Broken-Record Danzon"); José Valdés; and the dynamic Armandito Sequeira, a very musical, charismatic, and completely demented guy who had played drums with his illustrious uncle, Armando Romeu, in the navy band and at the Tropicana Club. Eddy Torriente was an enthusiastic admirer of Paul Gonçalves and played his alto sax with the very same swing as his idol. He was a careless cat with somewhat of a bohemian lifestyle. When he died, after falling off his motorcycle in the heart of Havana at dawn, he was coming from an all-night session playing tenor sax with a group of Cuban rural musicians, and inside his messy saxophone case, still attached to his old mouthpiece, was one of the reeds that my father had given him as a gift some months before.

We all mourned the death of that affectionate gringo who shouted "*Campeón del mundo!*" ("World champion!") whenever any asshole player appeared at the door of the Atelier nightclub with the intention of jamming.

And we learned much from the pianist Mario Lagarde, "El Americano." As he said in heavily accented Spanish, referring to the importance of harmonic knowledge in jazz, "If you don't know the chords, you can't play, seenyorr."

Mario was someone who felt insulted every time Armandito, Pepe, or any of the many potheads of the musical environment offered him some high-grade marijuana.

"That shit is repugnant to us *revoluucionnarrios!*" he said with indignation. In any case, one day a neighbor squealed on him (a story that was corroborated by gossips in the neighborhood), and the police went inside his house and seized an entire *Cannabis sativa* plant on his bedroom's little balcony, across the street from the Focsa Building.

"Cubans are terrible," he complained. "I asked for a rosebush, and instead they sold me a marijuana plant!" After that incident, the wise guys in our crowd would call him *el yerberito moderno* (the modern herbalist), in reference to a guaracha sung by Celia Cruz, or *el jardinero del amor* (the gardener of love), based on the title of a hit song by the Orquesta Aragón.

A powerful swing was injected into Havana nightlife by the two gringos of the Free American Jazz, along with Armandito, El Negro Nicolás, Pucho Escalante (recently repatriated from Venezuela), and Timor with his Jazz Tuesdays. I was happier than a mouse in a cheese factory the day when the Toad invited me to play Artie Shaw's Clarinet Concerto with his big band, a performance that I repeated a couple of times with Romeu at the Tropicana and on television with the orchestra led by the unforgettable Adolfo Guzmán, featuring the drummer Guillermo Barreto.

Bebo Valdés's cousin, Guillermo Barreto, was one of the few Cuban drummers who understood the subtleties of playing jazz with an authentic American swing, without whacking or none of that shit. In addition, he had a very special ear and, above all, an exquisite musical taste. His playing technique was low-key and understated, and to his credit, he never gratified himself (and disgusted us) by playing like the drummers now on the scene who sound like a clothes dryer with Michael Jordan's sneakers banging around inside.

Known as El Loro (Parrot) due to his constant chatter and parrotlike walk, Barreto was as comfortable playing in a big band as in a jazz combo, and he sounded just as good when playing timbal with groups devoted to *descargas cubanas* (Cuban jam sessions).

If asked today to provide a good example of what we call Latin jazz, I'd say there's nothing better than those delightful sessions with the Quinteto de Música Moderna, featuring Frank Emilio on piano, Gustavo Tamayo on *güiro*, Tata Guines on *tumbadoras*, Papito Hernández or Cachaíto on bass, and the unequaled drumming of Guillermo "the Parrot" Barreto.

Jazz was gaining so much powerful energy that the state-owned recording enterprise EGREM (just about everything was owned by the state already) released albums by Pucho Escalante and by Leonardo Timor's orchestra. I was invited to perform two solos on Timor's recording: the first an arrangement by Roberto Sánchez Ferrer of Urbano Gómez Montiel's "Canta lo Sentimental" (which had been popularized in those years by the great Cuban vocalist Elena Burke) and the second "La Gruta Blues," in honor of Mario El Americano and dedicated to the celebrated nightclub where he worked with his jazz group.

The troubadour César Portillo de la Luz was also featured at La Gruta. The author of "Noche Cubana," "Contigo en la Distancia," "Delirio," and many other immortal pages of Cuban music, César was one of the pillars of the fifties movement known as *filin*, which—like

Rio de Janeiro's bossa nova in the sixties—combined Cuban contemporary genres with jazz elements. (The word *filin* is a Hispanicized version of the English word "feeling.")

"What happened in Brazil with bossa nova had already been cooking for a long time before in Cuba," commented the Brazilian vocalist Flora Purim. Both *filin* and bossa nova were hybrid genres with a mutual affinity, and that is why at the social gatherings organized by jazz aficionados some *filin* musicians, such as Frank Domínguez, Miguel de Gonzalo, or the well-fed Aida with her spectacular, phenomenal quartet, were always bound to appear.

Rafael Somavilla had led, a little earlier, a heavy-duty orchestra at the Hilton's Caribe Lounge. The baton of that orchestra was later passed to the great pianist and composer Fernando Mulens, with a beautiful collection of arrangements that Somavilla (aka El Soma) had taken from recordings by Kenton and Johnny Richards. So my friend Amadito and I used to drop by to listen to the drumming of a creative and restless musician called Blasito, the younger brother of flutist Richard Egües. Sometimes we got lucky and they gave us a chance to jam in one or two of those cool charts.

The contrabassist working in that Salón Caribe was a very quiet and discreet young man, the last person you would have imagined would, in less than a decade, revolutionize popular music inside and outside Cuba with his band. I'm referring, of course, to Juan Formell and Los Van Van. Very few are aware of the curious fact that the first drummer of Los Van Van was none other than the prodigious Blasito, whom Emiliano Salvador, upon their first meeting, began to call the Roy Haynes of Cuban music.

There was jazz everywhere: El Pigalle, La Red, El Pico Blanco, and another club located on Neptuno Street called Descarga-Club, which featured Kiki Villalta alternating on piano and guitar, Tomasito Vázquez on that beautiful King Super 20 tenor that he bought from my old man years before, a redheaded drummer known as Zanahoria (Carrot), and a young and very tall bassist by the name of Luis Quiñones whom I'd met in the conservatory.

I enjoyed going to the Descarga, particularly to see Luisito, who played a very solid bass à la Ray Brown, and with whom I maintained a great friendship that extended to our families. The bassist is the son of the composer José Dolores Quiñones, who had moved to Europe many years before. His mother, Carmita, played piano by ear and was a versatile accompanist to singers who often played in piano bars. I earned my first pesos as a member of her group, Carmita y su Combo, playing boleros, guarachas, tangos, and fox-trots while trying to follow amateur and professional singers. I have very tender memories of Carmita, that sweet lady who was as naive and innocent as a young girl.

The entire Quiñones family was composed of musicians. Besides Luis's parents, his aunt Lourdes (aka Mayuya) played bass or *tumbadora* with the all-female Orquesta Anacaona. Even the grandparents were musicians who sang and played instruments from the rhythm section. The Quiñoneses were the most charming and generous family you could imagine. The door to their house in Buenavista was never closed, and musicians and friends came and went at all hours.

Through Kiki Villalta, I was able to establish a relationship with the extraordinary guitarist Carlos Emilio Morales, whom I'd watched admiringly on television playing with Felo Bergaza (La Fela!) and Fernando Mulens. In order for you to understand just how much I admired Carlos, I must tell you that the first time I saw that man play in person, my mouth dropped wide open in amazement.

Carlos "El Gordo" (Fats) Emilio (when I met him in the early sixties, he hadn't earned his nickname yet) is one of the most prominent members of the illustrious Cuban guitar tradition and is highly respected and admired by colleagues in the jazz, classical, and popular genres of Cuban music.

Born on November 6, 1939, in Marianao, Havana, Carlos Emilio was the son of a dentist. He attended medical school at the University of Havana and worked as a traveling salesman of medical products for several years. But it didn't take long for him to find his true vocation. He learned to play the guitar himself, with the aid of albums of Latin American trios, such as Los Panchos and Los Tres Caballeros.

Carlos Emilio Morales in my studio in New Jersey

After he discovered jazz, he became an avid record collector. Thanks to him, many of us were first exposed to the work of artists such as Chico Hamilton, Buddy Collette, Barney Kessel, Lee Konitz, Lenny Tristano, Wes Montgomery, Tal Farlow, Ray Brown, Charles Mingus, Oscar Peterson, Horace Silver, and Ornette Coleman.

He was soon taking classical guitar lessons and learned sight-reading. These studies enabled him to join the orchestra of Havana's Teatro Musical, where the prestigious classical guitarist Leo Brouwer worked as a composer. Brouwer was another enthusiastic admirer of El Gordo. Furthermore, El Gordo was the first to suggest to Cuban bassists that they could apply guitar techniques to the Fender bass with great results instead of trying to play that instrument like a contrabass. Carlitos del Puerto learned this technique directly from El

Gordo and later introduced it to a whole new generation of electric bassists on the island. El Gordo's unique style of playing has influenced not only guitarists but also many other instrumentalists of various generations of Cuban musicians. It's amazing that such a timid and humble man could have such a tremendous impact on our lives as musicians.

In November 1994, Messidor Musik, the German record company that had released some of my previous albums, approved my idea of recording with the Cuban pianist Bebo Valdés, who had been living in exile in Sweden since the early sixties.

This would be the first recording by El Caballón (Big Horse) in thirty-four years. I wanted to prepare something special for the occasion, so I came up with the crazy idea of bringing Carlos Emilio along with Chucho (Bebo's son) and the timbal player Amadito Valdés (no relation) from Havana to Frankfurt by air.

I knew very well that this adventure would be very difficult to accomplish. However, combining my anonymity with the tenacity of El Flaco (Amadito's nickname) and the efficient assistance of my good friend Barbarita and her German husband Bernardo (whose travel agency could handle any request), we were able to bring—within a remarkable three or four days—Amadito and Carlos to Frankfurt. This would be the first time in three decades that exiled Cuban musicians and their colleagues who remained on the island would record together.

Although Chucho canceled his participation in his father's first recording in more than three decades just a few hours before his flight was scheduled to depart for Germany, the CD *Bebo Rides Again!* bears witness to an extraordinary musical reunion. As the featured liner notes writer, Dr. Cristóbal Díaz Ayala, stated, "A first-rank guitarist and member of the group Irakere, Carlos Emilio Morales had soloing opportunities on this album that he rarely has when playing with his band."

Recording Bebo Rides Again! *at Studios Bauer, Ludwigsburg, Germany: Juan Pablo Torres, Patato Valdés, Bebo Valdés, Gerardo Rosales, Carlos Emilio Morales, Gabriel Machado, Göetz Werner, Amadito Valdés, and Diego Urcola (1995)*

In October 1995, taking advantage of the fact that El Gordo Carlos Emilio was going to come to New York on a cultural exchange, I set up a recording session for his first album as a soloist, to be joined by great musicians such as Harvie Swartz, Claudio Roditi, and Dave Samuels. The musicians participating in the project were thrilled. The recording session was to be held at the Old House Studio in Westchester, operated by the Argentinean pianist Daniel Freiberg. The musicians included Freiberg (piano), Harvie Swartz and Oscar Stagnaro on bass, drummers Mark Walker and Pat Forero, guitarist David Oquendo, Claudio Roditi on trumpet, and, as guest artist, Dave Samuels on marimba and vibraphone. Such great expectations were created by El Gordo's projected recording that *Down Beat* magazine scheduled an article that I wrote about the Havana-born guitarist for its March 1995 issue, which would appear around the time the CD was due to be released.

But as my grandmother Panchita Moreno would say, "The priest killed the big snake and then was frightened by its head." This Cuban proverb explains why, after agreeing to make the historic recording, El Gordo chickened out and canceled the session that we had prepared with so much love, time, and money, even though it would have brought together more great musicians and talent than he'd ever seen before in his life.

Around that same time, we received a call at my office from the record company Tropijazz, owned by the Dominican American impresario Ralph Mercado, proposing that I produce a recording at the phenomenal Fantasy Studios, located in Berkeley, California, with a group of Cuban musicians from both sides of the Florida Strait, including Chucho Valdés and his legendary father, Bebo.

"Look, Ralph," I told the impresario, with whom I had worked on numerous occasions, "I've recently read this beautiful thought on a postcard I got in the mail: 'A friend is someone who knows you well and, despite that, still loves you.'"

"And what do you mean by that, maestro?" Ralph asked me, intrigued.

"What I mean, my dear Ralph, is that despite the thirty-odd years that I've known my friend Chucho, I never exactly know what he's thinking, and generally what he says he's going to do turns out to be something totally different from what he actually does."

I explained to Ralphy that I had tried unsuccessfully to reunite the two Valdéses, father and son, for the German session conducted the previous year and that I couldn't imagine why things would be different this time. I had placed all my energy and hopes in that project and was deeply hurt by Chucho's sudden cancellation. Quite frankly, this time I would participate in the proposed recording only if there were a truly attractive financial remuneration.

Moreover, I didn't have the least intention of being an accomplice to the violation of the U.S. commercial embargo against the Cuban dictatorship, so I left it to the discretion of Ralphy and his staff to resolve such a politically sensitive issue. After outlining very clearly the specifics of our recording agreement, I went to San Francisco, where I joined the other participants. Among them were the New York–born recording engineer Jon Fausty, a veteran of thousands of Latin music recordings; the Puerto Rican coproducer assigned by RMM (Ralph Mercado Management), Eddy Rodríguez; and a group of musicians who could best be described with El Loro Barreto's frequently used saying: *Cuidado con los callos, mi hermano*. Although the literal translation is "Be careful with your foot corns, my brother," it actually means that one must be alert and vigilant when the cream of the crop is gathered in any given place because anything is bound to happen. The cream of the crop included the trombonist Juan Pablo Torres, who also participated in the Messidor session; Carlitos del Puerto; Angá, Irakere's former *tumbador*; Pachú, a trumpeter who came from Miami; Horacio "El Negro" Hernández on drums; the distinguished Cuban American percussionist Luis Conte (second cousin of the famous journalist Luis Conte Agüero); Bebo Valdés and —SURPRISE!—the one and only Chucho, who fortunately didn't suddenly bow out by saying that he had to change the water in his grandmother's fish tank or assist Geraldo Rivera in looking for Al Capone's hidden treasures in Chicago.

At the beginning of the two-day session, we received the pleasant visit of Andy Narell and his lovely wife Jenny, who lived in that area, and almost in unison and unanimously we decided that he would be the guest artist of the Cubanos on the album. The brilliant American musician played a version of Mexico-born Chelo Velázquez's "Bésame Mucho" that was "finger-lickin' good," as they say at Kentucky Fried Chicken.

Despite the political barriers in existence between Cuba and the United States during these last decades, once in a while we find cracks in the Sugarcane Curtain that allow us to experience a bit of Cuba and its culture. Cuban musicians such as Chano Pozo, Machito, Mario Bauzá, and others had created a great impact in the jazz community. However, during most of the sixties and seventies, we knew very little about the musical changes that were taking place in Cuba.

Irakere was the first group that recorded in the United States, circa 1979, and it is very difficult to express the impact made by their album among those of us who were interested in Caribbean music. The group possessed an explosive power. Their level of musical accomplishment and their compositions gained our immediate respect and admiration and left us in a state of amazement. Since then we have been able to listen to more of their recordings, but you still have to travel out of the country to catch their live performances. Twice I had the opportunity to listen to them when we played in the same Curaçao festival, and they were truly incendiary. I also had the chance to jam with them, and it was an unforgettable experience.

The 1995 album was recorded in San Francisco during a visit made by Chucho Valdés, along with other members of Irakere, to the United States. Paquito, as well as Chucho's father, flew to that city for the reunion. To be present at those sessions as a spectator was a tremendously emotional experience, but a greater emotion was created when I was asked to play in some cuts.

I know that I'm not the only one who wants to see these great musicians more often in the future. Meanwhile, we can enjoy a preview of the good vibrations created in those recording sessions.

—Andy Narell

For reasons known by all, relationships with people on the other side of the Straits of Florida are usually tense, if not chaotic, but in

Cuban recording at Fantasy Studios in Berkeley, California

the case of artists, the nightmare ends when the music begins. Irrefutable proof of that fact is the marvelous improvisation over "El
Manicero" ("Peanut Vendor") recorded in only one take by the piano
duet of Bebo Valdés and his son Chucho, as can be enjoyed on the
CD *Ninety Miles to Cuba.*

In the early sixties, there was also a little jazz network at the conservatory—Luis Quiñones, Carlos Emilio, and me. Carlos Emilio began
to study cello and flute with Fabio Landa and Raúl Ondina.

Among the other students, there were the pianist Adolfo Pichardo
and the drummer Armandito Romeu (son of Armando Romeu). Both
of these students worked in two different shows at the Tropicana.
Sometimes, when Armandito finished the show "Bajo las Estrellas"
("Under the Stars"), Quiñones and I would go into the Panorámico
(the former casino) to jam with Pichardo.

With this small group and Freddy Muguercia (a guitarist who stuck to us like glue), one afternoon I played in a concert presented, strangely enough, by the UJC (Union of Communist Youth) at the Payret Theater, along with Frank Emilio, Tata Guines, and the Free American Jazz. Leonardo Timor closed the show with his big band. Leonardo Acosta, who played alto on his recently premiered flügel-horn, organized a fantastic combo composed of Chucho Valdés (piano), Papito Hernández (contrabass), Emilito del Monte (drums), and Carlos Emilio (guitar), with the added presence of a photographer–bongó player named Manolo Armestro—also known as Calandraca.

This professional photographer, who took great delight in playing the bongó, had a very tragic end more than twenty years later. On his birthday, he organized a small party in his apartment, located on Forty-second Street in Marianao. As the guests were going down the stairs to leave, they heard the unmistakable sound of a gunshot. For some reason, Calandraca had taken his own life with a bullet from his old Colt .38 revolver.

Ironically my first real jazz concert was organized by the UJC in 1963 at the Payret Theater. It marked my almost religious initiation in this musical genre, although I had been first indoctrinated into the faith by my father when he brought home that Benny Goodman record. I was fully invested in the jazz priesthood seventeen years after this concert when I definitively arrived in my own promised land, the City of New York, in October 1980.

Leonardo Acosta wrote in a humorous letter:

> The jazz festival at the Payret in '63, well yes, it was kind of organized by the UJC, but I think I found the answer: the real organizers were at the time very young singers from Los Modernistas vocal quartet, who happened to be members of that Communist youth organization, with the help of Robert Williams, the first African-American civil rights leader that came to the land of "La Siguaraya." Later we had Stokely Carmichael here, and then the real Black Panthers, like your friend and many others I met, and finally the Pink Panther, who is probably still around!

At that festival, you forgot to mention the late Maggie Prior, the only Cuban singer (besides Delia Bravo, Armandito Romeu's mother) who kept on singing jazz forever and ever in the language of Ella, Sarah, and Carmen.

Now about my group. Actually it was Horacio Hernández's idea; he rang his cousin Papito, who phoned me, so I got Carlos Emilio on guitar. As you well say, "Charles" Ondina was not available, but El Gordo brought Chucho and also Emilito del Monte on drums. We played concerts at a place you wouldn't imagine, the theater at the Ministry of Industries, where Horacio worked at the time. Later on, we played at Bellas Artes. But at the Payret, Papito and Emilio couldn't make it, so we subbed with Armando Sequeira on bass and Macho Almirall on drums. End of story. I do have a photo of that group at Payret, and also one with Papito and Emilio.

Paquito and I crossed paths throughout the years on certain significant occasions. I first saw him as a kid, at Tito's music shop, where I used to go with saxists Pedro Chao and Tata Palau, my buddies. I heard him play at a jam in 1958 when I think he was ten. I was playing alto, Pedro was on tenor, and we had this terrific rhythm section with Frank Emilio on piano, Papito Hernández on bass, and Walfredo de los Reyes on drums. It was at Club Maxim's, and sitting at the bar was none other than Chico O'Farrill and friends. Paquito made me show him my old Buescher sax and he said, "Hey, man, who brought you this, Christopher Columbus?" There was his humor already! So then Tito asks us if we can play some tune Paquito learned, and there he goes, improvising in a style reminiscent of Benny Carter. Not bad, huh? Later on he played with Los Chicos del Jazz in a session organized by Club Cubano de Jazz at Havana 1900, with big Luis Quiñones on bass and Amadito Valdés Jr. on drums, while Kiki Villalta and Sergio Vitier (both guitarists) covered on piano and congas. That was around '62 or '63. Funny, in '58 I was in NYC and "discovered" Jackie McLean at Café Bohemia in the Village, and twenty years later (1978) Paquito introduced me to Jackie's son, Rene McLean, at the Rio Club in Miramar, La Habana. (Remember, Paquito?)

Other coincidences: in '63 we have this Payret festival, each one with a different group. Well, that same year comes this guy I had known in Mexico as a comedian (now a Hollywood film director), Alfonso Arau. We have lunch at the Polinesio and he offers me the first alto chair in the orchestra for the *teatro musical* he was organizing. I was working as journalist, had a recent raise in salary plus collaborations in magazines, and played only in jam sessions or concerts—just did what I wanted. "No more big bands for me," I said. So I remembered Paquito playing alto and clarinet in all these swinging jazz joints we had then and told Arau, "There is only one guy who can fill that chair, a jazz improviser and great clarinet player [I was a lousy clarinet player], and Paquito is just what you're looking for." His eyes popped out and he says, "You're the third guy who's told me the same thing. He must be incredible!" And so there we had Paquito and Chucho and Carlos Emilio together, and ten years later (1973) a big baby called Irakere was born.

Around '65 and '66 Paquito and I hung out together, used to go places like El Patio with some chicks to see this new group Tres Mas Uno (Three Plus One), a Cuban version of Modern Jazz Quartet in which Armandito Romeu played vibes and all these licks from Milt Jackson. And this drummer Joe Iglesias had a tenor sax he would lend us to blow. Later on we moved to the Flamingo, played duets and four and all, and one night we just blew the house down. El Negro Nicolas looked down at me from his six feet and exclaimed, "You and Paco are a couple of motherf—." Of course it was a compliment. Finally we organized in 1969 that three-day concert at the Amadeo Roldán Theater, with three pianos onstage and three groups: Frank Emilio with Cachaíto, myself, and Ondina; plus Amadito and Changuito on percussion and Eduardo Ramos on bass; and Paquito with Chucho, Enrique Plá, and Fabián García Caturla on bass. I wrote a piece inspired by Ornette's "Double Quartet" in which we both played alto and flügelhorn. Chucho was supposed to have written something for this grand finale of both groups playing together, but apparently he had a problem at the laundry or something, so he just took a look at my "score" (just a few bars) and told me, "It's OK, just like what I intended to do." I also wrote something called "Raveliana" based on two melodies by Ravel, and Paco played it with Chucho and a quartet at Bellas Artes. I remember Chucho changed the chords, took out the augmented fifths, and made it sound more like Chucho, not Ravel.

In a recent interview Paquito gave, I read the inevitable question of the biggest influences on him by other sax players. I remember we used to listen to everyone: Bird, of course, and James Moody and Sonny Stitt, and old-timers Johnny Hodges and Benny Carter, and also Konitz, Art Pepper, Lou Donaldson, Gigi Gryce, McLean, Paul Desmond. . . . And the tenor players too, from Hawkins to Coltrane. The journalist insists on Desmond, and I don't agree. (By the way, I met Desmond at Birdland in the fifties. He went to the bar and I introduced myself, which I never do, and he goes, "Incredible, you mean they know ME in Havana?" Beautiful person, and we had three gin and tonics.) And there's a lot of Bird in Paquito and everyone else, including Konitz and Pepper. One thing in common is a humorous zest for interpolations. I find people like Phil Woods and Bobby Watson more in the same groove as Paco, and I also think of Dexter Gordon and Cannonball Adderley, even if Dexter played tenor, as possible influences. Because Paquito listened to everything. And these sax players I mention can play a ballad copying this lyricism and sheer joy and beauty and still you feel that swing. Now, Dexter and Cannonball have a special sense of humor and technique. For them it's just a tool subordinated to expressive needs, and there is drama and, yes, the blues and hard times that make you tell a true story. It's difficult for them to make ends meet because it's hard to communicate humor seriously.

Just a small part of this humor would be the use of interpolations by quoting a phrase of a well-known standard not related to the improvised discourse. Many critics tend to neglect or criticize this practice, which they consider to be in bad taste and showing a lack of inventiveness. They're wrong: such quotes belong to the classical tradition as well as to Afro-Cuban danzones and other styles. I remember Paquito's rendition of an up-tempo number

Clarinet duo with Phil Woods (Town Hall, New York, 1985)

where he quotes "Mona Lisa" three times, and you thank him for doing it. Cachao used to quote Broadway hits and even Debussy in his danzones. Bird quoted "Mon Homme" in his masterpiece rendition of "Just Friends," and Big Nick Nicholas gained immortality with his tenor solo in "Manteca" with his harsh, macho sound and unexpected quote of "Blue Moon." Dexter Gordon in a single CD quoted six tunes: "Fascinating Rhythm," "Fools Rush In," "Jarabe Tapatio," "In Other Words," "Poinciana," and "Take Me Out to the Ball Game." And I already mentioned Desmond, with his impeccable taste and lyricism. Paco goes further: he's the only one who actually laughs with his horn and who also has that facility to communicate that was a trademark of Cannonball. *My Sax Life* makes me think about my next book on jazz after *Cubano Be Cubano Bop: 100 Years of Jazz in Cuba* (English version), with a beautiful preface by Paco himself. (Yeah, this is a commercial.) Meanwhile, Paq's dreams of New York City really do come true, and every musical or literary success of his fills me with as much joy as if they were my own. Thanks, Paq-Man.

In the year 2002, the Smithsonian Institute in Washington asked me to write an introductory note for the English version of Leonardo Acosta's magnificent book on Cuban jazz. Here is what I had to say about this remarkable colleague:

The Jazz Grotto

It was one of those luminous nights in Havana in the early sixties, when our little gang of "Los Chicos del Jazz," cruising down Twenty-third Street, arrived at the nightclub La Gruta (the Grotto). We were going to listen to Free American Jazz, a group founded by pianist Mario Lagarde and saxophonist Eddy Torriente, two African Americans who had just established themselves in Cuba. It must surely have been Friday or Saturday, since the small club located in the basement of the La Rampa movie house was completely packed with jazz aficionados, or simply with curious people attracted by those musicians who had arrived from the mythical "Forbidden North." The rest of the quartet consisted of drummer Pepe El Loco and, on the contrabass, the composer Julio Cesar Fonseca, a picturesque character of the bohemian Havana nights.

Down at La Gruta, when we finally cut through the crowd and smoke, we found Eddy El Americano seated on one of the high stools at the bar with a very cold beer in front of him. "Hey, *campeón del mundo*," shouted the charming saxophonist, raising his frothy beer mug into the air. It was his signature salute to all those colleagues who came each evening to listen to his beat-up Conn alto sax, which he played in that old style inspired by his idol Paul Gonçalves.

Behind the bar, in the reduced space of the bandstand, and occupying Eddy's place next to his compatriot at the piano, there was a young, skinny man wearing glasses, looking somewhat like Paul Desmond. Hanging from his neck was an enormous silver-plated baritone sax made in Czechoslovakia.

Mario Lagarde counted off a medium bounce tempo and, following a brief introduction of Pepe's hi-hat, the group began to play his composition "La Gruta Blues." The first solo was taken by the saxophonist, who immediately caught our attention, mainly because with the exception of the few Gerry Mulligan, Serge Chaloff, or Harry Carney recordings that my father or Amadito Valdés played at home, this was the first time that we heard a baritonist playing bebop lines live! At that time I was almost a child and was fascinated with the musical language of that skinny guy with the enormous shiny saxophone who was none other than Leonardo Acosta.

"You're Tito's son! How's your old man doing? I haven't seen him in years," he said enthusiastically when I went to greet him at the end of the set. This was the beginning of a solid friendship that has lasted till today, and from then on I've deeply admired Leonardo's musical and literary labor. Along with Camille Saint-Saëns, Artie Shaw, Nicolas Slonimsky, and a few others, Leonardo Acosta belongs to that select group of musicians who also possess the ability to communicate through the written word. That's why I've always thought he was the most appropriate person to tell the story of what happened in the past hundred years of jazz music on our island. I hope you'll enjoy this new book of Leonardo's (which reads like a novel, as Nat Chediak would say) as much as I enjoyed his baritone solo that faraway evening in Havana at La Gruta club.

Verde que te quiero verde.

Green, how much I want you green.

—Federico García Lorca

THE ARMY

I wouldn't be surprised if Commander Raúl Castro, minister of the FAR (Revolutionary Armed Forces), were an avid reader of García Lorca because he wanted us green, and he made us wear green uniforms for the three long years of the longest compulsory military service on this planet.

The initial news about the establishment of the unpopular SMO (Compulsory Military Service) had the impact of a bomb being dropped. All of those possibly affected by the new law began to think creatively about how to avoid wearing green. There was an avalanche of medical certificates, flat feet, only-family-support conditions, helpless grandmothers, productive professionals in key positions, and every other excuse imaginable to avoid wearing the color favored by Lorca and by the closet *loca* (queer), according to the prevailing rumor about the sexual preferences of Raulito, the dreadful little brother of the Maximum Leader. But everything was useless—sooner or later, most of us, the young men between the ages of sixteen and twenty-seven, had to respond to the "call of the fatherland."

I received the dreaded military telegram in April 1965, shortly before I turned seventeen, while enjoying my stint with the Teatro

With my closest friend Felix Durán during our army days (1965–68)

Musical and finishing my studies at Marianao's Alejandro García Caturla Conservatory.

The truth is that the fatherland was calling me at a rather inopportune time. Influential parties such as Enrique Jorrín, Tony Taño, Félix Guerrero, and Rafael Lay—among other cultural celebrities—wrote letters to the military committee stressing my supposed "vital importance" in the construction of the new revolutionary culture. But according to an old Cuban proverb, *Cuando el mal es de cagar, no valen guayabas verdes* (rough translation: "When the shit hits the fan, there's nothing you can do"). In other words, I had to respond to the damn call of the fatherland, like any typical Cuban.

And you know what? After all that, I'm not sorry I did. The army is a unique experience in the education of a young man. Sharing living quarters with so many other different men teaches one to respect the space of others, willingly or unwillingly. Since our only other option was to be jailed for desertion, we took the course of involuntary cohabitation that was "generously" offered by the revolution.

Along with many other youngsters, I had to report early one morning to the stadium of the Pedro Marrero Brewery (formerly La Tropical Brewery), ready to depart for "a location in Cuba" (which could have been Africa or Bolivia) to comply with the military summons.

That morning my father, who even in pajamas didn't lose his commanding presence, unexpectedly informed me that it would be impossible for him to accompany me to the stadium to say farewell and that my mother would be in charge of transporting me there.

"Besides, it's not such a big deal," he abruptly added. "If all the kids your same age are going, who are you to stay home like a mamma's boy?" At home, Tito's orders were not discussed, so my mother and I climbed into our 1941 Plymouth and left, but about halfway to our destination we had to turn around to get something that I had forgotten at home.

When I opened the door of our home, I found my father sitting in my favorite armchair in front of our Admiral TV set, which was turned off, crying inconsolably over my departure. That was the only time that I saw the former sergeant major of the infantry cry.

I was assigned to complete military training at a unit called Barbosa, near one of the very few Catholic seminaries that were left on the island. Other fellow recruits were placed in a training school located in the area known as La Vaca Muerta (Dead Cow). This curious name was adopted after a spacecraft launched by NASA from Cape Canaveral landed on an unfortunate cow that happened to be grazing in the area. Not surprisingly, the Communists put together a tremendous spectacle featuring the rocket and the cow, parading the strange interplanetary object through the whole town along with images of the poor animal, "a victim of imperialist brutality."

A little later some of us were moved to the military unit at El Salado Beach. In keeping with the old adage "Necessity is the mother of invention," I found sooner rather than later three or four amateur musicians (fellow companions of misfortune) and organized a combo, with the idea of freeing myself from the military exercises, the Marxism-Leninism classes, and particularly the act of rising at break of day. The only professional musicians of that fledgling military combo were the very fine five-keyed flutist Joaquín Oliveros, who used to play that typical wooden Cuban instrument with Abelardo Barroso's Sensación Orchestra, and drummer Tony Valdés, who suffered from frequent bouts of depression.

Before Tony was drafted, he had been playing with Felipe Dulzaides's group, a popular musical attraction of the nightlife—or whatever was left of it—in Havana. As a new recruit, the poor guy's nervous condition worsened daily to the point where he began to slowly pull chunks of his hair out by the roots. The military camp was located next to the coast, and you could see in the far distance the Riviera Hotel, where Tony's wife worked as a showgirl at the Copa Room, and this made him even sadder. Tony's only moments of happiness came when our small combo played together.

We even had a local radio program transmitted at noon through the camp's loudspeakers. Fortunately (or unfortunately), the director of the training school, Lieutenant Campos, was crazy about Mexican music, so I had to set up an extensive repertoire of Mexican *rancheras* and *corridos*, but the only vocalist to be found happened to be a rock singer—a very hairy guy who looked like a cross between Fred Flintstone, King Kong, and Sammy Davis Jr. but who happened to be white.

With the combo known as El Saladito, we conducted "artistic tours" through other military units and provided entertainment at political events and parties organized in the homes of Commie big shots. That's how things went until one morning when someone came with an order to move me to Military Unit 3076, which was the military band of the general commanding staff of the MINFAR (Ministry of the Revolutionary Armed Forces).

A couple of days after I left, a fellow soldier told me that Tony, who was at the time a very strong young man, got up from his bunk during an after-lunch break and started screaming like a madman, throwing all kinds of objects and people through the windows. Everyone was scared shitless in his barracks. News of his crazy rampage spread quickly, and Lieutenant Campos declared a general alert in the camp. Several men were needed to restrain Tony and finally take the deranged drummer to the hospital. He never came back to that unit or any other military installation.

In those days, the military band was still sufficiently disorganized to give us a certain margin for mischief, and we played countless practical jokes in the big house where we lived on the corner of Luis Estévez and Parraga streets, in the neighborhood of La Víbora. Within a short time, the jokes reached such a level that the house became a menace for unsuspecting souls. Anything could happen there—an enormous toad was slipped under a pillow, a huge rat and all her progeny were slipped inside a tuba. . . . It was also common for a powerful gush of icy water to be flung through a window, disrupting a good night's sleep and making you leap in terror from your bunk bed. Or you could wake up from your siesta with a horrible rubber tarantula glued to your chest.

In the band dormitories there were some metallic cabinets

between our bunk beds that were held together by hundreds of tiny screws that could easily be removed. One smart-ass recruit decided to totally unscrew one of the cabinets, leaving it lightly suspended between the beds. As a result, when Sergeant Depestre arrived silently at dawn and tried to open the door of his cabinet, it collapsed like a house of cards and created the most infernal noise that could be imagined. The sergeant, fuming with anger, challenged to a duel "the son of a bitch who's responsible for this fucking shit!" Of course, everyone remained totally silent while concealing their laughter.

In those soldiers' quarters, I witnessed the most violent and furious tomato fights as well as some weird incidents, like the time when Soroa, a tall, blond clarinetist, was taking some pills that made his shit turn as bright green as a Heineken beer bottle. One time, after Soroa had used the bathroom, Pichardo—a trumpeter from Matanzas—entered and, upon discovering the large green feces that emerged halfway out of the water, it occurred to him to decorate them with little bristles that he pulled out from the yellow broom that was always left there to clean the place. A little later we heard a soldier named Matos come running out of the bathroom, pistol in hand, yelling at the top of his lungs, "*Coño*, there's a monster coming out of the toilet!"

Around that time, the whole country was canvassed to select the delegation that would represent Cuba in the Ninth World Festival of Youth and Students to be held in the city of Algiers in North Africa. The slogan selected for the propaganda campaign was "The Best Ones Go to Algeria." The best and the brightest of Cuban youth were selected according to multiple categories of the socialist society: sports, politics, culture, education, sheepish behavior, and informant networking.

Considering my well-deserved reputation as an incorrigible and mischievous practical joker, I assumed I'd never be chosen, and I was not even interested in being among the "best ones" chosen to go to Algeria. However, since I wasn't half bad at blowing the sax, I was selected to join the delegation's orchestra, and the military band issued a temporary relocation order for me so that I could join this new mission assigned by the revolution.

The delegation was housed in the luxurious Comodoro Hotel that years earlier had been a very beautiful tourist resort in the exclusive Miramar neighborhood, facing the Florida Strait. It was much more comfortable and romantic than the military school at La Vaca Muerta or that damned band directed by the idiotic Lieutenant Forneiro in La Víbora. Following my natural instincts, I got ready to pass the time as well as possible as a delegate on my new "international mission."

The first thing I did was to fall head over heels in love with a girl from Santa Clara who sang pretty well but played the clarinet as well as I play the *bandoneón*. Nevertheless, I believe that love is more deaf than blind, and to my ears, she sounded better than Benny Goodman. But the girl never paid any attention to me and later married some pretty boy who was a fencing champion and owned a nice 1957 American two-door sports coupe. And to top it off, the guy was a jazzophile like me, and he later became my friend, the son of a bitch. No hard feelings!

At the same place, I met two phenomenal musicians from Puerto Padre, the trombonist Juan Pablo Torres and pianist/drummer Emiliano Salvador, who was almost a child at that time. Both of them would much later gain international recognition. They hooked up in the cultural delegation with a very funny guitarist and great *sonero* named Cotán, who used to drink *aguardiente* like tap water and who I guess by that time had been surviving without a working liver for years. He was quite a character, a big guy with dark skin, a rusty voice, and reddish eyes. I'll always remember him with affection, not just for his musical talents but also for that special personal charm that radiates from some natives of Cuba's Oriente Province. If my mother heard this, she would say, "Well, of course, he's from the Oriente, right?"

I think the last time I saw Cotán was at the Club Rio. Somehow this clever troubadour found a way to stay in Havana after that crazy adventure in Algeria. There he formed a group with his son, who was a good jazz-rock guitarist. The band's name was Cotán and His Timba-Rock—a combination that to me is as surrealist as a group called Pavarotti and Led Zeppelin.

At the Comodoro, the artistic section had three musical groups: Cotán's group (with Emiliano and Juan Pablo), the all-female group from Santa Clara called Las Llitem, and a large orchestra that could switch from jazz to *charanga* or to whatever was needed, whose musicians included yours truly. The musical vibes were great. We spent our days rehearsing, jamming together, or climbing on the roof to spy on the girls in the showers with a telescope that Emiliano had brought.

But for an obscure reason that was only somewhat clarified later, the projected festival in Algiers suddenly got canceled.

Even in those days, the stories of Commander Efigenio Ameijeiras's boastful deeds remained fresh in our memories after he participated in the Algerians' little war against the Moroccans over some stupid territorial dispute. This was one of the first interventionist adventures conducted by the Havana government in Africa. When Algeria became independent from France, the island's government appointed as ambassador none other than the infamous Jorge "Papito" Serguera, who was previously the prosecutor responsible for dozens of death sentences by firing squad during the early days of 1959. In his new diplomatic mission, he would also be in charge of personally informing Castro about the latest developments in the young Arab state.

But Serguera was always a specialist in spreading misinformation, and this is perhaps why Castro, instead of sending him to face his own firing squad for the ridiculous mess he created in Algeria, decided to appoint him years later to head one of the most powerful mass media organizations in the nation.

Well, Papito created such a fuck-up in Africa that Fidel ended up saying horrible things in public about Ouari Boumedienne, a *güiro*-faced guy who was chief of the army. Right after he recovered from indigestion caused by a meal of very bad camel ribs and couscous, Boumedienne decided to stage a coup d'état to remove the recently inaugurated Ahmed Ben Bella, who was the first head of state of an independent Algeria. Afterward, Boumedienne threw Ben Bella in prison for about twenty years and swore on Allah's holy name never to eat camel ribs again.

At the same time, our Maximum Leader called one Buterflika (the Algerian minister of external relations) every name in the book, only to learn a few days later that the whole spat was due to a misunderstanding provoked by the stupidity and arrogance of Serguera.

After this tempest in a teapot was resolved and the festival was canceled, it was necessary to decide what the hell to do with an entire mountain of equipment, vehicles, time, propaganda, and exemplary (and not so exemplary) youngsters and oldsters housed at the Comodoro Hotel. And while waiting for the top hierarchy to come up with a solution, we were sent to Sierra Maestra to plant new trees throughout the Mayarí pine groves, which, it was claimed, had been decimated because of careless deforestation over many years.

The entire delegation was ordered to encamp in a location of the legendary mountain range, under the great tent of the National Circus. It made me recall my days as a member of Troop 16 of the Boy Scouts, until the new government decided that those ideas "imported from the perverse and brutal North" were not compatible with the ideals of Marx. Thus, the scout organization was dissolved, and then the concept of the *pioneros* (pioneers) was imported from the USSR. Whereas before we said, "Scouts always ready!" the slogan was now changed to "Pioneers for communism, we will be like Che!" Years later, when the Communist system collapsed in Eastern Europe, the mischievous Cuban writer Guillermo Cabrera Infante said, "Well, now that communism is finished you'll be asthmatic like Che."

But I enjoyed that expedition to the mountains of Mayarí. At age seventeen, that whole adventure and the circus tent was equivalent to an enormous troop of Boy Scouts camping under the moonlight, under the biggest camping tent ever imagined. I was in high spirits and determined to have a good time. Naturally, planting pines—an exhausting, boring activity, totally against my natural desires—was what I did the least. I spent hours taking afternoon naps under the shade of luxuriant trees, drinking rum, and chasing after the girl from Santa Clara (although I got no more than a telephone number from her!), while the spiritless "exemplary youth" (as the government propaganda put it) broke their Leninist asses carrying bags of soil and digging holes with pickaxes and shovels under a scorching sun.

However, I must admit that I got a little carried away and provoked the civic attitude (meaning informant reaction) of some of the exemplary assholes. So upon my return to the capital, I was publicly expelled, along with a couple of other seditious musicians, from the immaculate bosom of that flock of human sheep who were scheduled to travel immediately on the gigantic Russian ship *Gruzzia* to Bulgaria and the USSR.

After I returned to the military band of the general commanding staff, the next two and a half years of my life were marked by professional frustrations, abuses of power, intimate friendships, military funerals, gratuitous enemies, cans (many cans!) of Baltic sardines, good musicians, conductors (horrible, as usual), terrible (very terrible) musicians, sugarcane cutting, incredible jokes, (in)voluntary work, and all of that in exchange for seven pesos—the generous salary assigned by Raúl, the Lorca-inspired *loca*, from her closet at the MINFAR's penthouse.

As a young man forced to become a soldier under adverse conditions, I learned to cohabit with others, which is the best way to learn about mankind and become a man. Particularly in a place where your partner on night-watch duties—or even the one sleeping in the adjacent bunk—can be your friend or your worst enemy, and sometimes, in such a political system, you cannot tell the difference.

It was there that I heard for the first time the horrors of the political prisons in my own country, narrated in a low voice by a fellow recruit with whom I became good friends at the beginning. He had several relatives in different jails within the immense gulag that the entire island had been turned into by the Communists. From his lips, I heard frightening tales of bayonetings, massive beatings, tortures, and men who had been living and sleeping for years on top of their own and their cellmates' excrement. Fifteen years later, in Madrid, I heard the exact same stories from the mouth of Rodolfo Rodríguez and in the testimony of other former political prisoners who had been recently released from Cuban jails. An account of their ordeal was eventually published in the moving book *Against All Hope*, by the Cuban poet Armando Valladares, who spent twenty-two years in many of those diabolically repressive prisons.

But it appears that few pay attention to someone else's suffering, and I always run into some shithead who insists on talking to me about the good things that the Cuban Revolution brags about. Like that Spanish journalist who asked for my "impartial opinion about the education, public health, and revolutionary work conducted by Fidel in favor of the Cuban proletariat." I advised him that since it was still during business hours, he should contact the Israeli embassy and ask the distinguished ambassador for his opinion regarding Volkswagen, Hitler, and the economic prosperity of the German people during the Führer's mandate.

All dictators, whether right wing or left wing, always do some positive things in the beginning. Later on, they lose their heads and start fucking with everyone's existence.

"Hey, Cantinflas, drop that little black cornet and finish peeling the potatoes. . . . Shit, it's almost time for lunch and the people will be here any minute!"

I never knew the reason why Piloto, the military band's cook, called me Cantinflas, after the comical character created by the Mexican actor Mario Moreno. I'm convinced that he didn't know my real name. I suppose that such a humble *guajiro* (rural peasant) never suspected how much affection my father had for him ever since he had first gotten off the number 100 bus right in front of my house to relate stories to my old man about his son "Cantinflas," the kitchen helper. According to my father and other more or less reliable sources, the truth is that it was the cook himself who really looked like Cantinflas, considering his inelegant clothes, his very short pants, and his tendency to tuck in his shirt only halfway. He wore an old Colt .45 revolver that he never removed from his waist, not even when he was cooking. The trumpeter Andresito Castro asserted that if Piloto ever pulled the trigger, the gun would shoot out a bunch of split peas and sardines that had been trapped in its barrel for years and years.

Piloto had a very peculiar concept of geography. We were able to verify this on a certain occasion after a shipment of canned meat arrived. This *guajiro* began to read the label in a loud voice, pronouncing the words clearly and very slowly: "Made in Bulggoria . . . *Coño*, look, it's Mexican."

A favorite form of punishment of the bandleaders was to assign a recruit to be the kitchen boy, so I spent a great part of my brilliant military career with my friend Piloto, who may not have been the ideal person to be chef at the Ritz Hotel but was a truly unforgettable character for us all.

Around that time, Lieutenant Rolando Forneiro—the head and director of that musical-military unit—devoted himself to snagging every talented young musician he could find. As a result the band's quality improved from near pathetic to almost symphonic, mainly because of the young musicians assigned there against their will.

Among the other staff members, there was a private named José Luis Oropesa who was a catalyst for all the musical talent because he could orchestrate very well. He transcribed symphonic works of Shostakovich, Tchaikovsky, Weber, and Mayakovsky that we performed in concerts. But as far as jazz was concerned, forget it. Particularly after one evening when Lieutenant Forneiro showed up unexpectedly while we were in the middle of a jam session and ordered:

"Stop that immediately! I don't want to hear another note. *Compañeros*, jazz music represents the enemy!" With those words, he turned off the Russian hi-fi that played albums by Bird, Dizzy, Kenton, and Miles. Thereafter, we had to listen secretly to Willis Conover's shortwave jazz program on the Voice of America.

That was a very difficult time for young people because the government relentlessly persecuted every foreign manifestation of creativity, and jazz was specifically included. Unfortunately for me, jazz was one of the things that I most loved ever since I was an infant.

At theaters and other cultural centers, a frenetic witch hunt began against homosexuals, too. Many valuable professionals in the performing arts were targeted, so we were left without makeup specialists, choreographers, beauticians, dancers, hairdressers, scenographic directors, and wardrobe consultants. Without those individuals, it was practically impossible to conduct any opera, ballet, or cabaret shows.

As part of a highly virulent speech delivered in Moscow on November 2, 1962, an apoplectic Nikita Khrushchev said, "Some of these so-called modern dances are completely improper, and judging from these experiments, I'm justified in thinking that you are pederasts, and for that you can get ten years. . . . Gentlemen, we're declaring war on you!"

Later on, after biographer Peter Watson gained access to the shadowy KGB archives, he found out that Khrushchev personally had signed a death sentence against ballet dancer Rudolf Nureyev at that time, one year after the secret trial for Nureyev's defection in Paris in 1961.

Back in Cuba, it was truly painful for us to stand by and witness the terror and the injustice committed against unfortunate gay people who had worked with us for so many years, whose performances were as good as anybody else's but who were now fired and treated like criminals only because of their sexual preferences.

Within that whole tragedy, a very funny incident took place that made all of us feel happy because it involved a conflict between a very beloved and admired person and a completely despicable one.

It was said that a very talented writer and theater director in Havana had a varied menu of sexual habits and could implement them with a genital organ that looked like a clarinet and delighted ladies and ephebi alike. Well, one afternoon, in the middle of a re-hearsal, a goon arrived from the CTCR (Confederacíon de Trabajadores de Cuba Revolucionaria). He convened an urgent meeting with all members of the theater troupe, including the well-endowed director, in order to inform them that the "citizen" in question, as ordered by who-knows-who, had been immediately dismissed from his job. "Any questions?" asked the repugnant myrmidon, after finishing his speech, as he dried the sweat from his forehead on the sleeve of his olive green uniform.

But since everyone knew what the very respected director was up to and the sorts of adventures he was having, no one dared to say anything. Finally the director himself asked very calmly, as if he was curious to know why he was dismissed, "And can you tell me why, *compañero?*"

"What do you mean, 'why,' *compañero!*" the Commie cried out, visibly upset. "Everyone here knows about your homosexuality, and the revolution only wants real men in its cultural cadres. Do you understand me now?"

"Real men?" replied the director with a sneer. "That's precisely what your wife always tells me when we're in bed, that I'm a real man, unlike you, so I don't understand how you can accuse me today of being a faggot," he concluded triumphantly.

"I've read your manuscript, and although that incident didn't happen exactly as you recounted, so many years have passed that it's not worth it to dwell on ancient and painful wounds," the artist in question once wrote to me in a beautiful letter. "Although I can tell you God wished that the only son of that man who wanted to offend me and cause me so much grief has turned out to be the most flamboyant queer imaginable. He's always seated in the first row of my presentations, when he's not screaming hysterically at the ballet."

Twice a week, I was given a release to attend harmony and clarinet classes with Félix Guerrero and Enrique Pardo at the García Caturla Conservatory, which was located a few blocks away from my home in Marianao. This helped to relieve my feeling that I was involuntarily confined at the band building, although band duty was much better than serving in a combat unit—not to mention being sent to the horrible forced labor camps of UMAP (Military Units of Assistance to Production) in Camagüey Province.

Labor fields that resembled Nazi concentration camps, the UMAP were especially created not to so much to produce goods as to repress certain sectors of the country's youth who were not eligible to serve in the armed forces. This repression was aimed directly at those who were openly homosexual or religious.

WORK WILL TURN YOU INTO MEN, threatened the enormous billboards located at the entrances to the camps, which were surrounded by barbed wire. It was as if the cruel labor camps would make their inmates doubt the sacred existence of Buddha or Jehovah, or make them renounce their most intimate and private sexuality.

Thousands of valuable young men—including political dissidents —were forced to serve in this satanic project. Among them was one of the most brilliant and contradictory characters in my country's entire musical history, the Bayamo-born troubadour Pablo Milanés.

Pablito, as everyone calls him affectionately, sang for some time with Los Bucaneros (Buccaneers), a great vocal group, led by the pianist Robertico Marín, along the jazz lines of the Hi-Los. Pablo also worked with a quartet of young black men who belonged to a

Seventh-Day Adventist church. Their group was called Cuarteto del Rey (Quartet of the King), and the king in question wasn't Elvis, the King of Rock and Roll, or Tito Puente, the King of the Timbal, but Jesus Christ.

He was one of the younger members of the *filin* movement that appeared in some Havana nightclubs. These were songs about love and romance and took many elements from jazz, particularly in terms of harmony. It was a music born from the romantic Havana nights of the fifties and early sixties.

I remember a certain night when through the door of the Cabaret Caribe's kitchen, where musicians got together between shows to have a cup of coffee, there appeared none other than Che Guevara, accompanied by Anastas Mikoyan, an Armenian who was the minister of industry of the USSR (whose grandson would much later become one of the first post-Stalinist Soviet rock promoters and the founder of the popular and successful band the Flowers [*Tsveti*]). In our country Guevara held the same position as the Armenian in Nikita Khrushchev's administration. By that time Guevara had successfully fucked up every single industry that had crossed his path since his arrival. This man was so irresponsible that, although he'd never set foot in Cuba before, he had the balls to impose a revolution upon the natives of a country that he didn't know. He also even ordered the execution of many Cubans during his tenure as military chief at La Cabaña fortress in Havana. But thank God (and the CIA, I guess), all that is left of that twisted character are several thousand T-shirts with his face on them, available mainly at Cuban tourist stores for purchase with American dollars only!

After the greetings, welcoming remarks, and a little forced joke made by the arrogant Argentinean adventurer, Cuco—an old-guard Communist who played the tenor (quite badly) with the show's orchestra—asked the Soviet visitor, half in Spanish and half in Russian, what he thought of Havana.

"Very beautiful!" answered the politician enthusiastically, adding more calmly, this time through an interpreter, as if making sure that his sincere words were well understood, "Never lose the lovely nightlife that you have here."

A few years later, in 1970, when the nightclubs were closed, the government ended up annihilating the nightlife that enchanted Mikoyan and so many visitors. They killed the bohemian lifestyle and that pretty star-eyed black girl that symbolized the city in the seductive lyrics of César Portillo, and in her dark arms, in silence and dreaming about past glories, the Americanized *filin* died as well.

Dressed in a fashionable Continental-style suit and wearing glasses similar to Paul Desmond's, there appeared in the penumbra of the small club Karachi a very thin shape of a young singer who intoned with a delicate and very clear voice, "*Soy tan feliz . . . nada me preocupa en el mundo!*" ("I'm so happy . . . nothing in the world worries me!")

That was the last time that I saw the great Pablo Milanés in freedom. A little later he was sent, along with thousands of young men, to serve three years at the tenebrous UMAP camps set up to "assist the harvest" in Camagüey Province.

Gossips specializing in Havana nightlife (whatever was left of them) claimed that while recovering from a suicide attempt at the concentration camp, Pablo composed "Mis Veintidós Años" ("My Twenty-two Years"), a song recorded by Elena Burke that became an anthem of hope for those who were able to emerge physically and mentally healthy from that inferno.

> *Y en cuanto a la muerte amada*
> *Le diré, si un día la encuentro*
> *Adios, que de ti no tengo*
> *Interés en saber . . . ¡Nada!*

> With regard to beloved death
> I will tell her,
> If one day we meet,
> Good-bye—about you I wish to know . . . nothing!

Inexplicably, Pablo ended up offering his enormous talent to his own tormenters, becoming the official singer of a system that just a short time earlier had applied its whole repressive power against him. He placed himself at the service of a dictator whose devotion to art never went beyond the showgirls at the Tropicana. One time I found him near the studios of the former CMQ television station, and I asked him why I had not seen him on television for such a long time.

"Hey, Paco, my friend !" exclaimed Pablo when he saw me, with that simple and friendly manner reminiscent of *filin* nights. "No, brother, there's no more television for me," he said firmly. "Shit, every time I take them a new song, Papito [Serguera, the director of national radio and television] has to listen to it first. Between him, the security goons of the revolutionary ethics commission, and the party, I'm forced to make changes to the text. They're worried that this or that could be misinterpreted. I'm between the sword and the wall. The problem is that when everything is worked out, the song has become outdated. No way! Papito and his television can go to hell!"

The top-ranking leaders always made sure that the least qualified individuals headed the cultural institutions. Like when Commander Jorge "Papito" Serguera was named head of the ICRT (Cuban Institute of Radio and Television), which was as irrational as appointing Anastasio Somoza as director of the School of Jazz History and Improvisation at the University of New Orleans.

Commander Serguera could be described as an ill-mannered, imperious, abusive, narcissistic, sexist, arrogant, incompetent, skirt-chasing beast. After his triumphant and almost Messianic entry into the complex world of the mass media, he quickly specialized in making as miserable as possible the lives of thousands of office clerks, actors, cameramen, political policemen, maintenance workers, elevator operators, musicians, orchestral conductors, script writers, sound technicians, broadcasters, doormen, dancers, librarians, wardrobe mistresses, transcribers, hairdressers, choreographers, piano tuners (and untuners), cooks, rural poets, makeup specialists, drivers, watchmen, and so many other employees of that gigantic enterprise, which aimed to exasperate (even more) the rest of the population from one end of our island to the other through radio and television.

In a very short time, this commissar earned a variety of nicknames, such as the one given in contempt by the jokers of the rock group Los Dada, who called him El Barbero de Sevilla (Barber of Seville) in just revenge for his obsessive assault against beards and long hair, which were so fashionable among the youth of that time. Not surprisingly, the prohibition against beards didn't extend to the untouchable Barbudo de Cebolla—a nickname applied to the Maximum Leader due to his *barbudo* (long-bearded) appearance and *cebolla* (onion) smell—and his sidekick, Che Guevara, and other authorized long-haired characters that we all know.

One of Serguera's favorite sports was the indiscriminate pursuit of songs whose content was deemed harmful to the development of the new society. One of the first songs targeted by his ideological rifle was "Anduriña," a very popular tune recorded by the Spanish duo Juan y Junior, whose simple lyrics narrated the story of a little girl who walked out of her town and never returned, having become lost in time. The final chorus repeated mournfully, "*¿Anduriña, dónde estás?*" ("Anduriña, where are you?") Well, that little song was taken off the air. Why? It was claimed that thanks to the great work of the CDR (Committee for the Defense of the Revolution, the organization located on every block, whose purpose was to spy on the neighbors), along with the devoted and sleep-deprived combatants of the Ministry of the Interior, "neither Anduriña nor anyone else can get lost so easily, because we know where everyone is here," according to Papito's own words. "Anduriña" was the first of an endless blacklist of forbidden songs, many of which were exquisite musical jewels that could never be enjoyed by our people.

Among the many men who fell under the orders of the unyielding commander Serguera was Armando Calderón, who earned his bread for a few decades with the unusual job of providing voice-overs while silent movies played on TV. As old footage of Buster Keaton, Charles Chaplin, Laurel and Hardy, and other actor-comedians of that time rolled, the old man would make them speak, and even sing, with a proper voice.

Calderón would give his characters funny names like the Marquise of Clothespins, Balloon Face, and the dog Tribilín. They would almost always, near the end of the episode, find themselves in the most incredibly ridiculous and far-fetched of situations. At the end of his show every Sunday, the imaginative performer always ended with his lively "And that's all for today, my little frieeeeeeends!"

Well, it seems that one afternoon (and maybe it was because Armando Calderón was exhausted, or because he had had one glass of rum too many, or simply because Balloon Face, Tribilín, or the policeman Cat Whiskers was involved in such a complex and confusing situation), the poor man, his mind overwhelmed, brought his show to a decisive close, live and on national television, screaming at the top of his lungs, "AND THIS HAS TURNED INTO SOME FUCKED-UP MESS, MY DEAR LITTLE FRIENDS!!!"

In the pages of a Spanish newspaper the incomparable Cuban author Zoé Valdés observed, "I've recently finished reading a kick-ass book written by the illustrious Cuban musician Paquito D'Rivera. . . . And in his *Sax Life* the saxophonist tells that story about Armando Calderón, who instead of closing the show with his personal slogan 'And that's all for today, my little frieeeeeeends!' shouted, 'AND THIS HAS TURNED INTO SOME FUCKED-UP MESS, MY DEAR LITTLE FRIENDS!!!' . . . Of course those professional oppressors took it as a direct attack to the regime, and they told Calderón to go fuck himself and canceled the show—as to be expected. The phrase echoed among the people and has since become part of daily slang."

Frequently, humble individuals from the streets have inspired innumerable pages of the Cuban popular songbook. Among them one finds El Caballero de Paris, Candido el Billetero, Malanga, and so many other individuals who have been immortalized thanks to the creativity of our popular composers.

One of those characters was a black man called Bulé. It's said that he was already old when he was appointed to the position of General Manager-Technician for the Maintenance and Environmental Hygiene of Radio Progreso, which, translated to any language, living or dead, means "the guy who gets a salary for sweeping and mopping the floors, cleaning the toilets, and taking out the trash" from the Radio Progreso station in Havana.

But old Bulé took his job very seriously and didn't hesitate to exercise his environmental-hygienic authority by preventing anyone, even the Pope, from walking on the resplendent floors under his care until they were totally dry.

"Bulé is the one in charge here!" he vociferated like a general speaking to his troops and menacingly grabbed his mop and bucket, which gleamed under the sun like a military Roman shield.

Without knowing it, the intriguing character inspired the members of the orchestra Ritmo Oriental to create a delicious guaracha that soon made us all sing in chorus the catchy refrain that went "*Bulé . . . Bulé . . . aqui él que manda é Bulé.*" ("Bulé is the one in charge here.") But since the *Cubanos* tend to fight fire with fire, it eventually occurred to someone to refer to the Maximum Leader of the Revolution as Bulé, and the little joke, as witty and dangerous as it was, spread like wildfire.

"Bulé is going to make a speech today," the people used to say, since most of them didn't know of the existence of the old radio-station employee. "Let's see what he is going to take from us this time to send to some friendly country."

I can't prove that it was as a result of this curious incident, but what is certain is that the creators of that catchy tune had to, as we say in Cuba, *pasar el Niagara en bicicleta* (cross Niagara Falls on a bicycle) in order to board an international flight and go on tour, despite the fact that they were the best and the most popular dance orchestra at that time. And I repeat, "the best and the most popular," because those are terms that don't necessarily go hand in hand. Well, that could be the theme of another book with many more pages than this one.

Finally, Papito Serguera's foolish actions were so frequent and came in so many different colors that (as if following the tradition founded by Lenin in 1918) he fell apart, provoking one of those tantrums typically thrown by the commander-in-chief, who, as punishment, shipped him off to be ambassador to a capitalist country in Europe. What was never clarified was whether this punishment was intended for Papito, for the embassy employees, for the European country, or for all of the above.

In those days, Fidel gave one of his trademark dressing-downs on every radio and television station to Enrique Lusón, publicly firing him from his position as minister of transportation, a position as useless in Cuba as being named secretary-general of the platypus hunter's union in Greenland. The situation of public transportation is so chaotic that neither Lusón nor Henry Ford could resolve it, even if assisted by the Puerto Rican astrologer Walter Mercado and his colleague Arcadio, the famous sorcerer of Guanabacoa.

As Rolando Laserie would sing, "*Pasarán más de mil años, muchos más*" ("A thousand years and many more would pass") after Enrique Lusón left his ministry with more headaches than triumphs. And as far the public bus system—it's as bad as ever!

After years of repression, suddenly, in 1967, the cultural higher-ups decided to form an enormous big band with the best possible musicians to play "all types of music," mainly jazz and rock (???!!).

Who the hell can explain this abrupt change after so much pressure had been applied precisely against those types of music and their cultivators? That was the million-dollar question, and if I'd had the answer, it wouldn't have made a difference. The thing was that we had a jazz orchestra, and we were free to jam, at least until the

big boys changed their opinion, ordering us to exchange electric guitars for balalaikas and saxophones for helicons or something worse.

Let's not forget that back in 1929, when Ernest Krenek's jazz
operetta *Jonny Spielt Auf* was officially authorized to be performed
at the Nemirovich-Danchenko Theater in Moscow, the proletarian
ideologues succeeded in closing the show and then launched a campaign to ban the saxophone from the Soviet Union. But now it was
swing time for us, no questions asked, and that's how the Orquesta
Cubana de Música Moderna (Cuban Orchestra of Modern Music, or
OCMM) was born.

Dear Paco,

It feels almost like a century has passed since you asked me to
contribute an anecdote from the good old days in Havana for your
book. Perhaps you won't remember these things that I have jotted
down in this article, but I could add some additional details that I
remember clearly. To cite an example: I remember perfectly the
first session where Carlos del Puerto showed up. Anyway . . . here
goes, with admiration and friendship always.

Three Decades of Paquito

I moved restlessly in the auditorium seat, apprehensive about the
unexpected. I somehow felt that I was about to finally know why I
had this mysterious urge to go that concert after all. Only an hour
before I had sat at home, playing with the idea of attending this big-
band event, yet not quite making up my mind to get up and drive to
the Amadeo Roldán Theater in Havana's Vedado neighborhood. But
it was Saturday night in September 1967 and my procrastination
finally gave way to my instinct. After all, it was the first concert of
the newly created Cuban Orchestra of Modern Music, and judging
by its announced program and some well-known musicians in it,
there would be some live jazz.

There's a special place for big-band music in my failed musician's heart. As a jazz fan, I of course enjoy improvised combo performance and the spontaneity of individual solos. And because I'm a jazz fan, the predictably harmonious chords produced by brass ensembles over the rhythm of piano, bass, and a spectacular set of drums always put a smile on my face. It must have been this special touch that moved me at the last moment (when it was almost impossible to get to the concert on time) to turn to my twelve-year-old son, Carlos, and ask him if he would go with me. Sure. He was always ready for this kind of invitation.

And now, sitting in the audience, I knew it had been worth it. The musical arrangements were solid, the performance masterful. Yet we were not ready for what we were about to witness. The band was in the middle of a daringly fast version of "The Man I Love" when a young kid in his teens, extremely thin and wearing glasses and a crewcut, got up from his seat in the saxophone line, walked around behind the other players, and took the spotlight in the forefront, by the piano. At a designated dramatic riff, the youth jumped into his solo with such striking force that I had to grip the arms of my seat as if taking off in a jet fighter. But my ride was just beginning; I had heard nothing yet. After he gave one run to the melody itself, he embarked on various rounds of swift phrases built on incredibly agile fingerings, astonishing intervals executed by nimble fingers at the fastest tempo. The deep notes made his alto sax sound like a tenor; his highest pitches resembled a soprano saxophone ascending to peaks that cracked beautifully at the very top. All that with a remarkable sense of swing. Never losing beat no matter how many notes he managed to squeeze into his bars. Never sacrificing feeling to technical execution but taking his music on a journey from heart to mind to lips to fingers and out the bell of the instrument that two decades before had made history between the lips of Charlie Parker.

Of course, Parker came to mind. So did John Coltrane, Jackie McLean, Cannonball Adderley. All were present in the amazing performance of a seventeen-year-old: Paquito D'Rivera. It was the first time I saw him. I then learned that he had been a child prodigy and had performed at age eight with the symphony orchestra and later played as a guest of some Cuban jazz bands. At the time of the 1967 concert he was serving, like every other youth on the island, his mandatory time in the army and was allowed special leaves from the barracks to play with the new national band.

The next time I saw Paquito, he was swimming in the Riviera Hotel pool on a Sunday afternoon. A group of us had organized a jam session at a private home, and drummer Enrique Plá, Ernesto Calderín, and I went in my car to pick him up. We wanted him to come and play. As we approached the hotel we spotted him through a wire fence. Plá whistled to him, and he came and talked to us. He was wearing a red bathing suit and a black beret and was in his usual good mood. He was so skinny in his swimsuit that we teased him and asked him if he wore his skeleton on the outside. Paquito told us to wait for him and later joined us in one of the bars in the lobby of the hotel, where we had a few drinks before going to our jam session that Sunday afternoon. For years there were many, many other jam sessions in friends' houses and concerts of smaller groups where we enjoyed Paquito's marvelous music and his extraordinary sense of humor. I have never seen anyone with so much genius behave with so little ego. Modest, friendly, gentle, jovial, he was almost shy.

After completing his military service, Paquito also became a conductor of the big band, and his performances packed the concert house again. Some members of the orchestra, including Paquito, subsequently gave birth to the Modern Music Quintet. Later Paquito was a founder and codirector of the group Irakere, whose first concert was to become yet another landmark in the history of Cuban modern jazz. In the late seventies, at a time of high political antagonism between Cuba and the United States, Irakere came to the United States, played at Carnegie Hall, and won a Grammy.

The last time I saw Paquito in Havana was in 1979, when he was hosting one of the Jazz Mondays at Johnnie's Dream, a classy and spacious lounge by the Almendares River on the Miramar side. I was there helping jazz critic Horacio Hernández tape a session for his radio program. Months later I left Cuba and emigrated to Spain, all the time lamenting that one of the best jazz saxophonists in the world would waste his talent in a country that didn't appreciate his music. I was of course wrong. In 1980, during an Irakere tour, Paquito defected in Madrid and asked for political asylum. I ran into him one afternoon at the International Rescue Committee headquarters, where we were both being processed for U.S. visas. He flew to New York, I flew to Miami. We didn't see each other again until 1981, when he came on his first visit to the Cuban exile capital and with his Havana–New York ensemble packed a concert hall. What a coincidence and privilege for me to be the *Herald* reporter who covered the event!

In the following years Paquito became an important part of the American jazz scene. As a recent arrival, he was signed by Columbia and featured at the Newport Jazz Festival of 1981. There, he shocked the jazz mainstream by playing friendly mano a mano sessions with established alto saxophonists Phil Woods and Arthur Blythe. His memorable "Lover Man" of that festival stands among his best ballad executions ever, and his take on "Ornithology" carried so much strength that you must understand it as the genuine catharsis of a man who had just gained both political and artistic freedom.

Paquito's presence in the mainstream, however, has been on and off. He has opted to remain longer in the bubbling domain of the Latin jazz boom, where he has played a major role not only as the versatile musician he is but also as a mentor to a younger generation of Latin jazzists—Danilo Pérez, Claudio Roditi, Michel Camilo, Daniel Ponce, and many others—who received from Paquito the push they needed to launch their own successful careers.

Of the dozens of albums he recorded as leader or guest in all these years, my favorite continues to be his first in the United States: *Paquito Blowin'*. Although it has never been reissued on CD, some of its numbers later appeared in *The Best of Paquito.* And two decades after his group Irakere won the coveted Grammy, Paquito received the 1997 award in the Latin jazz category with his album *Portraits of Cuba.*

Is this a big deal to him? Something to brag or get cocky about perhaps? Nah! He may not wear his skeleton on the outside anymore, and he is closer to the half-century mark than to the age of that kid who stunned a Havana audience with his solo of a Gershwin song. But Paquito is still just Paquito—a warm *abrazo*, an enormous heart, and all that talent.

Carlos Verdecia

¿Tengo lo que tenía que tener?

Do I have what I ought to have?

—Nicolás Guillén

THE ORQUESTA CUBANA DE MÚSICA MODERNA

The truth is, I couldn't tell you, even under duress, why the hell the Orquesta Cubana de Música Moderna was established, so you'll have to wait until someone who was there decides to write another book or something like that, OK?

The surprising thing is that all of a sudden the government began to import electric guitars, amplifiers, U.S. drum sets, two Selmer saxophones, a Farfisa organ (that always sounded horrible in Chucho's hands, mainly because, as a great pianist, he hated any plastic shit), mouthpieces, accessories, and all those "imperialist instruments" that just a little earlier had been regarded as taboo.

Due to orders from up high, several key musicians were removed from their workplaces to participate in the project: the trombonist Linares, Cachaíto, and Luis Escalante came from the National Symphony; Chucho and Carlos Emilio came from the Teatro Musical; and others came from television orchestras—Pucho Escalante, Oscar Valdés Jr. and Sr., Andrés Castro, Barreto. . . . And at the head of this formidable ensemble, they placed none other than the legendary Armando Romeu, who had led the Tropicana Orchestra for twenty-five years.

Around that time, I was still playing in that fucked-up military band (remember?), but I got lucky when the head of the army, Commander

A poster for the Cuban Orchestra of Modern Music,
or OCMM

Raúl Castro, decided to take a military course in the USSR and left behind as acting chief one of the few Communist big shots who had a certain affinity with performing artists—Commander Juan Almeida. Despite my record as a mischievous practical joker, Almeida ordered my military unit to authorize my transfer to the new orchestra, as Romeu and the others had immediately requested that I be named soloist and lead alto of the new band.

At that time, I also performed occasionally with the National Symphony Orchestra, as well as in opera and ballet events, since we were sharing more or less the same venues. I remember as a very special highlight the concert in which Leo Brouwer presented his work Arioso a Charles Mingus, written for jazz group and symphony orchestra. I played alto in that work as a member of the group of soloists, along with Rafael Somavilla (piano), Orlando "Cachaíto" López (bass), Guillermo Barreto (drums), Leo Brouwer (electric guitar), and Manuel Duchesne (conductor).

To inject a more political tinge, the Communists arranged a debut performance of OCMM in Guane, a small town located in the westernmost region of the island (homeland of the great exiled Cuban five-keyed flute player José Fajardo), where a bunch of young students were working "voluntarily" in who-knows-what agricultural plan. But since we were delighted with our new jazz orchestra, for us it was the same to play in Guane or in Outer Mongolia, so we attempted to fuse Engels with Count Basie as well as we could.

Tours were organized throughout the entire country, including some tumultuous concerts at Havana's Amadeo Roldán and Karl Marx Theaters, where people would kill to go inside and listen to songs by the Beatles; Ray Charles; Blood, Sweat, and Tears; Chicago; and other foreign artists—the same songs that until recently could have resulted in serious sanctions. Further, it was even ordered that similar jazz groups be formed in the provinces of the interior.

On a certain occasion, my friend—the conductor, composer, and arranger Tony Taño—had obtained a special permit from my military unit to allow me to record some solos for an album with music of the acting commander Juan Almeida. Almeida always enjoyed the music world in Cuba (particularly the female vocalists). He was also a terrible songwriter, but when his tunes were arranged by Taño, Somavilla, and all those musical lions, they sounded as if they were written by Michel Legrand (well, let's not exaggerate). Because the commander had been pleased by the instrumentals that we recorded, Tony took advantage of the occasion to suggest to his friend Juanito that I be released from the active military service, which I was scheduled to complete six months later.

*   *   *

Very early the next morning, I was called to the office of my unit chief, who handed me a citation ordering me to appear in person at the building of the general commanding staff, in Revolution Square, that same afternoon at 1400 hours. I had no goddamn idea why I had received such an unexpected summons and was frightened that my constant practical jokes had finally come to the attention of military headquarters. I obeyed the instructions and appeared at the exact time and place specified in the order.

"Francisco Jesus Rivera Figueras?" the soldier assigned to the reception area of the ministry asked me.

"At your service, comrade, but this time I didn't do anything, I swear to you," I tried to joke around unsuccessfully with the stone-faced military officer, assuming that he knew all about my notorious history as a practical joker.

"Sign here and go to the top floor. The comrade minister is waiting for you in his office," he said very seriously.

"What did you say, my brother—comrade minister who?"

Without looking at me, the unimposing soldier dressed in olive green handed me an entry pass while pointing toward the private elevator of the minister of the Revolutionary Armed Forces of Cuba.

Tony Taño was there, sitting in a comfortable armchair next to the one I was ordered to occupy, in front of the desk occupied by Commander Juan Almeida, who was one of the very few blacks within the inner circle of absolute power around Castro. On the other side of the desk, the military chief was turning the pages of a file that appeared to be my military record. By some miracle I didn't shit in my pants.

After a few seconds of silence that started to turn awkward, I dared to speak to the high official:

"Did you like the album, Commander?" I asked shyly, referring to the recording of his songs I made with Tony Taño. Another long silence ensued, even more disturbing than the previous one, until the commander, without taking his eyes off the documents, commented very slowly and calmly:

"Tomatoes thrown at the post? . . . Spraying pressurized water

. . . throwing eggs inside the garrison . . . a nest of mice inside the tuba. . . . Hmm, this is a very interesting file," he said while taking a cold look at the orchestra conductor and then at me.

I was almost certain that those words marked the beginning of the end. The minister took a final glance at my problematic file, breathed deeply, handed me a paper that had been at the side of his desk since I arrived in his office, and told me authoritatively, "Take this paper and have it stamped outside, and then give it to the head of our military band. And get out of here before I change my mind." He had approved my dismissal from military service.

"*Sí, compañero Comandante!*" I responded, getting up energetically. I had never complied with an order with so much enthusiasm.

From that day, I was able to devote myself exclusively to orchestra work. One fine day, shortly after the OCMM was successfully formed, we heard about the upcoming World Expo '67 in Montreal, Canada, and that the Cuban Communist government wanted to participate by building a pavilion that would exhibit the "accomplishments" of the revolution, taking one of those big-time shows that didn't cost them anything, featuring beautiful *mulatas*, *rumberos*, magicians, and everything else including the kitchen sink, and, last but not least, a heavy-duty big band, the new orchestra led by Romeu and Somavilla.

Immediately, the cultural commissars gathered an enormous troupe. We were quartered in some houses in Miramar, and for a month they made us rehearse the gigantic show at the Karl Marx Theater. But I was already a bit doubtful I would join the tour because my parents were waiting for authorization to definitively leave the national territory along with my younger sister, and it wasn't likely that the authorities would allow me to travel with such a delegation to a capitalist country like Canada. (They'd never see my ass again, and they knew it!)

As it turned out, when I thought that everything was in order for my trip, the higher authorities surprisingly issued new instructions, indicating that Chucho, Paquito, Carlos Emilio, Cachaíto, and Enrique Plá were to be replaced by other musicians and that we were to remain in Havana as part of the Cuban Jazz Quintet getting ready for a very special appearance at Warsaw's Jazz Jamboree.

This sudden change of ballparks was like having a bucket of ice-cold water thrown on our heads. As usual, we had to remain silent and start rehearsing our quintet for that "important event" in Poland—which as it turned out, we never attended, just as three other members of the orchestra didn't attend Canada's Expo '67: Adalberto Lara (aka Trompetica, meaning "Little Trumpet"), the trombonist Modesto Echarte, and the trumpeter Jorge "El Negro" Varona. These three musicians didn't board the plane due to a direct request made by Manuel Duchesne, the appointed conductor of the National Symphony Orchestra and a very influential character in the cultural politics of our country. Duchesne later admitted making the request, but he never explained why he arbitrarily prevented those musicians from taking that flight.

Upon returning from Expo '67, the orchestra participated in many important events, such as the Varadero '67 Popular Song Festival, which felt as refreshing as drinking a capitalist Coca-Cola in the middle of so much socialist tension. Among the many international artists who attended the festival was Poland's Novi Quartet, a very good vocal jazz group that featured Adam Makovich as pianist. (Years later, he became my neighbor at New York's Manhattan Plaza Building, located at Forty-third Street and Ninth Avenue.) Another festival participant was the phenomenal Georgian singer July Shogely, who came with her husband Boris Richkof, a Russian pianist with a style similar to Oscar Peterson's. Around midnight, he would sit down behind the piano at the lounge of Varadero's Hotel International, backed by Cachaíto on bass along with Enrique Plá, who kept playing as if he were tied to his brushes. (Yeah, in those days it was still possible to find a drummer with a set of brushes inside his gig bag!) They kept playing until the following morning.

With the orchestra we recorded a few albums with an excessively varied repertoire. Our enthusiasm began to wane as soon as we started to accompany pop singers and variety shows and to participate in commercial recordings. Besides, the eternal wish to travel that dominated the minds of Cubans could not come true with such a large orchestral format. So when a Cuban variety show called *Saludo Cubano* was formed in 1968, a nine-piece group was extracted from the large orchestra to accompany it on the road. The extravaganza included Pacho Alonso, Los Bucaneros, Carlos Puebla, Ela Calvo, and Orquesta Aragón, among others, and we would tour through Bulgaria, Romania, Hungary, and some of the republics of the now defunct USSR —the friendly countries, as they were called by the hierarchs. After that trip, I realized that with friends like that, you don't need enemies.

Although I was happy about my upcoming trip to Eastern Europe, I was also saddened by the idea of being separated for almost three months from a beautiful girl who was driving me crazy (at the same time I was driving her thickheaded father crazy). The love story took place as follows:

I had, like almost everyone else, an involuntary father-in-law-to-be (and by this I mean against his will and paternal authority), Julio Colón. The Colón family was originally from Santa Clara, Las Villas Province, which along with Camagüey is one of the most racist regions on the island. The singer, painter, and multiinstrumentalist Bobby Carcassés courted Cecilia, the older sister of my girlfriend María Eugenia, and eventually married her, after a stormy, thunderous, and impetuous engagement. It was around that time that the extraordinary and unjustly underestimated composer Gilberto Valdés was in Havana. He was a pioneer, among other things, of the incorporation of Afro-Cuban elements into symphonic music, and he was returning from New York, seduced by the aroma of revolutionary palm trees. Back before Gilberto's fleeting palm-tree dream turned into a Red nightmare (which made him turn around and go right back to the concrete jungle), I visited him several times at his residence, which was said to have been given to him by Ernesto Guevara. His house was located in the exclusive neighborhood of Miramar, close to the Colón residence, and that's why I can't exactly remember now if it was at Gilberto Valdés's residence or at the Colón residence where one night we personally met Commander Ernesto "Che" Guevara, also a personal friend of Papá Colón.

"The pleasure is mine, young comrade," the long-haired adventurer with a star on his beret responded to my greeting, without much enthusiasm. Then he added, without the least interest, "And what do you do?"

"I'm a musician, Commander," I replied respectfully.

"No, no, no—you don't understand," he said, this time with an ironic smile and in a louder tone of voice, as if he wanted to be heard by everyone in that living room. "Not music—what I meant was the type of work you do, my dear boy."

They all laughed "spontaneously" at the humor of that Argentinean asshole: "Ha ha ha!"

Oh yes, that son of a bitch is so funny, I thought to myself but didn't say. Otherwise, you would now be reading Homer's *Iliad* or *Playboy* magazine, not my book.

"When it involves a white man and a black woman, it is called race mixing, but the other way around it is known as rape," a black American sociologist once said.

"But how is it possible, my child, that when there are so many men in this island, you find one who, on top of being a Negro, is also a musician?" Don Julio Colón bitterly complained to his daughter.

That was my first direct encounter with discrimination, either racial or professional. Discrimination—based on economic, racial, occupational, sexual, or political reasons—has caused excessive grief to humanity, and there are still too many individuals today that, like this unwilling father-in-law-to-be, have yet to comprehend what this planet is about. On a certain occasion, I was in Miami listening to an interesting program transmitted by Radio Mambí when a listener called in to express his opinion about the difficulties that would be faced in the reconstruction after Castro's downfall due in particular to the increasing growth of the island's black population since 1959. Such a stupid and harmful comment motivated me to write an article entitled "Rapsodia en blanco y negro" ("Rhapsody in Black and White"). It was published by the *Miami Herald* and widely discussed on local radio programs.

"Hey, *músico!*" howled the gentleman with a large mustache and silver hair while getting out of a flashy white Cadillac with a red interior in the parking lot of Bermúdez's fruit stand at the corner of Flager and Fifty-seventh Street in Miami. He wore a beige guayabera (a light shirt originally worn in the rural regions of Cuba), loose linen pants, and more gold around his throat, arms, and fingers than Liberace and the boxer Macho Camacho combined. "Allow me to introduce myself. I'm the grandson of Colonel Martiñán, Conde de los Pozos Dulces and Marquis of God-knows-what," he said.

"And I enjoyed your article in the *Herald* very much because we were never racist at home," Colonel Martiñán's grandson added with a reaffirming gesture. "I want you to know that at our farm in Camagüey, sometimes even the Negroes used to sit down and have breakfast at the kitchen table, along with my mother and sisters." (How liberal!) "And as additional proof, let me tell you that many years ago, my father found this sickly little black boy who had been starving in the streets of the town, and he felt so sorry for him that he brought him home. Since then, the little Negro was part of the family, like another little brother who used to wear clothes that his spoiled little white brothers didn't want anymore because they had been worn for so long. That's how generous my father was, and the little Negro was so grateful that on many occasions we could see him as he lay down by my father's feet while the venerable old man was smoking his pipe and reading *El Diario de la Marina*. I wish that you could have seen how faaaat Bemba (Fat Lips) became thanks to Papa's care," said the Cuban as a form of a happy ending.

What a moving story! Isn't it true? And that remark about how faaaat Bemba became . . . *Coño*, maybe they were stuffing the little *negrito* to eat him on Christmas Eve, or what?! And the worst damned thing is that they expel all that verbal diarrhea in complete earnest because, unfortunately, the immense majority of racist jerks do it unconsciously. They are ignorant assholes that cannot see beyond their noses.

Like that old bitch who wanted to praise Brenda by telling her, "Oh, my dear, what you need to do is not to say anything about being from Puerto Rico because you don't look Puerto Rican at all." Brenda, who was raised in Brooklyn and is totally bilingual, didn't know whether to say *gracias* or fuck you!

Racism is a cancer that metastasizes and sometimes results in contradictory situations. Such was the case of Mario Bauzá, who had to leave Cuba partly due to racial problems that existed in the musical scene of our country in the thirties and who became a voluntary exile in the United States, where, at the time, racism was written into the law. The Dorsey brothers were very admired by the Cubans, particularly at that time, and Mario himself remembered with bitterness how he was walking on Broadway once and met the saxophonist Jimmy Dorsey. During his conversation with Dorsey, the famous American bandleader commented, "Mario, it's a shame that you're black because you're such a good musician."

Five decades later, a young and illustrious black musician was teaching a master class at the Berklee College of Music in Boston. "What can I do to improve my sense of swing when improvising?" asked one of the students who participated in the crowded workshop.

"Well, my young friend," joked the well-known musician, "To do that, I think that you would have to be reborn with a little darker skin."

If I'd been there to hear his unfortunate comment, I would have asked the lecturer why there is such a double standard. Does that mean that in order to play the music of Haydn, Ibert, or Hummel well, you have to be born again in Europe, and with less melanin? What about Wynton, Jessye Norman, and Andre Watts? I think that all you need is talent and dedication, nothing more or nothing less. The same devotion and respect (do I need to say it again?) that many talented U.S. musicians of all races have NOT shown toward Latin American music, by the way!

But racial discrimination is even sadder when it takes place among people with common roots, as when some compatriots speak in a deprecatory manner of artists from other nationalities who interpret our Cuban rhythms when, in reality, people such as Oscar D'Leon, Andy Gonzalez, Giovanni Hidalgo, Johnny Pacheco, and even the Japanese Orquesta de la Luz or the Dutch group Nueva Manteca have a better flavor and sense of *clave* than some Cuban-born musicians do.

On the other hand, the jazzmen from the North are too busy looking for their brothers on the Dark Continent and apparently don't realize that the closest children of Mother Africa are not in Botswana or Cameroon but in Cuba and Brazil, cultures that they have ignored, if not caricatured, for years and years despite the existence of large communities of Cubans, Puerto Ricans, and Brazilians in New York, Miami, Montreal, and many other cities on the North American continent.

Shit, it seems that no one wants to remember that those unfortunate black slaves that arrived in Louisiana and on the South American coasts and whose blood and sweat planted the seeds of the gigantic trees known today as jazz and Brazilian music were the siblings of those who possibly left in the next caravel that sailed from the African Île de Gorée bound for beautiful Cuba.

The trip to Eastern Europe with *Saludo Cubano* in 1968 would be my first trip outside of Cuba since we returned from New York in 1960. The country's situation was going from bad to worse. Everything was based on promises and sacrifices to achieve a shining future that each day receded farther from view. But Castro always spoke of the USSR as the example to follow for the future of our fatherland. At last, during my first visit to the "workers' paradise," I would have the opportunity to closely observe the legacy of the great Lenin. I must confess that I was deeply impressed by everything I saw, and particularly by what I didn't see, during our stay in the formerly powerful nation founded by Vladimir Ilyich Ulyanov, which happened to be his real name. His nickname has inspired countless jokes, like, for example, "The Marx Brothers and the Lenin Sisters." In Cuba, he was known also as "the little old man who invented misery." I bet Lenin himself never discovered his real importance as the precursor of the little cap associated with the *conguero* Patato Valdés. Of course, under Lenin's cap, one could never have found the charm possessed in surplus quantity by that famous percussionist.

Obviously, the small and ambitious Russian didn't have any business talent either, and this incapacity transformed him into the most transcendent, idiotic, harmful, arrogant, charismatic, dictatorial, ignorant, and influential political dwarf of the entire twentieth century, besides having the dubious distinction of being the first successful Communist, and without the least drop of humor. The Bolshevik chief died without suspecting how much influence his fastidious Marxist style would have on future obnoxious totalitarian leaders such as Muammar Gadhafi, Wojciech Jaruzelski, Osama bin Laden, Hugo Chávez, the Ayatollah Ruholla Khomeini, Saddam Hussein, and Daniel Ortega. Only a cretin who is not capable of understanding a joke could have taken seriously the book of (German) jokes written by Engels's bearded friend and, on top of that, have put them into practice, creating that tremendous fart known as the October Revolution. What a mess! But all that aside, the truth of the matter is that our Eastern European tour was tons of fun.

In August 1968, the departure of the Soviet TU-114 airplane that was going to take us to Moscow (via Algiers) was canceled a couple of times due to a dangerous heat wave that flagellated Algeria. Between one thing and the other, we arrived at the Algerian capital two or three days behind schedule. Finally, after getting roasted under the Algerian sun and drinking our first Cokes in eight or nine years, we left the suffocating lobby at the Algiers Airport, took off from the airport, and headed toward the workers' paradises (!?).

Besides the journalists, some Cuban embassy personnel, and the official Soviet reception committee, we were very happy to find waiting for us at the airport the great Russian jazz pianist Boris Richkof, husband and musical director of the Georgian singer July Shogely, whom we had met the previous year at the Varadero '67 Popular Song Festival. Contrary to the image that we had acquired from the books of Gorky and Tolstoy, and from those horrible Russian television cartoons that sometimes made us wish for a dreaded blackout (those same cartoons that were used by parents to threaten their children, "If you don't eat all your food, I'll turn on the Soviet cartoons"), when we arrived in Moscow, it was as hot as Algiers, hotter than hell. And, on top of everything else, the air-conditioning chapter could not be found in the Marxist-Leninist repair manuals, so we had to endure the welcoming speeches and drink half a bottle of vodka per musician while toasting the "sacred friendship between our peoples" under a scorching sun that reminded me more of Che Guevara's "voluntary" sugarcane-cutting expeditions than the melting capital of the fifteen Soviet republics.

After pledging eternal love and fidelity to the noble and invincible cause of socialism and almost reaching the border between hallucination and alcoholic coma, we boarded buses that took us to the Russia Hotel, one of the largest, most uncomfortable, and most poorly designed hotels on the globe, located right in the area of the Kremlin, Red Square, Lenin's Tomb, and the extremely beautiful St. Basil's Cathedral, built during the rule of Czar Ivan the Terrible. According to legend, Ivan the Terrible gave orders to remove the designing architect's eyeballs to prevent him from building a similar cathedral anywhere else. And I'm certain that if the bloody monarch were still alive, he would probably have done the same with the miserable asshole who drew the plans for the Russia Hotel.

How could I have imagined that twenty-three years later, in 1991, I would return to that hotel as a guest artist with Dizzy Gillespie's quartet. "Hey you, *Cubano marricown*," said Dizzy, who learned his entire repertoire of scurrilous words in Spanish from Cubans. "My friends from the Baha'i religion have organized a little tour for me through East Berlin, Russia, and Czechoslovakia. Would you like to come along?"

Those were the days just after the Berlin Wall collapsed, and there was a general euphoria in all of Eastern Europe. We played in the German capital at a theater where I had previously performed with Irakere, and we stayed again at the Under der Linden Hotel, where it took them two and a half hours to prepare a beefsteak with French fries.

When crossing from the western to the eastern side of Berlin, it seemed as if when the dividing wall collapsed the complete eastern section had fallen flat to the ground. Such was the impoverished condition in which the Russians and their allies—led by the idiotic Erich Honecker—had left the area assigned to them when the formerly powerful nation was divided by the victors at the end of World War II. And let's ask those who insist on blaming all the present misfortunes of my country on the American embargo: Whom would they blame for the economic and social disaster found in more than one-third of the whole of Germany, one of the richest countries on earth?

Since the first stone of that mournfully celebrated wall in Berlin was laid at dawn on August 13, 1961, until its dramatic collapse thirty years later, more than forty thousand people were sentenced for attempting to escape or helping those who did. The average sentence just for assisting someone to escape ranged from five years to life imprisonment—that's including parents who helped their children flee from that infernal place. Between 1961 and 1989 more than a thousand people from approximately thirty nations were incarcerated for helping German citizens to escape from the zone of Soviet occupation.

Thousands went through fields mined with explosives; leaped into the abyss from tall buildings, bridges, and moving trains; dug tunnels; jumped over barbed wire; or hid in the mudguards or other compartments of tiny European cars. Some even built their own escape vehicles, such as personal submarines, hot-air balloons, and other extremely risky and dangerous floating and flying homemade contraptions. A wide collection of these incredible artifacts is on display at the Checkpoint Charlie Museum, very close to what was an important military post for controlling movement of authorized personnel from East to West Berlin. "The total length of the barbed wire used by the Communists to impede the escape of the people from their territory was enough to cover the entire circumference of the Earth" reads the pamphlet handed out at the entrance to the museum by the no-man's-land.

Some managed to survive that odyssey, but hundreds died either in their attempt or in the jails of the improperly called Democratic Republic of Germany. Many of the cruel and arbitrary orders to jail or execute captured escapees came directly from the pro-Soviet dictator Erich Honecker, and I can only imagine the reaction of those victims and their families when, for humanitarian reasons, the newly unified German government allowed the old tyrant to travel to Chile for treatment of his cancer, along with his daughter, the wife of an ex-collaborator of the wasted socialist president Salvador Allende, who also had a suicidal daughter, married to a high-ranking officer of Fidel Castro. "God raises them and the devil piles them together," as the old Cuban saying goes. Sons of bitches all of them!

"And here we receive the clear/the enwombing transparence/of your beloved presence/Commander Che Guevara. . . ." It was a sunny afternoon in the east of Berlin, and a little folk group from the Andes, with their ponchos, *quenas*, and *charangos*, intoned the sad melody Carlos Puebla dedicated to the "Heroic Guerrilla Man." A few meters from them, PROLETARIANS OF THE WORLD, FORGIVE ME! declared the graffiti at the pedestal of the enormous bust of Karl Marx, that mourning Santa Claus dressed in black who, instead of saying "ho-ho-ho" and leaving presents, sang the "Internationale" and took the consumer goods to the *diplotienda de área dólar.* (This could be literally translated as "diplo-store of the dollar area," a code phrase used by Cuban Commies to refer to those business establishments where only Yankee currency is accepted.)

From Berlin we traveled to Prague, the beautiful capital of Czechoslovakia, which had recently elected in a democratic manner the writer, theatrical celebrity, and former political prisoner Václav Havel, who attended our concert accompanied by the U.S. ambassador, the prodigious actress Shirley Temple Black. She had kept all the friendly charm that she had radiated many years before as a child star on the big screen.

When I was introduced by Dizzy before playing my piece as soloist, I approached the microphone to read in Czech some words that the great Czech saxophonist and recorder virtuoso Jiri Stivin helped me to write: "Dear Mr. President, it is a real honor for me to perform for a man who is a true example for Cuban artists, and I have faith that very soon we shall also have our own Václav Havel as our democratically elected president."

With Dizzy Gillespie and Czech president Václav Havel in
Prague (1991)

From Prague, we flew to Moscow, which I had not visited since 1978 to 1979. Before I left the hotel to perform at a large theater (everything there is large), Dizzy invited me to come along with him to a press conference—a large one, of course—attended by radio, television, and newspaper reporters from various countries.

"I was born in South Carolina on October 21, 1917, and I'm proud to celebrate my birthday along with that of the Bolshevik Revolution," said the illustrious trumpeter, with that characteristic facility to talk nonsense found among famous Americans, particularly when talking about international politics.

"And my name is Paquito D'Rivera," I riposted. "I was born on June 4, 1948, in Havana, Cuba, and I beg you, for the love of God, now that you have finally freed yourselves from the Bolsheviks (who came to power in this country the same year as Dizzy's birth—a fortuitous event for the gringos), that you manifest your solidarity with the pain and struggle of Cubans, as we have suffered for thirty years from the same contagious Marxist-Leninist disease that tormented you for the last seven decades."

I don't think Dizzy was too thrilled with my somewhat abrupt remarks during that press conference, but since Americans don't tend to mix friendship with politics, and I have (almost) learned to put that wise system into practice, my good friendship with him continued as before, without any major consequences.

That reminds me of what I once wrote in a letter to the maestro Armando Romeu: "The Commies already deprived me of too many things, and I'm not going to allow them to deprive me of your valuable friendship. Therefore, you and your brother Mario can express your gratefulness to Fidel while I shit on his mother's heart, but that doesn't in any way affect the beautiful relationship that has bonded me and my family to the Romeus, which I regard as my own family."

On the other hand, black Americans have been—and still are—so humiliated that any opportunist who hypocritically shows solidarity with their cause is able to dazzle them. Which prevents them, of course, from contemplating the sad reality of blacks who live in those countries "liberated from imperialist exploitation."

A good example is the case of Anthony Bryant, a former Black Panther who on March 15, 1969, hijacked to Cuba a National Airlines plane flying from New York to Miami. Due to a slight error in his calculations, instead of being welcomed with open arms, he was confined to a prison cell for more than a decade, and that's where he acquired first-hand knowledge of the horrors of the Tropical Gulag.

"*Mira, mi socio*," said the charismatic ex-hijacker in his Cubanized Spanish while we had breakfast very early in the morning at my New Jersey home. "I thought that I had landed in paradise, but God sent me to hell for twelve years." His face still reflected the terror that he had endured.

After his release from prison many years later, Tony wrote a passionate book entitled *Hijack*, in which he narrated his odyssey and that of thousands of Cubans, Americans, and people of many other nationalities who are trapped in the web of Castro's cruel and inhuman political prisons, which differ from Mao's or Stalin's only in terms of the weather. Commented Tony in his book:

> The Communists aren't worried about anyone as much as they are about blacks. The black they want most is the black American. The black American is the most controversial ethnic group alive. It is the most loved and the most hated, the most known and the least understood. But one thing is certain: the black American is the cream of the world's crop.
>
> They've suffered through and survived a horrendous experience and now they set the social atmosphere in the U.S. which reflects on every other society on earth. Everything that affects black America is felt around the world. You could almost say that the future of the world will depend on them. That's why the Communists are trying so hard to capture them. If the blacks in the U.S. can be made to believe that the Communists are their saviors, then the rest of the black world will follow their lead and humanity will be swept into the darkest days of its history!

On this 1968 tour throughout the Soviet bloc, Chucho Valdés and I were roommates and inseparable friends. One of the first things that we did, as soon as we acquired some rubles, was to buy one of those clocks with a little bird that comes out and sings "cuckoo" and two toy machine guns with plastic bullets. We used to wait on our beds for the clever bird to come out and BANG!

There was truly very little to do there. After we saw the Bolshoi Theater, Red Square, the Kremlin wall, the cosmonauts' museum, and a few other historic sites, Moscow became a boring, dirty, dusty city without any attractions. It didn't take long for me to understand why the Soviet minister of industry, Anastas Mikoyan, was fascinated with Havana in the early sixties (that same fabulous "City of Columns" that fascinated the writer Alejo Carpentier).

Coming from the airport, we were shocked to see so many women working in construction jobs: greasy, fat women with dirty handkerchiefs tied around their heads who were performing the heaviest and least feminine duties. The stench from their armpits could be smelled from the moving bus. That same practice of using women for hard labor (excluding the stench from their armpits) was rapidly tropicalized and transplanted to Cuba when students were sent to the useless agricultural cordon around Havana and other rural locations to perform what was contradictorily called voluntary work.

On the second or third day after our arrival in Moscow in that summer of 1968, we were bored to death, so we went down with our instruments to the hotel's awful restaurant and started to jam with the musicians who worked there. Suddenly some guy showed up who seemed to have a certain degree of authority. In a harsh tone that everyone understood, he told us to stop the music. Without any explanation, the Russian musicians were ordered to pick up their instruments and leave immediately. Something very similar happened years later at the Riviera Hotel when the state security agents prohibited the pianist Felipe Dulzaides from inviting the Canadian musician Moe Koffman, who was visiting Cuba as a tourist, to come up to the stage and play with us. Surely they wanted to prevent the distinguished flutist from infecting us with his imperialist music. . . . Isn't that a lot of shit?

From Moscow, we traveled to Baku, capital of the former Soviet republic of Azerbaijan, at the edge of the Caspian Sea, from where we could see the coastal lights of Iran. Many Soviet citizens escaped by this sea despite the fact that it is mined with explosives. Shit, the truth is that you have to be really desperate to want to escape to Iran! Well, a former girlfriend of Leonardo Acosta was caught by the Cuban coast guards when crossing the Windward Passage, at Cuba's easternmost point, trying to escape to Haiti! (These are the accomplishments of socialism.)

In Baku, we stayed at a very antiquated hotel called Intourist (the Soviet government's tourist agency), crawling with KGB agents who denied entry to anyone suspected of NOT being a foreigner.

There was a radio with two stations: the national Russian-language station and a local one that transmitted only Middle Eastern–style music and, I suppose, speeches of Lenin and Brezhnev translated to the native language.

During our stay in Baku, we played at an outdoor "green theater" and later at the opera, where the orchestra's main clarinetist became speechless when I showed him my 1959 Selmer centered tone clarinet (which is the clarinet I had used all my life until in 1997 I received a marvelous rosewood instrument made specially for me by Luis Rossi, the wonderful Argentine clarinetist, educator, and clarinet maker, who has lived in Santiago, Chile, for twenty years). The Soviet clarinetist, who played phenomenally on the stick with holes that he had, never before had closely examined a high-quality instrument like that French clarinet, which was a present from my father.

Something similar happened to another Russian clarinetist in Havana during the first years of the revolution, when he got into an automatic 1954 Chevrolet Bel Air, owned by his Cuban colleague Musiquito (Little Musician) Gelabert. The Moscow-born clarinetist could not figure out how that automobile could be driven without a stick shift and how a plain musician from the television orchestra who didn't exactly speak about the government in an affectionate manner was able to drive such a car. What the Slavic visitor has probably never heard is that shortly after his visit, Musiquito—a professional loved and respected by everyone—was removed from his position as lead saxophonist and clarinetist of the orchestra of the television station CMQ precisely as a result of his manifested antipathy toward the new "dictatorship of the proletariat."

A few years later, when food was becoming scarce, Musiquito got some fuel on the black market and headed to the countryside in his Chevrolet. He removed the inside panels on both doors, and he stuffed the spaces with bunches of plantains he had purchased on the black market from a farmer after having sworn that he would never reveal his source to the authorities if he got caught. . . . Well, it wasn't Musiquito Gelabert's luckiest day, and somehow the police nabbed him and proceeded to confiscate the contraband plantains hidden in the interior of the car as well as the car itself. It's somewhat hard to believe, but the saxophonist was tried and sentenced to a year and six months of hard labor on an absurd charge to the effect of "criminal possession of and illegal trafficking in green bananas." How do you like those bananas?

One of those days while staying in Baku in 1968, we boarded a train to go to Zakatali, a small town at the foot of the Caucasus Mountains, where we encountered a gigantic reception with a marching band, cannon shots, flags, and all kinds of shit. From our vantage point in the train, our attention was captured by a tall, lank, very old man dressed as a Cossack, with a huge, dirty, gray mustache, riding a horse that looked like Rocinante (Don Quixote's *equus caballus*). A little later, when we got close to that intriguing character who appeared to have escaped from the novel *The Brothers Karamazov*, we became aware that both the scrawny beast and its owner smelled like a combination of Rocinante, Don Quixote, Sancho and his burro, and even Cervantes himself, all together but dead!

Since the maestro Somavilla was functioning not only as musical director but also as political representative, he wanted to be the first one to jump off the train, even before it had fully stopped, while shouting in broken Russian, "*Spasiva, bolshoi, spasiva, tovariches!*" When, surprisingly, the old horseman who smelled like the ass of a wooly mammoth grabbed him by his shoulders and gave him, as is the custom in those regions, an extremely dreadful kiss on his mouth, it almost caused the Matanzas-born pianist to throw up. The worst thing was that on the following day, the town's daily newspaper published on its front page the photograph of Somavilla with all those filthy hairs from the Cossack's monstrous mustache in his mouth.

Chucho and I stayed at the home of a married couple affiliated with the party. They stuffed us with rice and raisins and sugar until we were ready to burst. One night they organized a party for us in the countryside, in the style of the ancient Cossacks, with typical music, a horsemanship competition, a beer-drinking bear, and a roasted goat with two cornets on its horns and beaming lights inside its eyes and its asshole.

When we returned to Baku, we had a couple of free days, and two of Orquesta Aragón's musicians hooked up with some Azerbaijani girls, resulting in a dangerous entanglement with the girls' brothers. It was not acceptable in that region for women to have any type of relationship with foreign men, and the brothers came around the hotel to challenge the Aragón guys to a fight. But then the KGB bloodhounds intervened, and we never saw the vengeful brothers again, and we saw their sisters even less.

St. Petersburg, the former Russian capital that was later renamed Leningrad, is the most beautiful Russian city of them all, in my opinion, and the one that maintains the greatest artistic tradition. There we went to various art museums and to the winter palace of Czar Peter the Great (who was the only man I know of whose shoes were wider than Les McCann's and bigger than Shaquille O'Neal's). Also in Leningrad we ran into Balkanton on tour, the Bulgarian orchestra led by Dimitri Ganev and featuring the enchanting vocalist Yordanka Hristova, whom we had met in the Varadero '67 Popular Song Festival.

During a morning rehearsal at the Komsomol location, several young musicians who were interested in the jazz scene approached us. Some spoke a bit of English, as they explained, "to be able to read the *Down Beat* magazines that we get every once in a while and the liner notes of the American albums that are brought back by the musicians who travel outside." (Or, as the Cuban saxman El Negro Nicolás would say, "They're not outside, they're traveling inside the free world.") Right away, we asked them about the jazz clubs that existed in Leningrad and questioned them about Benny Goodman's tour in 1959 and the Tallinn Festival on the Baltic Sea. They looked at each other in a silence that became embarrassing, and then one of them spoke up: "Yes, it's true that Goodman was here with his big band, with Phil Woods, Zoot Sims, and Mel Lewis, and then Charles Lloyd arrived later with Ron McClure, Jack De Johnette, and Keith Jarrett to play at a festival in Tallinn, Estonia, but that doesn't mean that we have a jazz scene here or anything like that. In fact, that was the first and last Tallinn Festival, and forget about any jazz clubs here in Leningrad." After we promised to get them tickets for the scheduled show of *Saludo Cubano (Cuban Salute)*, we said farewell.

A long time later, I read about the Charles Lloyd Quartet's tour of Estonia in *Jazziz* and *JazzTimes* magazines from 1997:

> "It was truly close to apocalyptic when the four of us set foot on that stage that night in Tallinn, 1967. It was as if the gates to freedom had been, through music, opened, and that audience shown the path to light," said Charles Lloyd. "It was like the end of the world!" a young audience member commented after the first set, which lasted fifty minutes and received an eight-minute-plus ovation after which the authorities, turning on all the lights in the auditorium, ordered an intermission.

There would be no more jazz festivals in Estonia until 1989.

Lloyd and his quartet were without a doubt conveying a hidden message of free thought. American jazz was their form of music, and the content was the voice of democracy and freedom, which, if allowed to exercise its full potential, would indeed end the Communist world—a world of oppression and control over all forms of expression.

To arrive at that liberating moment when Lloyd and his quartet played onstage was not as simple as it seems. Oddly enough, everything started when they were invited by a group of Estonian jazz fans to a festival in Tallinn. Lloyd wasn't enthusiastic about it, mainly because of the poor pay offered and the long trip. Then, through sources, he found out that he was a persona non grata there and that his music wasn't exactly appreciated by the Russian cultural officials. When he learned that, Lloyd changed his mind and decided under the cover of artistic ambassadorship to travel there without any overt political motives.

Upon the quartet's arrival, the authorities suggested a number of activities for them: visits to clinics, TV appearances, and the like, all of which of course excluded any appearance at the festival. The musicians would not accept such repression, and the four of them staged a protest on behalf of artistic freedom. They lay on the ground and would not move until they were allowed to perform for their fans at the festival. They even went as far as accusing the authorities of racism, knowing that the government would be embarrassed by such a charge on their soil because Communists often boasted that they were free of that capitalist evil. The authorities had no choice but to let the Americans play. "When we played over there, it was like the shackles were removed. Something happened between this group and the audience. It was like the shackles fell off and they could not go back on," Mr. Lloyd said.

The Charles Lloyd Quartet played once again thirty years later, in 1997, at the Jazzkaar Festival in Tallinn. There is a plaque in the medieval town hall in Tallinn commemorating the historic first visit. Having survived and finally escaped from a totalitarian regime in which jazz was considered a four-letter word, it is a relief to read that a well-known artist like Mr. Lloyd denounced the horrible repression against jazz musicians and their fans that he witnessed during his historic journey to the (thank God) now defunct Soviet Union in 1967. On the other hand, it is absolutely intolerable that a few colleagues still insist on lending their fame and reputations to support some of the most cruel dictatorships that remain, or, at best, they play the game of the nonpolitical artist and ignore the atrocities.

Back to Leningrad and *Saludo Cubano* in 1968. About an hour later, we were surprised to find the same young musicians who had approached us earlier standing in a corner of the theater lobby, listening to the authoritarian words of the Russian agent who had accompanied us as a representative of the Soviet artistic organization Gosconcert. To make a long story short, that was the last time we saw the young Russian musicians.

Mel Lewis told me a very funny story that took place during that historic tour of Benny Goodman and his orchestra through the USSR in 1962.

It has been said that although Goodman was highly admired as an artist, his employees didn't exactly adore him. Phil Woods, who played the lead alto and clarinet, sat in the middle of the first row of the orchestral formation, and the bandleader used to place his brand-new Selmer clarinet (recently delivered by the French company for that tour) on one of the two clarinet stands that Woods had placed on both sides of his alto stand. While Goodman conversed with the audience and introduced the numbers to be played by the soloists, Woods quickly began to exchange old pieces from his worn clarinet with new ones taken from Benny's Selmer. Over the course of a few weeks, by the end of the tour, Woods had totally exchanged his old, battered instrument for a new one, and the sour-tempered bandleader was left with only his mouthpiece.

"Look at the shitty instruments they make in France. I've only used it for two months, and this damned clarinet is already black and stained and looks old," complained the King of Swing while Mel Lewis almost died laughing because he knew the real story.

Years later I asked Phil Woods about what happened during the USSR tour with Benny and his new Selmer clarinet, and he swore it wasn't true, but anyway, it's a great story to tell, isn't it!

After Leningrad, we were taken for a few days to the sleepy coastal city of Odessa, where it rained all the time and we couldn't do much sightseeing. We performed our usual show, returned to Moscow, and from there flew on to Sofia, Bulgaria.

Before we left Odessa, the sun came out briefly, and we took some black-and-white photographs in front of the statue of the great poet Aleksandr Pushkin (who looked like a cross between former Argentinean president Carlos Menem and Pedrito, Celia Cruz's husband). Years later I discovered some verses by the great Russian poet that for obvious reasons spoke very personally to me:

> From all sweet things that gave me pleasure
> since then my heart was wrenched aside;
> freedom and peace, in substitution
> for happiness, I sought . . .
> —*Eugene Onegin*

Sofia is a small city, but it had a certain charm in comparison to all the cities that we visited in the former USSR. It has narrow streets with yellow paving stones that seemed to glitter at night. (I've never seen the same paving stones anywhere else in the world.) Bulgarian women were quite good-looking and very close to the female prototype that appeals to Hispanic American men.

In Sofia, we met our old friend Bobby Carcassés waiting for us at the horrible Vitosha Hotel, where we were housed by the Kultural Kuban Kommissars to save money (our money). Bobby had visited Bulgaria in 1959, around the time that he was working in France and Italy. Before returning to Cuba, he had married a Bulgarian lady with whom he had a daughter, and now he was given a chance to spend some time with his wife's relatives.

There were two of us assigned to one small and uncomfortable hotel room without a bathroom. In the mini-beds of that little hotel, I acquired a case of *Phthyris pubis* (meaning "crab louse") that provoked my first pubic (not public) shave, as I was assured that it was the only way to get rid of the troublesome insects. I was later told that one can also use beer and a handful of sand—after the bugs get drunk, they immediately stone each other to death.

I believe it was Dancho Capitanov, the trumpeter of the orchestra Balkanton, who took us one afternoon to a rehearsal of the jazz quartet Focus 65, led by the illustrious pianist, composer, and arranger Milcho Leviev. The group had a very special style, similar to that of Free Flight, who worked with Leviev years later in Los Angeles. The other members of the Bulgarian group were Pepe on drums, Simeon "Banana" Chterev on flute, and the Austrian Hans Rettenbaker on contrabass.

Milcho, a raging anti-Communist (like myself), couldn't put up with the political system anymore and managed to escape to the Wild West in 1970, leaving behind his job as leader of the radio/television orchestra and his wife and child. He didn't get to see his daughter until many years later, when she was already a grown woman.

When he returned in 1980, somewhat apprehensive that he would suffer retaliation for having escaped ten years earlier, he was welcomed as a national hero by the musicians, the jazz enthusiasts, and the public in general. They had been following his career through Willis Conover's shortwave program and through the recordings brought back by those who "had gone inside" (the free world).

After settling in the United States, he worked with the orchestra of trumpeter Don Ellis, who loved to play in those extremely rare, odd meters that are so common in Bulgarian music and that Milcho handles as easily as we Cubans can play a mambo. But the best thing about this charming little Bulgarian is that he has a special gift for Latin music, samba, and American jazz as well. All of these factors have made my friend Milcho a successful artist.

Years before Paquito came to Bulgaria, in the early sixties, when I was leading the radio and television orchestra, the bossa nova arrived like a gigantic wave and we played it constantly. One day, the secretary-general of the Communist Party in the radio industry asked me to come to his office, where he told me:

"Comrade Leviev, stop playing bossa nova."

"Why is that?" I asked.

"Well, do you know who imported the bossa nova from Brazil to the United States?"

"Mainly Stan Getz, right?"

"Correct," said the cultural commissar. "But who sent Getz to Brazil?"

"How would I know? I suppose his manager sent him, right?" I replied.

"See what I mean?" stated the official. "You musicians don't know anything about politics. The CIA sent him!"

"The CIA? What for?" I asked, a bit confused.

"What for? To sabotage the cha-cha-cha of our Cuban brothers."

That was his unexpected response. This incredible story is true, and what I regret the most is that I never had the opportunity to relate it to Stan Getz, who certainly would have been very amused.

—Milcho Leviev

▼▼▼

In Bulgaria, we visited the towns of Gabrovo, Plovdiv, Pleven, Xacobo, and Vidin. The latter is a border city by the Danube River. The opposite bank of the river belongs to Romania.

In that town, we were served, along with our supper, a type of sulfuric water similar to the Vichí Catalá that I tasted once (and didn't care for) in Barcelona. That Bulgarian water smelled like the fart of a *charro*.

In the middle of the night, I woke up feeling as if there were two alley cats fighting inside my stomach. Since there were no bathrooms in the hotel rooms, I ran out of my room in my underwear, hurrying to the communal bathroom located at the end of the long hall.

Imagine how surprised I was to find Oscarito Valdés (future singer and percussionist of Irakere) sitting on the only available toilet while our drummer Enrique Plá and Rafael Lay (leader/violinist of Orquesta Aragón) evacuated their intestines in a noisy duet inside the bathtub and trumpeter Varona raised his ass to get a better aim at the lavatory.

Since I couldn't find a pot to shit in among the crowd of nocturnal defecators pressed together in the narrow bathroom, I exited immediately and grabbed one of the standing ashtrays that were located along the hall. Thank God I was quick because the three remaining ashtrays were rapidly occupied by other distressed parties that came out of their rooms for relief. The first to desperately grab the improvised chamber pot was the flutist Richard Egües, who had enough time to drag it inside his room. Moments later, the tall and distinguished Svetla, our Bulgarian interpreter, sat on top of the second one, and I'm not sure if the third one was occupied by the well-fed Carlos Emilio or the singer Ela Calvo since that last provisional latrine was located at the other end of the hall and I couldn't see clearly into the semidarkness because I didn't have time to put on my glasses in my mad race to dump my uncomfortable load.

On the following morning, there was a fetid odor in the entire hotel that could be smelled for several blocks. We found out that night at the lobby that the massive defecation had affected everyone in the hotel. All the guests danced to the same tune!

Romania and Albania are the poorest countries in Europe, and it's not a coincidence that both nations had been part of the Communist bloc since the end of World War II.

My friend Eloy Oliveros, who's a very bright guy, especially when it comes to political jokes, says that while other great powers declare war, send thousands of troops, and destroy your country with their bombs, the Soviets declared peace, sent four or five economic advisers, and turned your country into a shit-hole at record speed regardless of the country's geographic, demographic, racial, or climatological conditions.

One time the Polish leader Lech Walesa was asked for his opinion about the Communists in Arab countries, and the Nobel Peace

Prize recipient replied, "To be honest, I don't know too much about that, but I have no doubt that if Marxists took over Arabia, they'd even run out of sand in the desert."

I have very little biographical information about the tyrant from Tirana who put the screws on the suffering Albanians, but it is well known that the Romanian dictator Nicolae Ceaușescu was as brutal and bloodthirsty as his compatriot, the fanged Count Dracula. The only difference is that the head of the socialist state and his aristo-Marxist-Leninist wife preferred to eat Beluga caviar, Cuban lobster tail, or breast of wild pheasant stuffed with Spanish langoustines and to drink French champagne, instead of their victims' blood, as they toasted the triumph of the proletariat. The man had a lifestyle similar to that of his Haitian colleague, the arrogant Jean-Claude Duvalier, in his Caribbean Romania. But the Romanians didn't wait for the Americans to remove the blood-sucking Nicolae and take him away to some beautiful beach in southern France as they did with Baby Doc. Without wasting any time, he, along with Madame Ceaușescu, was summarily executed by an improvised firing squad on a narrow street in old Bucharest.

Like the rest of the countries "liberated" by the Red Army, Romania was a very gray and sad place, with a shocking difference between the ruling class and the underclass comparable to some regions of Latin America. However, in Chiapas the indigenous sympathizers of Subcomandante Marcos, who have been undeniably abused and reviled for centuries, are not locked up in dark and stinking dungeons filled with rats and sewage to be interrogated about "that suspicious picture of Che Guevara hanging from the wall of your hut."

In his little-known book *Viaje por los Países Socialistas* (*Travels through Socialist Countries*), the Colombian writer Gabriel García Márquez relates some of the atrocities committed by the state as well as the immense tragedy created by the Communists in Eastern Europe.

I met briefly with Gabo—as Fidel Castro and other friends affectionately call García Márquez—before my country's nightclubs were closed, at a table located in the Hotel Nacional's Club Parisienne. I think he was there for one of those Jazz Tuesdays initiated by trumpeter Leonardo Timor in the sixties.

I have since realized that the Colombian novelist is a traveling contradiction. I remember that the author of *A Hundred Years of Solitude* commented in a certain publication that he kept in his house a painting by one of the Laguardia brothers, who were executed by a firing squad by the order of his friend Fidel Castro. They were condemned for their association with the drug- and diamond-smuggling operation of General Arnaldo Ochoa in the late eighties in Angola. The distinguished novelist is someone capable of making the most fucked-up remarks, such as referring to those harsh dictatorships controlled from Moscow as participatory democracies. (I guess that's what he meant by magical realism.)

As reported in a ten-page article in the May 6, 1996, issue of *Newsweek:* "For Gabriel García Márquez, the boundaries between his imagination and the real world keep shifting. And that's OK with him." And I would add: it shows, doesn't it? Even now I can't understand how the creator of *The General in His Labyrinth*, after saying the most horrible things about capitalism—cursing and vilifying the miserable Yankees and heaping praise on the marvelous Cuban educational system—could then move to Mexico and send his children to the most expensive schools in the United States.

"A bon vivant Taurus, now Gabo seems to better appreciate good painting, beautiful women, luxury hotels, silk shirts, good wine, conch in garlic sauce and caviar [oh yessss, caviar!]." That's how the novelist is described by his compatriot, writer, and close friend Plinio Apuleyo Mendoza, who is quoted in the same article. Mendoza continues: "'Champagne?' he asks, and not for ostentatious reasons. He simply has a satanic weakness for Dom Perignon." A close friend of Castro, García Márquez and the dictator often stay up talking until the wee hours of the night or go fishing on one of Castro's yachts (and occasionally Robert Redford joins them). The vision he has of Cuba is formed from the heights of power. Shit, with a life like that even Rush Limbaugh would join the Communist Party!

*   *   *

I don't remember much about Romania, except that we were housed at the Victoria Hotel in the country's capital, Bucharest, and that I had a very beautiful and sweet girlfriend named Mariana Basilescu. I also remember that some musicians whom we met at the hotel, upon seeing our interest in jazz, invited us to a concert given by a Romanian pianist called Iansi Korossi. Not only was he a great pianist, but he also wore his eyeglasses in a rather peculiar manner, with the earpieces covering his ears rather than tucked behind them.

Romanians are always being teased about Transylvania and the vampire Dracula, and since there are not too many of them (either vampires or Romanians), that whole mysterious atmosphere makes them a bit exotic.

Well, what I intend to say is that it would be very strange to enter Victor's Café in New York and find an aunt of Nicolae Ceauşescu eating black beans and rice, *picadillo* (ground meat with dry red wine and spices), and fried green plantains while drinking a Materva (a Cuban soda). And it would be even more bizarre to run into a vampire (Romanian, of course) having a beer with Willy Chirino at the kiosk of Radio Mambí at noon and in the middle of Miami's Calle Ocho Carnival. You dig?

In fact, after that trip, I didn't get to take a close look at a Romanian until many years later, when the Romanian-born impresario Jacques Braunstein contracted me to perform, for the first time, in the National Theater of Caracas, Venezuela.

My relationship with Jacques began through our common friend, the Guantanamo-born trombonist–music educator Pucho Escalante, who lived there (not in Transylvania, but in Caracas) for many years. Ever since my debut at the National Theater, when I was accompanied by a group of the best Venezuelan musicians, I have returned many times to that beautiful South American country, where I always feel at home. Also I don't think they allow ugly women to come out of their houses, or they deport them to Mongolia, because it's very difficult to find an unattractive Venezuelan woman. Plus their cooking is unbelievably good!

There I met great instrumentalists of every musical genre and recorded with national performers such as Soledad Bravo, and then in 1997 I recorded my suite entitled *Aires Tropicales* with the magnificent Cuarteto de Clarinetes de Caracas (Caracas Clarinet Quartet). On that same album made for the Musicarte label we recorded a version for clarinet quartet of my *Wapango* and also the enchanting waltz by Antonio Lauro entitled "El Niño." When the album was released we gave a spectacular concert in the Teresa Carreño Theater. Performing in the concert were the clarinet quartet; my jazz quintet; my wife, the soprano Brenda Feliciano; and the Simón Bolívar Symphony Orchestra under the direction of Pablo Zinger. The main part of the program was a tribute to Gershwin and Lecuona. My son Franco provided excellent arrangements of the three Gershwin piano preludes and two danzas by Lecuona for clarinet quartet and alto saxophone.

Through Jacques Braunstein I met composer Aldemaro Romero, who years later would compose Concierto para Paquito, a concerto for saxophone and clarinet in which the solo instrument alternates with each movement. Also through him I met the pianist Pedrito López and Frank "El Pavo" (Turkey) Hernández, who was Aldemaro's drummer through the beginning of that style called *onda nueva* (new wave), which was a very innovative movement on the Venezuelan musical scene in the seventies. Throughout the years I've enjoyed a beautiful friendship with the enthusiastic "Roma-zuelan" impresario, whose love for jazz and good music rivals only his blood-sucking passion for sensual women, and there are enough of them in Venezuela to satisfy a whole army of Romanian vampires.

Christopher Columbus made three trips to America, and Paquito made four or five to Venezuela. I believe that it was on his second trip when I was able to bring along the great innovative trumpeter/composer Dizzy Gillespie. Both of them are part of this story, although Dizzy is the central character.

I was waiting for them in the arrivals area at Maiquetia Airport when I was asked to speak to an official of Venezuela's department of immigration (DNEI). He told me that Dizzy didn't have a visa and couldn't enter the country. Fortunately, I had a copy of the telegram sent by the Venezuelan consulate in New York authorizing his entry (a document that Dizzy never picked up, God knows why).

When I went to see Dizzy, he was with a guard from the immigration department and almost dying of laughter. After I greeted him, I asked him what he was doing, and he showed me a pack of cards and replied, "I was playing whitejack with my friend." (The remark about "whitejack" had to do with the fact that Dizzy, being black, loved to make jokes about the name of his favorite card game.)

I felt a great sense of relief when the director of immigration authorized Dizzy to enter the country, and as soon as we left customs, the maestro said, "Hmmmm."

"What's wrong now?" I asked him.

"I forgot my camera on the plane," he responded.

We went back to the airline offices and were told that, unfortunately, nothing had been found. I insisted that they look, and an airline official was sent to check under the seat occupied by Dizzy and inside the overhead bin. Thirty or forty minutes went by before the man returned without the camera. We didn't know what to do. It was difficult to leave without the camera. We had to find that camera!

After we finally gave up and were walking to the car, Dizzy again uttered, "Hmmmm."

"What's wrong now?" I asked.

"He asked me to open the trunk of the car. Then he picked up his bag, opened it, and . . . surprise! The camera was there.

And Paquito, with a habitual smile on his face, nodded his

head as a sign of acquiescence, and said, "What can we do? More than that was lost in Cuba."

The following day, mysteriously, Paquito's words and the story of the camera appeared on the front page of the cultural section of a prominent Caracas daily.

I'll never know which is bigger: Paquito's smile or his heart—a kind and noble heart that can be also patient and understanding if needed.

—Jacques Braunstein

On October 29, 1968, we flew on Czechoslovakian Airlines (CSA) to the romantic city of Budapest. My darling Mariana came to say good-bye at the Bucharest International Airport, accompanied by her sister Victoria. She had tears in her eyes, and we promised that we would meet again without fail the following year in Europe.

But, like the lyrics say in Roberto Cantoral's "Bolero," distance is often equivalent to forgetfulness, and in any case, it wasn't my fault if I couldn't return to that sad and legendary country any earlier than 1994, when I performed at a jazz festival during a European tour with my quintet, which was composed at that time of Helio Alves (piano), Ned Mann (bass), Ed Uribe (drums), and Diego Urcola, the young and talented Argentinian trumpeter who replaced Claudio Roditi in my band.

Those were the years after the old and useless political system was crumbling in Eastern Europe, and although we were in Bucharest for one night only, we saw that the Romanians had not yet woken up from the long, horrible Red nightmare that seemed lifted from none other than the famous vampire story set in remote Transylvania.

The Hungarian capital really consists of two cities: the old Buda, and the newer Pest, which are divided by the Danube River. We stayed in

Caricature of my quintet, by Edi

the modern area, at a hotel called Beke (which means "peace"). At the time I didn't understand why the taxi driver laughed so loud when I asked him to take me to Hotel Béka (which means "frog"!).

Like the Basque and the Finnish peoples, the Magyars have a language that is unrelated to other European tongues. I think that it is one of the few idioms in the world in which a piano is not a piano but a *szóngora*. The food was very special too, and their typical music, mostly of gypsy origin, in fact inspired great composers such as Franz Liszt and Johannes Brahms. They had very unusual instrumental groups composed of clarinet, violin, viola, contrabass, and a native instrument similar to an open piano called the *cimbalon*, designed to be struck with special drumsticks. I was especially impressed by the technique and performing passion of the clarinet players. And I must mention the violinists' fourth string, which will make the hair on your soul stand on end as you listen to melodies rooted in the depth of the musical heart of that enigmatic nation.

Budapest had a small but interesting jazz scene. One afternoon we were taken to the Béla Bartók National Conservatory, where the School of Jazz was headed by the pianist and composer Janos Gonda, whom we knew through his recordings, just as we'd heard of guitarists Gabor Szabo and Attila Zoller, violinist-violist Csaba Deseo, and bassist extraordinaire Aladar Pege, among other Hungarian jazz players.

On the night of our last show, which culminated almost three months of touring through Eastern Europe, we were taken to dine at an elegant restaurant with typical Hungarian food. After sipping his Turkish coffee, Maestro Somavilla sat by the *szóngora* (piano) and played some breathtaking variations on Ernesto Lecuona's immortal "Siboney," like nothing I've ever heard, before or since.

This admirable artist—who was as close to a perfect, professional musician as they come—unfortunately composed only one song in his entire life, the ephemeral guaracha "El agua del pon-pon." Nevertheless, he possessed the innate talent and skill needed to arrange and orchestrate the most terrible "anti-melodies" and make them sound as if they'd been written by Tom Jobim, Rachmaninoff, or Billy Strayhorn.

According to those of us who had the privilege of working with El Soma—whose idols were Johnny Richards, Nelson Riddle, Billy Mays, and our compatriot Chico O'Farrill—any orchestration that he did (almost always at top speed) had a stamp of guaranteed quality. The term "arranger" acquired a whole new dimension in the hands of that notable Matanzas-born musician, who was also such a formidable and reliable conductor that you needed to worry only about playing correctly what was written on your score.

"You can't make any mistakes with that guy, even if you want to," the trumpeter Luis Escalante said half jokingly and half seriously. Somavilla had an easygoing and modest personality and dressed in a very simple manner. Sometimes he even dressed a bit carelessly, which occasionally made him the target of musicians' jokes.

Once he had just returned from a tour of several European countries during which he bought a pair of sandals that were already

falling apart. A trumpeter named El Guajiro (Hillbilly) Mirabal—
who was as ugly as he was funny—exclaimed during a rehearsal:
"Hey, Soma, did you walk all the way from Paris, or what?"

"Yes, Guajiro, and I was accompanied by Farrés," replied the
maestro without thinking twice, making a reference to the lyrics of
"Madrecita" ("Little Mother"), a song composed by Osvaldo Farrés.
It was Somavilla's elegant way to tell Guajiro "Yo' mama!"

I can't say for certain if we laughed harder at El Guajiro's joke or
at the maestro's clever response.

It was past midnight, and we were scheduled to depart Budapest at
seven o'clock the following morning. As we were going up the stairs
inside the hotel, Chucho and I were discussing the European custom
of leaving your shoes outside the hotel room at night and picking
them up, shined and cleaned, the following morning.

In the hallway outside our rooms we saw shoes of all kinds,
colors, and sizes, and the pianist—not me, I was only his helper—
came up with the idea of switching the locations of all of the shoes
on every floor of the hotel. I can't even remember how many floors it
had. As we say in Spanish, "*Juventud, divino tesoro!*" ("Youth, divine
treasure!")

The reader can imagine the tremendous chaos we found in the
lobby very early in the morning, where a multitude of guests were
complaining all at once about the loss of their footwear. Chucho and
I roared with laughter when a silver-haired giant with balloonlike
reddish cheeks began shouting in some unknown language while he
showed the confused receptionist the high-heeled shoes belonging
to the singer Mirta Medina that had mysteriously appeared in front
of his door!

"These aren't my husband's shoes!" clamored Mirta, referring to
her husband, Raúl, and looking with amazement at some large, clumsy
boots that looked more like skis and surely belonged to the red-
faced giant who spoke in a strange tongue. Suddenly, Chucho and I

With Leo Brouwer, Guillermo Barreto, Cachaíto, Rafael Somavilla,
and the Orquesta Sinfónica Nacional de Cuba under Manuel Duchesne
(Amadeo Roldan Theater, La Habana, 1965)

had to stifle our laughter when we met the stern gaze of the maestro Somavilla, who was observing us attentively while holding in his hands a little girl's pair of pink shoes.

From Budapest we took a long train trip to the Hungarian-Soviet border, where we transferred to another train that took us to Moscow, where we would catch our Aeroflot flight back to Cuba.

    I don't wish to spend too much time discussing what Gabriel García Márquez has already described in his book of travels through the so-called participatory democracies, but just to give you an idea, let me tell you that switching from the Hungarian train to the Soviet railroad system was like transferring from the Orient Express directly to a freight train.

During our brief stay in Moscow, we had the chance to visit the imposing red marble mausoleum in Red Square, in front of the Kremlin, where thousands of people from all over the world came daily to view the mummified cadaver of the leader of the Soviet revolution.

One of the musicians in the band who was also a member of the Cuban Communist Party was in front of me in the long line. Behind me was one of the *compañeros* from Cuba's State Security Department who were in charge of our delegation. Finally, upon arriving in front of the glass casket that displays the body, I said to the immobile Bolshevik, "Damn, maestro, you finally convinced me!"

The musician standing in front of me was surprised to hear my words. He shook my hand firmly, and with a certain mixture of affection, agitated emotions, and relief (relief owing to the rat that stood behind us), he enthusiastically replied, "I congratulate you, my brother. You're one of us at last. Welcome!" Fortunately, it didn't even occur to my friend that we were talking about two very different things. The old revolutionary lying in his glass casket not only convinced me but also made me an early adherent of the theory immortalized by a famous Cuban comedian who was born some years after Lenin and some miles farther to the west:

"Communism is such a piece of shit!"

Quite a number of recordings were made by EGREM in the late sixties, particularly of pop music. At that time, the singer, author, and arranger Raúl Gómez (who had left the group Los Bucaneros to form with his wife the duo Mirta y Raúl) composed a song entitled "Donde el cielo va a encontrarse con el mar" ("Where the Sky Meets the Sea"), and he wanted a combination of nothing less than a harp and a bagpipe.

The only person I knew who had a Galician bagpipe was a friend of my father's, an instrument repairman named Rodolfo Posada. Adalberto Lara (Trompetica) took me in his car to Posada's famous shop in Havana's El Cerro neighborhood, where we examined the bagpipe. One small problem was that this contraption looked as if it had been last used at the baptism of Hernan Cortés. The bellows were dried out, punctured, and useless. Thus, for the recording, it was decided that I would play the melodic part with the bagpipe's main pipe (known in the Galician language as the *punteiro*) while Trompetica— who is skilled in the technique of circular breathing—would maintain the pedal-base holding note with the bass pipe (*bajón*). Like all of Trompetica's adventures, there was a lot of fun involved.

To play the harp, Raúl brought over from the television orchestra a very tall and dignified girl named María de los Ángeles Córdova, who had no choice but to laugh at the bright thoughts of the mad trumpeter. Since my wacky friend was always such a ladies' man, I thought that he would make a pass at the girl, but it didn't happen like that. I was the one who ended up falling in love with the harpist, whom Trompetica named Arpa "Harp" Romeo in reference to the Italian sports car.

After some stormy tempests between María and my Santa Clara–born former girlfriend (the one whose father didn't accept me because of my status as a black musician), I decided that the best thing to do was to get married before things really exploded. After María and I got married, she came to live in our house in Marianao. A little while after that, my father received authorization to leave the country definitively and be reunited with my mother and sister.

Our marriage was a true disaster that lasted only a few months. Once I came home early in the morning, and both María and her harp were gone. Later, I found out that she'd learned that I had fallen in love with a certain architecture student, and that was the last straw. I also ended up marrying the architect. That relationship, although it had its stormy periods, lasted many years—and also produced my son Franco.

I learned a lot in that Orquesta Cubana de Música Moderna working alongside so many excellent musicians, particularly Armando Romeu, who organized free classes in his home on harmony, orchestration, dodecaphonic music, and new areas of musical knowledge that he shared with us as soon as he could. Armando even created an ingenious system for learning to speak a Chinese dialect by using the common system of musical notation. He also learned to write music in Braille for the sole purpose of helping his friend, the blind pianist Frank Emilio Flynt.

In those years (in the late sixties), symphonic activity was at its peak, and almost every month foreign conductors were brought to Cuba. Whenever they planned to perform Ravel's Bolero or works with parts for alto or soprano sax, I was called to play the solos. This was also the time when Leo Brouwer debuted his Airoso a Charles Mingus for symphony orchestra and jazz quintet as well as many other chamber and large ensemble works. It was a period when culture seemed to flourish. However, since this revival was created artificially and only barely tolerated by the government, which wanted to present to the outside world a pseudoliberal image, it didn't last for long, and we were left only with pleasant memories.

Before long, Armando Romeu, Somavilla, Tony Taño, and other men who lovingly and devoutly wrote music and led the marvelous orchestra known as the Orquesta Cubana de Música Moderna surrendered, little by little, to the many obstacles that they found in their path, and the reins of this crazy horse were finally handed to yours truly. How do you like that, my dear reader!

At one time a disturbing rumor was being spread to the effect that Castro was thinking about abolishing all professional arts, as he had previously done with sports, and let me tell you, my friend, everyone in the business was scared shitless.

I was horrified to imagine the hands of the concert-master violinist of the Stonecutters National Syndicate Amateur Symphony Orchestra as he played Symphony no. 11 by Shostakovich under the direction of the union leader Blás Roca (the Rock). Or the amateur ballet dancers of the Sugarcane Cutters Brigade Nguyen Van Troy rehearsing *Giselle* on location at the sugar mill after spending ten or twelve hours cutting burnt canes, Australian style. And tell me how this sounds to you: Georgi Dimitrof Vocational Workshop for Playwriting and Acting at the Institute of Slavic Languages for Mentally Retarded Political Refugees. But fortunately, the tyrant with the long beard was never too interested in artistic activities, and he soon forgot about the whole thing.

My appointment as bandleader of the OCMM was met with great enthusiasm, and I wrote and arranged plenty of new material and helped organize some concerts.

The national music administration, headed at that time by Julio Bidopia, a professional bureaucrat who had come from the INDER (National Institute of Physical Education and Sports), created a National Jazz Commission composed of Chucho Valdés (who smelled a rat from the beginning and never attended any meetings after the first), Armando Romeu, Horacio Hernández (who had a brand-new jazz program at the classical radio station CMBF that was canceled without explanation, with Hernández forced into retirement), Roberto Toirac (an engineer and founder of the dissolved Club Cubano de Jazz that brought Sims, O'Farrill, and Getz to Cuba), the multidimensional Bobby Carcassés, and Leonardo Acosta, a brilliant writer and bebop pioneer on the island. Chucho, with his characteristic apathy, played with reluctance at one or two events accompanied by Carlos Averhoff, Enrique Plá, and Carlitos del Puerto. Perhaps Chucho was somewhat frustrated with the poor support from the authorities. With his different jazz groups he gave a few concerts at the Palace of Fine Arts, where the only official support that he received was provided by his friend El Gordo Julio Vásquez, director of the small auditorium.

On the other hand, we were totally ignored by the shitty cultural commissaries upon our return from the Jazz Jamboree '70 in Warsaw. These were decisive factors that killed the great pianist's desire to participate in anything that smelled like jazz.

Emiliano Salvador, Leonardo Acosta, Bobby Carcassés, El Negro Nicolás Reinoso, Romeu, Leonardo Timor, and I organized performances at the Liceo de Calzada, the Amadeo Roldán Theater, and particularly at Johnny's Dream Nightclub (later to be known as Club Rio), thanks to the enthusiasm of our beloved and unforgettable friend José Molina, the manager of El Johnny, who became a sort of protector for musicians, even when there was a change in the political climate and jazz was regarded again as imperialist music.

In 2004, the Cuban authorities opened the brand-new Irakere Jazz Club at the former Johnny's Dream locale. "This is an old dream come true, and it will serve to enrich the lives of the new generation of Cuban jazz musicians," said Chucho Valdés at the inaugural ceremony. What he failed to mention was that the tickets to get into the new venue are available for American currency only.

The idea to organize the first Havana Jazz Festival was born during the meetings of that 1970 commission. Pablo Menéndez, an American guitarist who resided in Havana (the son of Barbara Dane, a blues singer who is well connected with some of the pro-Commie musicians in the United States), tried to invite bassist Charlie Haden. The authorities in charge of culture didn't take to the idea. They thought that a gringo, no matter how far to the left he might be, always remained a gringo.

Almost twenty years later, Haden managed to be included in the Jazz Plaza Festival in Havana, but unluckily for him it was in 1988, when the Cuban authorities, for the umpteenth time, denied exit visas to my son Franco and his mother, whose documents were already in order for our reunion in New York.

My letter, directed sarcastically to Comrade Karl, was published in various jazz magazines around the world:

> I've been following your amazing career for quite a long time, and I see that finally you've recently performed at the Jazz Plaza Festival in the formerly beautiful city of Havana (or whatever is left of it).
>
> So I wonder if it would be interesting for you to know that while

you were playing your odes to Che Guevara and to Fidel (who naturally didn't attend your concert, or any other concert), my son and his mother were visited by the political police in order to confiscate their passports and retain them there, in the "Island of Liberty"(!?), against their will and violating our most elementary family rights. It is now eight years that we've been trying to get them out.

Merry Chrismarx,
Paquito.

Before he published it, Michael Fagien, publisher of *Jazziz* magazine, sent Haden a copy of my letter, offering him the right to reply. However, the bassist's only response was to call the publication by telephone, furiously demanding that they abstain from publishing my justly written grievance. But the letter was published, and the musical community became aware of the injustice that was committed. I publicly express my gratitude to *Jazziz*, *Down Beat*, *Latin Beat*, and other specialized publications for their gesture of solidarity with our family.

Jazz is an art that represents in itself the most clear definition of what democracy and collective and individual freedom are about. The political system that prevails in my country is the very antithesis of this concept because it has no respect for the rights of others, particularly their right of free expression.

Charlie Haden keeps playing (very well) his pieces, which are dedicated to social injustices around the world, but he has not written to this date a single quarter note to the memory of the victims of Stalin or to the thousands of youngsters that were assassinated in only one day by the troops of Deng Xiaoping at Beijing's Tiananmen Square. He didn't protest either when, a few weeks after that horrendous massacre, former president George H. W. Bush granted most favored nation status to China, giving it certain trade privileges with the United States.

*At home with Franco D'Rivera and Bulgarian singer Yordanka
Hristova (2000)*

By the late sixties, there were some jazz players from Eastern Europe who came to work with us, such as the Polish composer–valve trombonist–pianist Andrzej Kurylewicz, who brought drummer Janus Csinski, a very good bassist called Jacek Bednarek, and his wife—singer Wanda Warska. We also worked with a singer from Barbados called Less Carlton, for whom Somavilla wrote and recorded a marvelous collection of big band–strings arrangements. We also worked with the French-Mexican duet of Hilario and Miky, the Novi Quartet from Poland, and a few others.

But suddenly the official support for our music began to disappear. A new anti-jazz period had begun, and the cultural hierarchs' attitude toward jazz musicians turned hostile. Julio Bidopia, the same former sports administrator from the Dirección Nacional de Música, dissolved the commission created by the musical bureaucracy. (Chucho was right—the whole jazz project smelled fishy from the start.)

As the last straw, to top off those evils, Major Forneiro, who had recently moved his garrison to a big house located—very appropriately—on a street called Amargura, which means "bitterness" in Spanish, took several crucial players from my orchestra to play in his damned military band (the trumpeter Arturo Sandoval, drummer Enrique Plá, and bassist Carlos del Puerto), and he threatened but did not succeed at taking away my closest friend at the time, the restless Trompetica. Rumor was that Trompetica managed to bribe someone at the military draft board to "disappear" his papers, so he escaped service.

Because I refused to continue accompanying lousy singers with such a good orchestra, the musical administration decided that I should retire for a while to "rest" at home. The conductor's baton was given to a musician from Holguín, a disciple of Juanito Márquez by the name of Germán Piferrer, also known as Pife. As expected, later on El Pife also voted with his feet and is now residing and working in Miami, very close to his beloved teacher.

This forced retirement lasted for two years, during which the government gave us free education to teach our children to love Fidel more than anything else, free hospitalization in case we had a heart attack while cutting sugarcane or in case we decided to slash our veins while waiting for one of those infrequent buses in Havana, and, in my particular case, a relatively high salary to ensure that I wouldn't engage in any form of artistic activity, so help me God!

Negra bonita con ojos de estrellas
en tus brazos morenos
quiere vivir un romance
mi alma bohemia

Beautiful black woman with starry eyes
in your dark arms
my bohemian soul
wants to have a romance

—César Portillo de la Luz, "Noche cubana"
("Cuban Night")

IRAKERE

There she was, once again, our beautiful Cuban night, that pretty black woman the troubadour dreamed about, with starry eyes and as beautiful as any other Havana night. We agreed to meet at the Antillas Bar of the Habana Libre (formerly Havana Hilton) Hotel. All of us were dressed up in suits and ties, in fashionable attire made to order at Oscar's Tailoring Shop by Antonio López, the saxophonist and stellar tailor of Havana's musicians.

Today, I nostalgically remember that small group of youngsters, bursting with the enthusiasm that characterizes that age and filled with pride from a very early age for our noble profession. For many of us, music ran in our families. This was true for drummer Amadito Valdés, guitarist Sergio Vitier, percussionist Carlitos Godinez, bassist Fabián García Caturla, and pianist Remberto Egües, son of that giant of Cuban flutists by the name of Richard Egües, who was the most prominent musician of the world-renowned Orquesta Aragón.

One of the most picturesque characters, and the old-timer in our crew, was Nicolás Reinoso, who played tenor sax at the Habana Libre. El Negro Nicolás (Black Nicolás), as everyone called him, was a tall, good-looking young man whose distinguished appearance and exquisite manners made it easy to mistake him for an African prince

*Celebrating my fiftieth anniversary as a musician at Punta del Este
Jazz Festival (January 2004)*

or diplomat. Coming from humble origins, he always strove to elevate
his cultural level, learning several languages on his own.

He was constantly reading, in addition to playing chess every
afternoon at the UNEAC (National Union of Cuban Writers and Artists) with prominent authors and intellectuals. El Nícolo was able to
become, through his own efforts, a well-educated man, but he never
turned his back on his modest past. In fact, he was proud of it, and
although he spoke Spanish correctly, he wasn't embarrassed to use
street language in conversation. That's how he turned out to be a
cross between a literary expert and a street rumba dancer. He would
come up with the wittiest remarks imaginable in a graceful and
spontaneous way.

As we say on our island, plenty of rain has fallen since those
youthful nights in Havana, and the close friendship that binds me to
El Negro Nicolás has since reaffirmed itself. After I left Cuba in 1980,
we always kept in touch through the mail and common friends,
but we weren't able to see each other again until 1996. Our reunion

occurred during the inaugural Jazz Festival at Punta del Este, Uruguay, the country where he had moved years ago and married Marguerite, a German lady he'd met in our country after my departure.

Nicolás played his tenor saxophone at the first annual Jazz en el Tambo (Jazz on the Farm), a festival for which I've been artistic director since its inception. This is a unique event, created through the incredibly hard labor of "fighting winds and tides" by a passionate jazz fan named Francisco Yobino, the owner of a dairy farm (*tambo*), El Sosiego, in Lapataia, Uruguay.

In the remote Uruguayan countryside, halfway down a dirt path that leads to a hacienda where goats feed on grass and are milked, an eight-hundred-seat amphitheater was built by the farmworkers. Every January, on an enormous stage surrounded by green fields, we present the most celebrated international jazz figures, among them

With Francisco Yobino, producer of the Punta del Este Jazz Festival and owner of a dairy farm in Lapataia

James Moody, Clark Terry, Phil Woods, Dave Samuels, McCoy Tyner, Kenny Barron, Michael Brecker, Leny Andrade, Chico Hamilton, Eddy Monteiro, Zimbo Trio, Monty Alexander, Danilo Pérez, Roy Haynes, Joice, Ron Carter, Claudio Roditi, Jeanie Bryson, Ed Simon, Andy Narell, Terrence Blanchard, Brenda Feliciano, Cesar Camargo Mariano, Benny Golson, Osvaldo and Hugo Fattoruso, Raul Midon, Steve Turre, Jon Faddis, Luis Salinas, Al Grey, Frank Wess, Frank Foster, Romero Lubambo, Fareed Haque, Cedar Walton, Jaime Torres, Regina Carter, Renee Rosnes, Carlos Emilio Morales, Mausha, John Patitucci, Terri Lyne Carrington, Claudia Acuña, Nicolas Payton, Johnny Griffin, Billy Childs, Kenny Burrell, Slide Hampton, Chano Domínguez, Kenny Garrett, Rosa Passos, James Carter, Bebo Valdés, the Heath brothers, and Roy Hargrove.

Within a few short years, our festival has become the most important jazz event in South America. For the fifth annual celebration in the year 2000 I wrote the following for the program notes:

> Fine music, good wine, and diverse people with whom to share an interesting and animated conversation are factors that make my life joyous. Direct contact with nature fascinates me: to breathe the ever-fresh inspiration that hovers in the pure air, to improvise on standards or new themes, and to rejoice at the enchanting art of the best jazz musicians in the world in the amazing beauty of the Uruguayan countryside. In other words, it should be no surprise that I spend the rest of the year counting the days until I go back to the festival in Lapataia . . . and for an animal lover like me, it's also an ideal opportunity to be reunited with old friends: two-footed and four-footed alike!
>
> All this along with a velvety backdrop and a stunning starry sky in this small and hospitable South American nation, the luminous green pastures, and a sweet murmur whistling through the graceful eucalyptus trees spreading a fragrance over the lands of the tireless Francisco Yobino, the man who wished to repay with art and culture a land which years earlier had given him the chance to start a new life. The first festival of the new millennium celebrates

the fifth edition of this event, which we organize with so much love and sacrifice every year. We thank the musicians, designers, technicians, office workers, and other staff, who with their contagious enthusiasm and painstaking work allow the magic to flow every time the lights on that enormous stage go on, showcasing artists coming from the far corners of our planet who breathe new life into the creations of such diverse composers as Ellington, Gillespie, Piazzolla, Monk, and Jobim.

Later, after every concert, the magic continues at the jam sessions that spring up between local musicians and foreign visitors in the bar-restaurant of the hacienda. Here the warm notes from Nicolás Reinoso's tenor are often merged with the distant song of an early-rising rooster in a perfect communion between jazz and Mother Nature herself.

One evening back in the very early seventies in Havana's Antillas bar, Amadito came in to spread the latest gossip—the popular orchestra Los Van Van was going outside (which meant that they were going to tour abroad in the near future).

"Where did you say they're going, Amado?" Nicolás wanted to know.

"They're going outside, my brother. They're going to Europe," answered the drummer.

"Oh, what you're trying to say is that they're going inside, man."

"What the hell you mean by going inside, Nicolás? What are you talking about?"

"It's very simple, Amadito. If Formell's orchestra is going to tour Europe, it's because they're going inside. We're the ones on the outside, because we can't go on one of those birds of steel, not even by accident, you dig?"

You didn't have to wait long for the loud laughter created by our friend's clever remarks. Although the joke didn't really have a political tinge or anything like that (we talked only about music and girls), the reality is that, in Cuba, the simple idea of going abroad, even for only a few days, was (and still is, more and more) an obsession. The Cuban who catches a "steel bird" for the first time is not worried about whether it's going to drop him off at Chernobyl or in a canoe with an Israeli flag adrift in the Persian Gulf. What's important is to go out-side or, better said, to go inside (as rectified by El Nícolo).

This travel fever was a decisive factor behind the formation of the group Irakere, one of the most important Cuban bands ever. Irakere, which means "forest" or "jungle" in an African language, was the new name of our group, but it was nothing more than old wine in a new bottle, as the gringos say. We were, more or less, the same guys from the Teatro Musical, the army band, and the Cuban Orchestra of Modern Music, the ones who had phoned each other for years to find out what Willis Conover was going to broadcast on his Voice of America radio program *The Jazz Hour*.

Through Conover's show, we got to know the music of Woody Shaw, Gabor Szabo, Roger Kellaway, Joe Henderson, Catalonian pia-nist Tete Montoliu, Don Ellis, David Samborn, the Thad Jones/Mel Lewis Big Band, and many, many other artists whose records were not available in Cuba.

In the year 1970, we were somehow able to travel to the Warsaw Jazz Jamboree with the Quinteto Cubano de Jazz, which made its live recording debut on the local label Polsky Nagrania, featuring Chucho's piece entitled "Misa Negra," a jazz suite on Afro-Cuban folkloric themes. That's where we finally met the prestigious radio personality with the deep voice. Ten years later, shortly after I had arrived in the United States, Conover graciously invited me to his famous program, transmitted from the VOA studios in Washington, D.C., while I was in the nation's capital for my first performance at Georgetown's Blues Alley with my quintet.

What a great thrill it was to sit in that same studio and broadcast that music to Cuba while sitting next to the man who enlightened our lives so much during our years of deep isolation. I remember his first words before we began to record the program: "This is a musical program, and the best way to be political is by not talking about politics, all right? . . . Sssh, we're going on the air."

The small studio seemed to light up when he played the first measures of Billy Strayhorn's familiar standard "Take the A Train," the show's theme song, as interpreted by Duke Ellington's orchestra, which I had heard so many times through the speakers of my Russian short-wave radio in Havana (and through so many Russian radios in Russia, North Korea, Poland, Czechoslovakia, Hungary, Albania, Rumania, and Bulgaria). And then on cue came that deep voice, which seemed to emerge from the depths of that captivating music, making an introduction I knew as well as my own name: "Music U.S.A., part one. . . . This is Willis Conover speaking from the Voice of America's *Jazz Hour*. Today we will present music by Cuban saxophonist-composer Paquito D'Rivera!"

CADA NOTA ES UN "SALUDO DE BIENVENIDA" A UN NUEVO MUNDO DE MUSICA...PRESENTANDO AL GRUPO MUSICAL CUBANO *Irakere.*

A poster for Irakere

~❦~

"Listen Slim, I want to talk to you about something," Chucho Valdés said to me one afternoon while walking around the Amadeo Roldán Theater.

"Well, let me hear it because we don't have much time," I answered to my partner in arms, who was accompanied by Oscarito Valdés, the *tumbador* from the OCMM.

"Listen," he continued, "Oscar and I came up with the idea of forming a separate small band to escape from that big orchestra. It will take a divine miracle to travel with that thing. What do you think?"

"Are you kidding me? Really?" I replied, curious.

"Paquito, you know the story about all these sorry-ass little orchestras that spend their entire time traveling all over the place. Meanwhile, we can't even take the plane a few kilometers south to the Isle of Pines. Right or wrong?"

"Well, Chucho, we've talked about that a thousand times, and it's not my fault that these idiots in charge of the cultural affairs are a bunch of ignorant jerks who want to get rid of us. What do you want me to do?"

"What I want you to do is to keep your mouth shut and try to understand what we have in mind. All right? Oscar and I think there's good reason why these lousy third-rate musicians are enjoying the sweet life while we're going through hell as grounded personnel, even though we're the best musicians in the country. Don't you agree?"

"You asked me to be quiet, so I'm all ears."

"Let's get to the nitty-gritty. We want you to help us form a band with the heaviest personnel available, beginning with Carlos Emilio," he added, laughing and making reference to the 275-pound Havana-born guitarist.

Two years had passed since the Ministry of Culture decided to remove me from my position as bandleader of the OCMM. In a humiliating manner, they kept paying my monthly salary to keep me sitting at home, not doing anything. So I explained to Chucho and Oscar that if the object was to get the prospective group on an international flight, then I would be a liability if I were a member of the group. Their scheme would go nowhere if elements regarded by the cultural commissars as conflictive (as in the case of yours truly) were included, especially if we were going to play jazz, which all the *ñam-ñam* drums from Africa couldn't disguise.

"Bravo, that's exactly what we mean!" jumped in Oscar enthusiastically. "The point is that the word *jazz* can't appear anywhere. We're getting closer to the airport, right?"

"And you have to shut up and play the same stuff that you've played up to now or whatever you feel like playing," said Chucho. "We'll take care of the rest. In any case, didn't you say that these people don't care about what you think but only about what you say, and that the big shots in the ministry have turds in their ears, and all that other shit that you talk about? Well, listen to your own story and play stupid, bro, and when you least expect it, we'll be flying in a steel bird."

The first edition of Irakere originated in an improvised trio composed of Chucho, Oscar, and Carlos del Puerto. This trio played in restaurants and tourist resorts on the beaches of East Havana. It grew with the addition of Jorge Varona (trumpet); Carlos Emilio (guitar); Bernardo García (drums); Oscar's brother, Lázaro "Tato" Alfonso, on *tumbadoras;* and the author of these pages. In the beginning, I wanted to play only the small curved soprano that my father gave me on my fifth birthday because it was easier to carry on the infernal public transportation system (the few urban buses were almost always so crowded that we had to hang on from the outside, like human bananas).

Oscar, who owned an East German MZ motorcycle, never liked the sound of my little instrument, so he arranged its disappearance from the place where I kept it in the symphony storage rooms. He kidnapped it for more than twenty years, until another member of Irakere told me (after I was already settled in New York) that he had seen it at the percussionist's home. Therefore, I gave $500 to my

With Chucho Valdés in Helsinki, Finland (1977)

good friend Amadito Valdés in Germany, and he generously negoti-
ated the release of my esteemed instrument. Although it was in poor
condition after being handled for so many years by ignorant people,
it was fixed very well in New York by an Italian repairman for the
modest sum of $3,460.

The first Irakere recording was *Bacalao con Pan* (*Codfish and Bread*),
on which I played the baritone saxophone. It was the first time that
the batum-batá, a rhythm created by Oscar and his brothers, was
heard. It was a new combination of a low-register *batá* and a large

cowbell attached to *tumbadoras* designed to be struck with a bass-drum mallet. Those elements were fused with the trap drum funk rhythm, resulting in a very distinctive and peculiar groove.

The success of *Bacalao con Pan* was immediate, but that was irrelevant to our cultural overseers, who came up with hundreds of obstacles to prevent the group from acquiring official status. One of those overseers was Medardo Montero, a former sound technician who enrolled in the school for political leaders and was later named director of EGREM (Enterprise of Musical Recordings and Editions). When he heard our "Codfish," with bread and everything, he decided against granting official status to a musical group made up of "known jazz players," since what we were playing was nothing but the same jazz that we always played, disguised with Afro-Cuban chants and drums.

"That's slander!" protested Chucho, indignant to hear Montero's miserable truth.

Although he played too loud, Oscarito was always, like his father, the popular and venerable Viejo Oscar (Old Oscar), a competent percussionist. Besides, he proved to be very creative and efficient when it came to making the indigenous section (as Carlos Averhoff called it) sound its best, particularly in the case of the trap drummer Enrique Plá, who came from a freer, jazz-oriented school of musical expression and had a harder time getting used to the repetitive rhythms with few variations that are required for dance music.

Up until then, Oscar had never sung ("He still hasn't sung!" that SOB Carlos del Puerto would immediately say), but despite the fact that almost all of us had doubts about his vocal abilities, we had to admit that the persistent percussionist—the nephew of the famous bolero singer Vicentico Valdés—created a truly identifiable vocal trademark.

Perhaps because he was very conscious of his own vocal limitations, he searched in a very disciplined way for his own stylistic path, and he always sang exactly the same thing in every tune, as if it were a recording. This may seem like a joke, but he was always very consistent and even made the same grammatical mistakes in the same spots.

Very cleverly, Oscarito Valdés also knew how to surround himself with the necessary professionals who would take him, sooner or later, to the door of the coveted airplane that flew out of Cuba. His extraordinary willpower, persistence, and ability to manipulate his multiple contacts in this corrupt society—from local smugglers to high officials of the dreadful Department of State Security—were fundamental to the group's success. Without his efforts, the influential musical group simply would have never existed, despite the high professional talents of each of us. That reminds me of the famous Spanish proverb *Honor a quien honor merece* (Honor those who deserve honor). To this I would add "but honor them for what they did," no more and no less. There's a bad tendency to exaggerate or attribute false achievements to individuals that divert us from their true virtues (and defects).

Such was the case, for example, of that well-intentioned gentleman who said, during Mario Bauzá's funeral, that among the many other merits that truly graced Mario's musical résumé, was his "brilliant work as the principal clarinetist of the Havana Philharmonic, a position occupied by the great arranger while he lived in that city." In reality, Bauzá, who moved to New York when he was a teenager, was listed in concert programs printed in those days as playing the bass clarinet (a big difference), while the hazardous chair of principal clarinet was occupied by the maestro Andraca or other older musicians who had greater experience in the symphonic world, which was never Mario's forte.

And as to the comment that Bauzá was a great arranger, Tito Puente once told me that in all his years in the music business, he had never met anyone who actually saw an orchestral score written by Mario Bauzá. We cannot, however, take away Mario's merit as the architect of an entire musical era and a musical style that we know today as Latin jazz. Maybe he was not an arranger himself, but he was wise enough to surround himself with great professional arrangers, such as Arturo "Chico" O'Farrill, René Hernández, Ray Santos, and Jorge Dalto.

I don't know how a journalist from Buenos Aires could have

written these words: "A virtuoso of the sax and clarinet, Mr. D'Rivera is a also great flutist." Come on, man, just because I'm able to find my way on a flute with certain degree of grace, that's not an excuse to exaggerate. Shit, say Julius Baker and then you'll be talking about a great flutist.

On the other hand, on several occasions I've heard people refer to the extremely creative Thelonious Monk as a virtuoso pianist, which in my opinion is an understatement, comparable to calling Celia Cruz "an extremely beautiful soprano." There are some virtuoso pianists and beautiful sopranos around, but Celia and Monk are, as we say in Spanish, *harina de otro costal* (flour from another sack or, in an English equivalent, cut from an entirely different cloth).

Except for their common interest in mystical brotherhoods and other kinds of sorcery (in which Carlos del Puerto also participated), Oscar Valdés shared little with Chucho Valdés besides a last name. Oscar had as much interest in jazz as my readers may have for the hemorrhoidal ailments that might affect Osama bin Laden. So instead of looking for more concertlike gigs, he devoted himself to getting Irakere to play regularly at popular dances organized every weekend at the Tropicana's Mambí Hall. It was not really a dance hall but a former outdoor parking lot with a separate, ugly entrance where they had constructed an extremely high stage, supposedly to prevent rocks and other objects thrown by belligerent, culturally deprived, alcohol-dependent individuals from reaching the bands featured at that venue. There was a dance floor below, where some danced and others engaged in fist fights or stabbings, while the dreadful "white helmets" of the antiriot police were let loose on the crowd as the best *montunos* reached their climax (I must confess that I have never met riot police so repressively rhythmical and musical). Although it was right next to the world-famous Tropicana nightclub, Mambí Hall was separated from that renowned cabaret by tall iron grates and an impregnable Berlin-style wall that prevented the low-life elements that frequented the remodeled parking lot from frightening the foreign tourists who visited the "Paradise under the

Stars" located on the other side of Mambí's dancing cage. "If I can make it there, I'll make it anywhere," sang Sinatra, referring to the gleaming city of skyscrapers. In Havana, the specialists in dance hits said something similar about that "exciting" place: if a new song was a hit in El Mambí, it would be hot all over Cuba.

But the truth is that because our group was unique, the Mambí dancers were immediately impressed, and many stood as if nailed to the floor while they observed us attentively, with their mouths open, amazed to be so close to a band of such high musical quality playing supposedly danceable music in the very same "jungle." After "Bacalao con Pan," Irakere had a succession of hits, such as "Luisa," "Moja el Pan," "Adagio," "Misaluba," "Quindiambo," "Danza ñáñiga," and "Fiebre"("Fever").

We had to change the title of the last song because Commander Papito Serguera, the head of the national radio and television, felt that the original name was not appropriate for our society of healthy individuals, so we called it "38½" (which refers to the centigrade temperature for a fever) and recorded it under that new title. God, only Serguera could think of such things. Besides the Mambí Hall (or Vietnam Hall, as it was baptized by some wits, referring to its warrior-like riffraff), we had to play at many "voluntary" work projects, agricultural enterprises using the free labor of urban students, political meetings, and the like. We also had to record songs authored by Commander Almeida (although the truth is that he never asked us to do so) and write music dedicated to the "accomplishments of the revolution." This was the case of a beautiful danzón composed by Chucho, which he entitled "Valle de Picadura" ("Picadura Valley"). It had to do with an agricultural plan controlled by Mongo Castro, the dictator's older brother. And once in a while, we got lucky and played at parties at the residence of some Commie big shot, where there was always beer, imported booze, and food—the types of things we didn't have at home.

I particularly remember a big feast organized by a certain Comandante Curbelo to celebrate the fifteenth birthday of his daughter

Luisa (yes, the same one our hit song was named after) on the patio of his house, located behind the former school of the Ursuline nuns in Marianao. Between sets, Averhoff started filling up a small box with slices of ham and cheese, croquettes, pastries, and other provisions that he picked up from the tables with the intention of taking the food home to his wife at the end of the evening. After he had filled the box with leftovers, the saxophonist wrapped his precious treasure in the purple cloth that he used to clean his instruments and placed it temporarily in the case for his old Selmer Mark VI tenor, believing that it would be safe there from the combo's human piranhas.

What poor Carlos didn't suspect was that Enrique Plá had been watching him the whole time. As soon as Plá had the chance, he grabbed the small box out of the case, and then, with the help of other members of the group who were in on the joke, its contents were devoured and it was refilled with little pebbles, mud, a grass sandwich, a pair of small coconuts that fell prematurely from the palms surrounding the big shot's patio . . . and even a dry turd from the guard dog. When he finished, the drummer wrapped the small box again in the velvetlike purple cloth and returned it to the place where his cautious colleague had previously hidden it.

The next morning—RRRIIIIIIING. . . . I picked up my telephone. "Paquito, I shit on your mother, OK?" CLICK!

It was Averhoff, and I thought, *Coño*, what an injustice! I wasn't to blame, but my reputation had preceded me. I was reminded of the Cuban proverb *Cría fama y acuéstate a dormir* (Once you have a reputation, you'll never live it down).

My reputation as a practical joker has dogged me for my entire life. Once in the early nineties, when I was touring Japan with my quintet, we were checking out of our hotel in Osaka and contrabass player David Finck (a notorious son of a bitch practical joker), left a note (in Japanese!) for Tito Puente, who was scheduled to arrive with his band at that same hotel a couple of hours later to perform at the Osaka Blue Note Jazz club, just as we had.

"Dear Señor Tito Puente," wrote the bassist in that letter, translated by a waitress at the club, "Welcome to Osaka, but please be advised that we are aware of the fact that you and your Dominican saxophonist Mario Rivera are compulsive thieves.

"We in Japan are not used to that type of behavior and it won't be tolerated by authorities in this jurisdiction. Please refrain from stealing anything from the club, hotel, or local stores, or we will be forced to prosecute you and/or the Dominican citizen Rivera to the full extent of our laws. Be warned that we will keep an eye on you and your group."

The threatening letter was signed by a certain Captain Atama Támago; supposedly the chief inspector of Osaka's police department.

The embarrassed clerk at the hotel's reception desk at first refused to translate the slanderous letter to the famous *timbalero*. But when he finished reading it he started laughing, because the name of the police chief, Atama Támago, meant "Captain Egghead"!

A couple of months later, I was on my way to perform a classical clarinet performance at Carnegie Hall when I ran into Tito Puente walking down West Fifty-seventh Street in Manhattan. "Hi, *cubanito jodedor*," said Tito sarcastically. "Thank you very much for your Japanese letter. . . . Hmmm, very funny!" There was no way to convince Puente that I didn't have anything to do with that damned letter.

In November of 1996, Juan Pablo Torres invited me to participate in a benefit concert of the organization Amigos for Kids in Miami with other performers including Dave Valentin, Giovanni Hidalgo, Hilton Ruíz, and El Rey del Timbal (King of the Timbal, Tito Puente). Right before the sound check, I signed some autographs while conversing with photographers and women of all ages, from a thirteen-year-old girl to a group of venerable older ladies who were members of the event's sponsoring organization.

"Paquito get over here, we don't have much time and we still need to get changed," Tito yelled. He was already in place behind his instrument. I excused myself and proceeded to walk onstage while the ladies followed me with their gaze. I picked up my sax, and a very strange object inside the bell of the instrument caught my attention.

I put my hand inside to investigate, and in front of the cameramen and all those little old ladies, pulled out an enormous black rubber penis that would have put King Kong to shame. I nearly died of embarrassment, and Tito, of laughter. That was the revenge of the King of the Timbal for that damn Japanese letter. He was convinced to the grave that I had written it.

೪ൂ

After a long struggle, authorization was finally given to Chucho, Carlos del Puerto, Arturo Sandoval, Carlos Emilio, Carlos Averhoff, Jorge Varona, Oscarito Valdés, and Enrique Plá, who substituted for Bernardo García on trap drums, to leave the Orquesta Cubana de Música Moderna. The formation of Irakere was also officially authorized. Tato, the percussionist, could not get away from some commitments he had with an Afro-Cuban dance school or something like that, so his place was taken by Oscar's younger half brother, Jorge Alfonso (aka El Niño, meaning "Child"). He was a kid as affectionate and naive as his alias, with extraordinary physical power and a unique rhythmic concept, as well as a tremendous ability to play Cuban percussion.

(Years later, in New York, I was deeply saddened to learn that El Niño had committed suicide in public, dousing his body with a highly flammable liquid and immediately setting himself on fire during a celebration feast with religious overtones that was traditionally conducted every year in an interior patio shared by his family and many others in the marginal neighborhood of Pogolotti.)

Had it been up to Oscar, we would have spent all our time trying to promote simple guarachas on national radio stations and performing at popular dances, carnivals, and other street events. That was his social environment, but he knew that within our multitalented group, we needed to play other types of music. Therefore, two repertoires were designed—one for dancing and the other for concerts. For our concert performances, Chucho reorchestrated his exuberant Misa

Negra, and I contributed my two short Mozartian concertos, written for solos on soprano saxophone and flute, respectively, in addition to other more jazz-oriented pieces.

Although we generally avoided singers, there were special cases, like that time during the seventies when the cultural authorities brought Danny Rivera from Puerto Rico, along with Alberto Carrión, Lucecita Benítez, and Pedrito Rivera Toledo as musical director.

In those years, Cubans had very few chances to establish personal relationships with people from abroad. The foreign musical scene in Cuba basically consisted of a couple of little groups of Andean musicians, a protest singer-songwriter from Paraguay, and the Ballet of Uzbekistan, to give you some examples.

In other words, if "Liudmilla Trespatinova" arrived with the brass band of Red Cossacks from the Ukraine, for us it was as if Ella Fitzgerald and the Count Basie Orchestra had visited. (Note: The last name of the fictitious visiting Soviet artist is a wordplay based on the stage name of one of the greatest Cuban comedians of all times— Tres Patines.)

As a professional musician, with broad interests in the music field, I'm always willing to expose myself to any artistic expression that enriches my musical knowledge, but to forcefully shove down people's throats music of such specific ethnicity, absolutely alien to our national idiosyncrasies and character, is simply absurd!

"They also tried to impose on us all that sadness of the quena and charangos of Andean music—any subway musician with a poncho would become a star on Cuban TV," wrote Zoé Valdés in one of her novels. "What the hell did that Andean agony have to do with our capriciously festive nature? Why wish to dispense sadness in a place of gaiety? Why that unhealthy desire to make us think that we were closer to Quilapayún than to the Beatles?"

The deal was that between Siberian balalaikas and *quenas* from Machu Pichu, our musical horizon became more boring than a Kim Il Sung speech; when we worked with the magnificent Puerto Rican artists, we felt as if we were in a small oasis in the middle of a cultural

At home with Brenda and Danny Rivera in the early eighties

desert created by the overseeing bureaucrats. While they sang their praises to Castro's revolution, we prayed to Changó (the Yoruba god of thunder, fire, and drums) that the Ricans could stay so we could keep having nice meals at the island's tourist resorts.

I had the frequent pleasure of accompanying Danny Rivera, that giant of Puerto Rican song who earned the respect of the Cuban musicians. Years later, when I was already established in Manhattan, Brenda and I were happy to receive in our apartment this bright and handsome man with a sincere smile. That same night, he told me how, while staying in Varadero Beach, he and Lucecita, along with Carrión, managed to get hold of a boat in order to remove themselves from the coast and speak privately, without hidden microphones or indiscreet spooks who pried into their affairs day and night.

In November 1994, Rivera performed at a theater in Miami, and the Cuban exiles (who remembered how he eulogized the bearded dictator in the past) didn't hesitate in showing their disapproval to the Puerto Rican singer. I was saddened by the news because it was like witnessing a deadly fight between a dearly beloved friend and a close relative to whom I've been united for more than forty-five very painful years.

"Paquito, Cuba wasn't what I thought it was," he said with bitterness during that evening gathering at my Manhattan apartment. What I don't understand is why he didn't say the same thing to the journalist Agustín Tamargo when he was interviewed for a Miami radio station. I'm convinced that the immense majority of Cubans would have accepted his apology because rectification is the quality of wise men.

This kind of apology was made by the French actor Yves Montand, who denounced the atrocities committed by the Communists around the world. By the time of his death, he had earned the respect of thousands of his involuntary victims from back when he was an international standard-bearer of Marxism.

But Danny chose to remain silent, and the exiles decided to shout. . . . And the views of those who shouted could be considered as extremist as those of the Israeli musicians who have omitted from their repertoire the works of Wagner and have never invited Herbert von Karajan (the Führer's favorite orchestral conductor and a former member of the Nazi Party) to conduct an Israeli orchestra . . . only because he thought differently than they do!

The same happened to a New York–based theatrical writer of Cuban origin and unorthodox tendencies who presented her play *Coser y Cantar* (*To Sew and to Sing*) at a Latin American theater festival in Miami. It didn't take long for the powerful and distinctive voice of the clever Guillermo Álvarez-Guedes to pass judgment on it:

"Gentlemen, let's stop this foolishness. This liberal crap is fine in New York, but this is Miami. So they can go to fucking hell with that sewing and singing bullshit!"

In March and April of 2003, while hundreds of intellectuals around the world, including José Saramago, Joan Manuel Serrat, Mercedes Sosa, and Fernando Trueba, decided to publically denounce the more than twenty-year sentence against poet Raúl Rivero and seventy-seven other peaceful dissidents, along with the death penalty against three young Afro-Cubans just for stealing a boat, Danny Rivera signed a letter of support for Castro's regime, together with Rigoberta Menchú, Harry Belafonte, Gabriel García Márquez, and Danny Glover.

"When someone claims to defend human rights, you don't expect him to defend tyrants," wrote Myles B. Kantor in his great article "The Strange Conscience of Danny Glover," dated May 14, 2003.

> Actor and MCI spokesman Danny Glover has often blended art and political concern—against apartheid South Africa, for instance. He starred in *Mandela* (1987), *Bopha!* (1993) and *Boesman and Lena* (2000), all of which depict apartheid as a brutal system.
>
> It would seem that Glover cares deeply about freedom, especially the freedom of people of color.
>
> It would seem.
>
> Angel Moya Acosta, Dr. Oscar Elías Biscet, Iván Hernández Carrillo and Jorge Olivera were among eighty Cuban human rights activists convicted last month in a series of closed sham trials—"a judicial Tiananmen," in the words of opposition member Manuel Cuesta Morua.
>
> Acosta was sentenced to twenty years, Biscet to twenty-five years, Carrillo to twenty-five years and Olivera to eighteen years.
>
> What was their crime? Conscience, to witness evil and call it evil.
>
> These men share a racial as well as moral nexus: they are black. People of color are a majority in Cuba, and they aren't exempt from Fidel Castro's despotism.
>
> It is a crime for black Cubans to criticize this white tyrant, his henchmen or their dogma. Neither can they establish their own media or organizations. And like chattel on a plantation, they can't leave Cuba without a pass. (When Americans consider foreign travel, issues such as cost and scheduling are of concern. Cubans worry if they will be allowed to travel and harmed for the desire.)

Eusebio Peñalver, a black Cuban exile who was a political prisoner from 1960 until 1988—longer than Nelson Mandela (a Castro admirer), who was imprisoned from 1964 until 1990—observes, "There is no difference between the Cuban dictator and Stalin, Mao, Hitler, Mussolini, Idi Amin, Pol Pot, or any of the dictators who have terrorized the peoples of the world."

Former black prisoner of conscience Dr. Ramón Colás notes how the Castro regime "turned me into a modern slave, subjected to unjust laws, discriminatory practices which made me a non-person."

Black Cubans such as Dr. Biscet and Jorge Olivera have been fundamental to the Cuban human rights movement. Others include prisoner of conscience Jorge Luis García Pérez and dissidents in exile such as Vicky Ruiz Labrit and Marcos Lázaro Torres León.

Has Danny Glover denounced the sentences perpetrated against these heroic black Cubans? Has he denounced the systematic violation of black Cubans' human rights?

On the contrary, Glover's solidarity is for the man who subjugates black Cubans.

Glover signed a letter released last month entitled "To the Conscience of the World," which states in part:

"At this very moment, a strong campaign of destabilization against a Latin American nation has been unleashed. The harassment against Cuba could serve as a pretext for an invasion. Therefore, we call upon citizens and policy makers to uphold the universal principles of national sovereignty, respect of territorial integrity and self-determination, essential to just and peaceful coexistence among nations." Addressing this defense of Castro, the late Mexican poet and essayist Octavio Paz wrote in 1994 how many Latin American intellectuals, obliterated by the seduction of ideology, still defend Castro in the name of the principle of non-intervention. Do they perhaps ignore the fact that this principle is based on another, the "freedom of self-determination"? A freedom that Castro, for more than thirty years, has refused the Cuban people. Indeed, those who speak of self-determination in totalitarian regimes like Cuba's might as well speak of squares with three sides.

Totalitarianism's essence is the suffocation of choice by a colossal apparatus of terror.

With Glover there's also the irony of his call to respect totalitarian Cuba's "sovereignty" when he vigorously sought to destabilize apartheid South Africa. Apparently this "universal principle" isn't so universal for him.

Glover has also visited Cuba many times and met Castro. The state-controlled Cuban "newspaper" *Granma International* noted last May: "There's an intense relationship between Danny Glover and Havana. It was love at first sight, and not only has it stood the test of his frequent visits, but it is growing deeper and deeper, through discoveries and affinities."

Castro's black victims from Havana like Dr. Biscet, however, haven't been among those discoveries and affinities.

Black journalist Clarence Page writes of Castro's latest victims: "They look to us in their hour of need and to the other freedom-loving people on this planet. We must not let them down."

Danny Glover not only has let these heroes down, he also has allied with their oppressor. People who love freedom don't do that.

Getting back to Irakere, the group was gaining more and more popularity among both musicians and critics as well as among the dancing youth and the general public. We were in high demand and participated in the most wildly different spectacles throughout the entire country. For a long time, however, the only thing missing—apparently due to the damned stigma attached to jazz players that had followed us everywhere—was the anxiously desired summons to the international airport. Until the spring of 1976, when . . .

Mejor joven y rico que viejo y pobre.

Rather young and rich than old and poor.

—Miami-Cuban proverb

FASTEN YOUR SEAT BELTS!

It must have been in February or March of 1976 when rumor spread in the Ministry of Culture about an upcoming Cuban Culture Week to be organized in Eastern Europe. This time it was going to be a week in Sofia, Bulgaria, and another in Warsaw, Poland.

Among the participants were the writers Onelio Jorge Cardoso and Roberto Fernández Retamar; a cigar-maker; a pair of visual artists from the National School of Arts; some dancers from the National Ballet (Alicia Alonso wasn't among them because she travels only to enemy countries); the Grupo de Experimentación Sonora de ICAIC (Sound Experimentation Group of the Cuban Institute of Cinematographic Art and Industry), and . . . (shit, at last!) our own group, which not only performed independently but also accompanied the singers Farah María and Miguel Angel Piña.

I should note that one of the main reasons why Irakere was formed was precisely to avoid having to accompany any singers, but when we heard the word *fasten*—which was the code word used by Amadito Valdés Jr. and all of the musicians to refer to international travel—no one said a word of complaint about Farah and Miguel. The best thing about Irakere's association with those singers is that this was the beginning of many international tours together.

With Mario Rivera, Jon Faddis, and James Moody, performing with
Dizzy's United Nation Orchestra (1989)

The other combo, organized by the ICAIC, included the singer-songwriter Pablo Milanés; a pelican-faced, fat singer named Sara González, who sang dramatic political songs and told hilarious dirty jokes; Manuel Valera, who later worked extensively with Gonzalo Rubalcaba's Proyecto before going into exile and joining my United Nation Orchestra as lead alto player; and the unforgettable pianist Emiliano Salvador.

I remember that Emiliano had the strangest food cravings. On our 1976 tour in Bulgaria, Emiliano found some Spanish olives at a market behind the hotel in Sofia. Because he adored olives and they were very difficult to find in Cuba, he spent the very limited amount of pocket money that the Cuban authorities had given him, up to the last cent, to buy several bottles and devour their contents. At another time in Havana, I was present when a certain female vocalist, whom Emiliano didn't really like that much, seduced him by luring him to her bedroom with a gigantic bottle of Spanish olives. Emiliano, who was also a bit tipsy, wolfed down the olives with brine and was afflicted the following day with a case of gastritis that lasted an entire week. I know very well that when Carlitos del Puerto reads this, he's going to get a good laugh out of it. *Recordar es volver a vivir.* To remember is to relive those experiences! Isn't that true, Carlitos?

During the two years that Bidopia, Tony Henríquez, and the guys from the National Music Administration put me out to pasture at home, I formed El Trío with Carlitos and Emiliano, and we were together almost all the time. Although we knew we weren't going to earn a peso, we frequently rehearsed at the ICAIC premises, where Emiliano worked. We were able to develop a very creative repertoire in which Emiliano played (besides the piano) the drums with a modern jazz concept that was never achieved, before or after, by any other Cuban jazz drummer. This trio and another experimental project organized before by Nicolás Reinoso and Leonardo Acosta were the only groups that played free jazz on the island. Despite the constant mistrust and threatening frowns of the purist overseers who controlled many cultural centers, we managed to play voluntarily (voluntarily in the true sense of the word, that is, unpaid!) at universities, vocational schools, conservatories, and particularly at Club Rio, the venue that our friend José Molina made available on Mondays, which turned into the headquarters of imperialist music in Havana, the place where we gathered almost every night.

Since we had our free jazz trio rehearsals at ICAIC, I made friends with the guys from the Grupo de Experimentación Sonora and, as I was without work, even played some concerts with them. They had very good connections with other musical groups, intellectuals, filmmakers, and Latin American and European artists of the type they often referred to as the "festive left"—people such as the Brazilian filmmaker Glauber Rocha; singers Joan Manuel Serrat, Roy Brown, and Sonia Silvestre; the Uruguayan writer Mario Benedetti; and the Group Quilapayún.

▲▲▲

In my personal anthology of humiliations, which in these last five years has reached mythic proportions, I reserve a special page to record how certain foreign intellectuals assimilate and interpret Cuban reality after their short visits, during which they make little dance steps through institutions, cities, and small parties, and above all, have enlightening talks with bureaucrats and cultural pimps. Later in front of the international press they feel qualified to pronounce their definitive opinions, transcendental judgments, advice, recommendations, and even slogans for the inhabitants of this outraged archipelago.

The planeloads of Spaniards who now arrive on the island, happy and relaxed and showing old pictures of their fore-bears, also come to teach us many things along with their *cuates* (buddies) from Mexico and their business partners from Canada.

I remember the great poet Rafael Alberti. I can see him now wrapped in a dark sweater, inside a Mercedes-Benz (a kind of poet-mobile) looking at Havana through a car window, inaccessible and distant. I remember also his statements later in Madrid:

"Everything is working well in Cuba. Everything is wonderful."

Another cultivator of the genre, with fewer laurels but fiercer and more insistent, is the writer Mario Benedetti, who outdoes everyone in his concern for all that is Cuban. His is by far the deepest, the most profound concern. Here is what he said to a journalist who asked for his impressions of the country:

"I'm glad they reopened the farmer's market, because I lost count of the times when I had a government representa-tive close at hand and I insisted on reopening it, because the people had demanded it. I think that's always the case with people. Above all for Cubans who love eating so much."

I refuse to comment on this literary jewel from the author of *Montevideanos*. . . . I won't publicly offend this excellent Uruguayan writer in the same way that he offends us who live here. I have in my files many similar infamies, produced by lofty artists and academics, public scribes, cowmen, and murderesses who make up the fauna of the literary world.

—Raúl Rivero,
independent journalist, Cuba Press, 1996

▼▼▼

In April and May of 2003, a violent crackdown on Cuban peaceful dissidents took place, but many individuals as well as music organizations still insisted on promoting cultural exchanges with the forty-five-year-old dictatorship. In response, I sent the following letter to *JazzTimes* magazine:

North Bergen, New Jersey
May 23, 2003

As a regular reader of *JazzTimes* magazine, I've noticed that your publication is heavily promoting cultural tourism to (what is left of) my homeland, the beloved island of Cuba.

Although I'm totally convinced that my words are not going to change anything, at least I want to call your attention to the fact that last year more Cuban artists from both sides of the Florida Straits obtained more Grammys and Latin Grammy awards and nominations in the most diverse categories than in any other period in history. Among them were Celia Cruz, Omar Sosa, Nilo Castillo, Rey Guerra, Albita, Jorge Moreno, and Bebo and Chucho Valdés. I wonder if you guys are aware that, as usual, none of the distinguished exiled Cuban artists were mentioned at all by the cultural officials of the longest dictatorship on earth (forty-five years!), and while deservingly celebrating Chucho's many achievements over his career, nobody even pronounced the venerable name of his own father Bebo, who by the way went home to Stockholm carrying two of those awards for his formidable CD *El Arte del Sabor*, accompanied by three other compatriots, Patato Valdés, El Gran Cachao, and myself.

It's true that those days are gone when jazz was a "four-letter word" in my country and we had to hide to listen to Willis Conover's radio show, but please keep in mind that while you guys are jammin' with Cuban musicians, eating at restaurants where natives are not permitted, or visiting some school from Castro's famous free education system, only a few weeks ago, three young Afro-Cubans died by firing squad just for stealing a boat, and twenty-eight independent writers, among them the great poet and jazz fan Raúl Rivero, are serving over twenty years of imprisonment just for doing what they were trained for, writing.

Bon Voyage!

Paquito D'Rivera
Exiled Cuban musician and writer

Needless to say, this letter was never published.

Back in 1973 and 1974, the director and bassist of the ICAIC band was Eduardo Ramos, who had been appointed director of the second Festival of Political Song, in which national "protesters" and imported artists from oppressed Latin American countries participated. In the beginning, it was called the Festival of Protest Song, but the government big shots of "Kuhlture" decided that in a socialist country governed by the people there was nothing to protest, so they changed its name.

Most of the singer-songwriters at those events were of very poor professional quality, so Ramos, who had heard that I could arrange unarrangeable melodies, asked for my help and commissioned me to orchestrate eight or ten of those political-musical disasters.

Since I was sitting at home, involuntarily retired and eager to get back into music, I started working enthusiastically—and without charging a peso—on overhauling those songs, which by the way, had to be orchestrated for a large jazz band with strings.

After I don't know how many days of working hard until the wee hours of the morning, the day finally came to rehearse the arrangements, which would make up almost the entire program of the festival that same night.

While waiting my turn to step to the podium, I was approached by a classical pianist named Frank Fernández, who on top of being a member of the Communist Party also worked as an informant for the Dirección Nacional de Música (National Music Administration). He had been given the unpleasant mission of informing me, very discreetly, that as per orders from above, I would not be conducting the pieces I had arranged for that event and that another conductor would take my place at the concert.

Frank's words made me explode inside with frustration and hate. The only thing I could think of doing was to make a quick exit from the Amadeo Roldán Theater, the former stage for so many great international artists, now dedicated to the third-rate music of all those shitheads. To make it worse, they had looked down from their inflated political station and decided that I wasn't worthy of conducting my own orchestrations.

As in many other sad situations (and in many happy ones as well), I gave an SOS call to my friend Normita Rojas, who dropped what she was doing and met me.

> It was true. Paquito was extremely depressed when I managed to escape my new job as a psychologist and meet him in the park right across the street from the theater. He paced around and around the bench as I tried in vain to make him sit down and explain to me what the hell happened.
>
> "Normita," he finally said, almost crying from anger, "that asshole Frank Fernández has just told me that I can't conduct the fucking

music which took me so long to arrange—and I didn't charge them a peso for it."

"What did you just say?"

"Exactly what you just heard—the little comrades of the fucking Communist youth say that I don't have enough Communist aptitudes to conduct an orchestra in this festival of political songs."

"But it's OK to use your music, right?" I told him, "Shit, if you let them do that, you're a colossal shithead."

"But what can I do, Norma? All the music is on their stands and the concert is at nine P.M."

"What do you mean what are we going to do? Shit, there's no one in the theater right now, so let's steal the music. What do you think?"

"Normita, that's crazy."

"So what, one more crazy thing won't make a difference. . . . Let them cancel the concert, come up with other music, what the hell do I care, fuck them! Just leave it to me, I'll distract the watchman, and meanwhile you sneak in and 'rescue' your arrangements—and tonight we'll see who can conduct such a big orchestra if the musicians don't have scores. Ha ha ha!"

That's exactly what we did, and soon after we found ourselves in Paquito's house in Marianao, celebrating the great triumph of stealing from the devil, with none other than a bottle of *aguardiente* Coronilla (the most diabolical liquor in Cuba at those times). But because our unhappiness, powerlessness, and frustration were so great, not even the combined effect of the alcohol and a Chick Corea record could break the tension.

Suddenly, we heard loud banging on the front door. It was Eduardo Ramos accompanied by the bureaucrat from the UJC (Union of Communist Youth) who was in charge of the damned festival. Paquito was reluctant to open the door, and since he was a little drunk he threatened to break the guy's head in two if he didn't leave. I convinced him to open the door and talk to the guy, because talking is the best way to understand and be understood, not by throwing wild punches.

Paquito opened the door violently. He gave them the finger and shouted at them:

"Not even in your dreams! If I were soaked in my own blood, I wouldn't give you my music, so get out of here!"

The bureaucrat jumped back in surprise at Paquito's anger. Eduardo, who had always been held in high regard by Paquito, knew how unjust the festival directors had been with him. He said with affection:

"Relax, mulato, we come in peace. It's all been an unfortunate mistake, but the shit ends right here. You'll go back in the program tonight conducting your music. We'll wait for you to get ready and we'll all leave together. Agreed?"

Paquito calmed down and took a bath with a bucket of water we had to draw from an underground cockroach-infested water tank. His delirium vanished and the concert took place. The hideous songs that he arranged and conducted were a complete success.

But the story doesn't really end there. Years later the dictatorship made us pay very dearly for our "crimes"—because it's very difficult to get out of hell without getting burned.

Nights in Havana have a peculiar aroma of sin. It's difficult, if not impossible, to resist its lures. I recall one night in particular in the late seventies when we escaped in a gorgeous 1956 Oldsmobile hard-top driven by a chubby girl who came every Monday from the small town of El Cotorro to listen to jazz and have a few drinks at El Johnny. It was a Saturday, and finding a motel room at the beach of Marianao was almost as difficult as having a burger and French fries without a Spanish, Canadian, or Swedish passport in hand, so without a second thought the chubby girl started the enormous motor of her American car and headed toward the Havana Forest (a free zone for lovers). The passengers were Carlitos Puerto with a very pretty *mulata* named Yoyi; a man accompanying the chubby girl, whose name I've forgotten over time; and me, with my friend Sara, a very petite girl, full figured (not fat), as refreshing as a Coca-Cola, with blue eyes and the kind of smile that would cheer up a man in the deepest gloom.

The man who was courting the girl in the Oldsmobile had the privilege of using the car for his amorous rendezvous, while we had to settle for the woods and bushes. We jumped out of the car almost before it stopped and into the darkness, filling our lungs with the moist, perfumed breeze coming from the nearby river. Sara was, as always, in full lusting desire, and before I had a chance to take notice, she had peeled off all her clothes, unzipped my pants, and invited me to join in her erotic dance. Her naked body danced in the light of the full moon, which was like a magical halo, and I still remember that almost unreal gleam of her blue eyes that competed with the silver light of the moon pouring on the grass carpet. As if possessed, she drew me in, whispering in my ear how much it excited her to contemplate the naked body of Carlito's *mulatica*.

After choosing our love nests, we decided to leave all our clothes in a clear area of the forest. But as soon as we had left our last garments behind and turned around, a man came out of the thick vegetation, jumping and shouting:

"Hands up! You're under arrest for your immoral behavior—you know that's prohibited!"

And as he was saying that, he picked up all our clothes from the ground, and before we could recover from the surprising encounter, the guy disappeared into the tropical forest with the same speed with which he had appeared only a few seconds earlier, leaving us stark naked, in the middle of the jungle, like a double image of Tarzan and Jane.

The most difficult part was when Carlitos and I had to get out of the car naked at his house, which was close to a military post, while praying to the god Changó that we wouldn't get caught in the powerful searchlights if the soldier on duty turned them on. Then we'd have to explain to him what we were doing running around naked late at night near a military station. But we reached his house safely, and fortunately, María Elena—the bassist's wife—hadn't returned yet from the Tropicana, where she worked as a dancer.

In Sofia, Bulgaria, in that spring of 1976, we again met our old friend Yordanka Hristova, a beautiful woman inside and out, whom we had accompanied many times in Cuba and who could speak and sing in any language imaginable.

"What happened to you in the Havana Forest, darling?" That was the first thing that the Bulgarian singer asked me. She refused to tell me how she found out about our adventures in the bushes, and I'll never know who told her.

From Bulgaria we traveled on to Poland to perform at another one of those cultural weeks. I had already visited that country in 1970 to participate in the Jazz Jamboree, where we met the pianist Dave Brubeck, who had a phenomenal quartet back then composed of Gerry Mulligan, Jack Six, and Alan Dawson. Before both trips, the Cuban authorities had called a general meeting to warn us about the notorious ideological deterioration of the Polish people, their depraved capitalist tendencies, and particularly their anti-Sovietism. There was a joke going around Warsaw at the time that the Polish capital's best panoramic view was from the top floor of the big ugly building where Kongresova Hall (the site of the jazz festival) was located, because it was the only place in Warsaw where the arrogant wedding-cake-like building "donated" by Stalin could not be seen.

"You've already gone to New York, so now you'll have to go to the USSR as well!" our minister of culture, Armando Hart, decided (he didn't go with us, of course) a short time after we had returned from our first trip to the Concrete Jungle in 1978. I couldn't help but remember those words at the end of our "tour-ture" of the USSR, Lenin's fatherland.

We had such bad luck that our electronic instruments broke down and we had to camp out for several days at a hotel run by the Soviet tourist agency Intourist in a shitty little town called Krasnodar, where the only form of recreation that my roommate Averhoff and I had (when the electricity was working) was to look at the only two television channels available, the local channel and a national one, both in Russian, of course.

The following is an example of their programming (in black-and-white, not even in red, shit!) that began around 6:00 P.M., when I suppose the viewers got home from work. It went something like this:

> Channel 1: Comrade Leonid Brezhnev gives a speech for two hours and forty-seven minutes during a ceremony in which party cards are distributed to the distinguished workers of the Frederick Engels Processing Plant for Siberian Buffalo Hoofs. This is followed by a special performance of an 857-member chorus, accompanied by one accordion and two balalaikas played by Cossacks retired from the *kolkhoz Kalinin.* They interpret the anthems of each of the fifteen republics as well as the majestic Soviet anthem orchestrated by Dimitri Shostakovich. Then, in an emotional finale, the chorus leads the entire audience in a stirring rendition of the "Internationale," that glorious canticle of the world's proletariat.

> Channel 2: Canceled: the first Socialist Jazz Festival at the Kremlin. Appearances by the invited artists (Charlie Haden, Gato Barbieri, Pete Seeger, and Harry Belafonte) are also canceled, as is the presentation of awards and medals to Angela Davis, Jane Fonda, Robert Redford, and various intellectuals for their valuable contributions to proletarian internationalism, to be beamed by satellite from the Beverly Hills Marx-Lenin Golf and Yacht Club. In place of the canceled festival, a rerun is shown of the ceremony honoring the workers who process Siberian buffalo hoofs.

The only other alternative in town was to stand in an immensely long line to buy beers with labels that had an expiration date (after which they would turn into vinegar). The label of course, was in Russian, which disoriented Carlos Emilio, our beer-guzzling guitarist. When traveling, the musicians of Irakere stayed in double rooms, and since our first trip, my roommate was always the saxophonist

Averhoff, perhaps due to our instrumental affinity or something like that. Besides being a good musician, he's also great at repairing wind instruments, which really is not my forte.

Irakere's first real chance to "fasten our seat belts" was on a 1976 trip to Jamaica (as a capitalist country it was the best kind of "fasten" there was) to attend the Carifesta celebration, featuring artistic ensembles from the entire Caribbean area.

At that time, the democratically elected Jamaican president was Michael Manley, a leftist politician who loved music, particularly jazz, and who sympathized with Castro (what an absurd combination!). Unaware of Castro's contempt for artists, Manley invited him, along with part of his retinue, to the joyful Caribbean festival.

One of the "artists" Castro brought along was Teófilo Stevenson, the amateur world heavyweight boxing champion. During a little party in his room at the Pegasus Hotel, Stevenson got pissed off at the soprano Alina Sánchez and threw a big silver tray of French fries from the tenth floor, only because the singer had the nerve to refuse to go to bed with him. (If Teófilo had known what would happen later to Mike Tyson, right?)

More than twenty years later in Buenos Aires, I was reminded of that unusual story by concert pianist extraordinaire Jorge Luis Prats, who was performing with Cuba's National Symphony. He happened to be in Stevenson's hotel room the same evening and witnessed the whole spectacle of the flying French fries. At that time I was in Argentina to play three clarinet-piano recitals featuring the two wonderful Brahms sonatas in addition to music by Félix Guerrero, Ernesto Lecuona, the Argentinean Carlos Guastavino, and a couple of my own pieces. For my concerts in Paraná, Rosario, and Buenos Aires, I was accompanied by Aldo Antognazzi, a very fine pianist and teacher, who is an authority on Muzio Clementi's music. From Aldo I learned that this Italian composer has in his wide catalog much more than his few well-known sonatinas.

In order to catch up with Jorge Luis Prats (the grandson of saxman Rafael Prats, a very dear friend of my late father), I decided to stay some extra days in Argentina's magnificent capital city when I completed my engagements in that country. In Buenos Aires I attended concerts given by the Cuban orchestra at the Grand Rex Theater on the popular Corrientes Street and spent some time with my old friends from the symphony, some of whom I hadn't seen for more than sixteen years. Among them was a talented young tuba player called Tamara Depestre, the charming daughter of that unlucky sergeant with the military band who, you may recall, returned late one night to the barracks and became a victim of some humorous asshole who had the idea of unscrewing his Russian metal locker, causing the most infernal noise imaginable when it collapsed.

At one of those concerts, we had the great pleasure of listening to Prats's marvelous rendition of Beethoven's *Emperor* Concerto for piano. Afterward, Aldo Antognazzi invited the young virtuoso to his home and invited the even younger Cuban conductor to a little party they held in my honor, and that talented son of a bitch sat at the upright piano that Antognazzi keeps in his living room and played a whole collection of Cuban danzas by Saumell, Cervantes, and Lecuona that took everyone's breath away.

After that 1976 Caribbean celebration, the next time I saw the former Jamaican president Michael Manley in person was at New York's Blue Note Jazz Club circa 1989 or 1990 on a night featuring his distinguished compatriot, the jazz pianist Monty Alexander.

After the show, the politician went backstage to say hello to Monty, who played marvelously that evening, as usual. I also went over to congratulate the pianist and was tempted to tell the former head of state that during the twenty-one years that I had endured the Communist system on their neighboring island, I had never heard that his bearded friend attended any piano performances of Peruchín, Frank Emilio, or Zenaida Manfugás, although his sister Josefina Castro was married to the classical pianist Silvio Rodríguez Cárdenas. However, I didn't wish to tarnish such an exquisite evening by mentioning Silvio's antimusical brother-in-law.

In Kingston, the different delegations that attended the Carifesta '76 stayed in the vacant rooms of a university dormitory because the students were on vacation. After we arrived in the reception area, something unexpected happened: when the names of the colleagues rooming together were called out, I was surprised to hear my name along with Enrique Plá's instead of with that of my usual roommate, the saxophonist Carlos Averhoff. I also saw that Carlos didn't react, as if he already knew something. Before I could complain about it, Plá quickly came over and said into my ear:

"Look, bro, there's an order from above that, as a militant Communist, I have to round out your political education, and I've got to be at your side all the time, so now you know what's going on . . . you know it's not my fault." And the truth was that it wasn't his fault. That is the arbitrary manner in which that fucked-up system functions.

Plá continued to be my roommate against his will (and mine) during our next tour of Italy, where we performed at the festival of the daily *La Unita*, organized by the Italian Communist Party. From there we went to Finland, where my friend Esko Linnavalli, a Finnish pianist I'd met in Havana a few years earlier, made arrangements for me to record with the great Danish bassist Niels-Henning Orsted Pedersen, whom I greatly admired. The session almost didn't happen due to stupidity of the political agents in the delegation, who wanted to talk about money and all that crap. In any case, money meant absolutely nothing to me compared with the dream of being able to play with that extraordinary musician and to record my first jazz album.

After discussions went back and forth among those in charge, the contentious recording was finally made, and the Finnish musicians were able to get Oscarito Valdés to join the session as percussionist. The Finns were the ones who made the suggestion to me, in front of the maestro Somavilla (a great and dear musician but, contradictorily, a member of the Cuban Communist Party), that I should include the piece entitled "Hasta Siempre," composed by Carlos Puebla and dedicated to none other than Che Guevara. At the time, there was no way in hell that I would have dared to say anything less than "Of course, what a great idea!" That's why, when I read in 2003 that Chucho Valdés had ended his concert in Buenos Aires's Teatro Colón with a piece dedicated to Che Guevara, I understood his position and felt sorry for him.

Finally, against all odds, *Paquito en Finlandia* (*Paquito in Finland*), produced in Helsinki by the small Finnish label Love Records, was recorded in a few hours. It was my first album as a jazz soloist, thanks to the unselfish efforts of my Finnish brother Esko Linnavalli, who played piano in that session. During that same trip, Irakere also recorded its first album outside of Cuba, and we even arranged to obtain our own sound system with an engineer named Matti Sarapauti, a Finnish Humpty-Dumpty whom I had met in Cuba, along with Esko, Otto, Pekka, Baron, and other Finnish musicians.

In the Finnish language, the polite way of asking "How are you?" is something like *Mite senolle kullo?* If you pronounce those words together very quickly, you'll understand (if you speak Spanish) why soon after I arrived in Helsinki, I was so shocked the first time a Finn said to me "*Mitesenoleculo*" (which sounds pretty much like "Stick it up your ass" in the language of Cervantes). How do you like that?

From the cold Suomi—which is what Finns call their country—we traveled to Communist East Berlin. As soon as we reached the hotel's front desk, not only did Plá, my twenty-four-hour shadow, disappear but also I was surprised to discover that I had my own private room for the first time.

Despite everything, Plá's company never disturbed me. He's a great drummer who loved the same things I did and from whom I didn't have anything (or almost anything) to hide.

A few years later, in May of 1980, after my escape in Madrid, when my colleagues in Irakere realized that I wasn't planning to board the plane and the shit hit the fan, Plá said very calmly, "Wait a minute—*coño*, everyone knows that Paquito didn't like it there. Why are you surprised now? Stop fucking around. What had to happen finally happened, so don't give me that shit, OK?"

Arturo Sandoval told me this story during our trip with Dizzy Gillespie on the first European tour of the United Nation Orchestra, back in 1991, during which he requested political asylum in Italy.

Sandoval was a last-minute replacement for Jon Faddis, who wasn't able to make that gig. When Dizzy told me Sandoval would be joining us in Copenhagen, I didn't believe it would happen, because with me as a prominent member of the band, it would be very unlikely that the Cuban authorities would allow our reunion.

"Arturo is very aware of his political role as a true representative of Cuban culture," said Dizzy, without suspecting what was soon going to happen.

But there Arturo was, to our surprise, using that same Schilke trumpet that I had sent him with the journalist Don Lucoff when he traveled to Cuba (which was coincidentally a present from Jon Faddis and his friend Lew Soloff). Because of the good relations his family had with the upper echelons of power in Cuba (the trumpeter was a member of the Communist Party, and his father and wife were long-standing party militants), he not only was able to get permission to join us in Denmark but also managed to obtain an authorization (which was extremely difficult to get) for his wife and son to join him in London during his vacation in the British capital, where they would remain until the end of the tour, under the generous care of Pete King (the manager of Ronnie Scott's Jazz Club) and his spouse. In fact, it was arranged for Arturo's family to remain in the home of that British couple until the tour was over.

In Rome, on the stage of the ancient Coliseum, I met up with the exquisite drummer Max Roach, who was touring with a beautiful orchestral format including choir, string quartet, and jazz group.

"Now Dizzy has the two sides of the Cuban political spectrum in his band," the famous percussionist said philosophically when he saw Sandoval and me in the same orchestra, without suspecting that a few days later the two sides would turn into one when the trumpeter would request political asylum, thereby joining the two million Cubans who are wandering around the world "without a country, but also without a master," as José Martí once said.

But Max never made a comment about Sandoval's defection, just as he never said a word about the video I sent him years later, a documentary made by the Cuban director Jorge Ulla entitled *Nobody Listened*, which is a dramatic denunciation of the horrible experiences of Cuba's political prisoners.

Such double standards make me ask myself how it is that the twenty-something years of prison imposed on Nelson Mandela by the racist South African regime constitute an important matter but the thirty-something years spent in prison by Mario Chanes, the Cuban who has been confined longer than any other political prisoner on the planet, are irrelevant. Perhaps it's because Chanes is nothing more than a white counterrevolutionary, Fidel's enemy. But at the same time, Fidel's whiteness is forgiven due to his friendship with Mandela.

When the South African leader came to visit various cities in the United States, he had already made a stop in Havana, where he praised the Cuban dictator for his alleged achievements. That motivated hundreds of angry Cubans to threaten to sabotage the official reception prepared for the black leader in Miami, which convinced Mayor Xavier Suárez to cancel the celebration in his honor.

The situation caused the indignation of the area's African American population, who saw it as a racial offense against them instead of understanding that it was a response to a just grievance on the part of the Cubans. This added even more tension to the already strained relations between Hispanics and African Americans in South Florida.

And to make matters worse, a few days later, as if competing with Mandela's very ill-advised praise of Castro before visiting Miami, an organization of Cuban exiles stupidly invited, with great fanfare, none other than the ultraconservative politician and former member of the sinister Ku Klux Klan, David Duke, to visit the city. In short, it turned into a contest to see who would commit more foolish actions, and, in my opinion, the contestants ended in a stalemate. I leave it up to the reader to decide on the winner, or to any psychiatrist interested in the field of stupidity.

When there were only a few concerts left on Dizzy's United Nation Orchestra's 1991 European tour, the authorities in Havana smelled something funny, so they ordered the immediate return to Cuba of the entire Sandoval family. The overtly threatening words of this notice terrified Arturo. At that time we were in Italy, and I decided to stay close to the panic-stricken Arturo in order to support him as much as possible, just in case something happened to him or his family in England. At the same time, the orchestra's manager, Charlie Fishman, also known as El Pescao (Fish), mobilized all of Gillespie's contacts in the White House and at the Immigration and Naturalization Service to get the Cuban defector out of Italy (and his family out of London) and to arrange for their reunion in the United States. El Pescao Fishman spent enough money on his telephone calls to pay off Brazil's external debt!

Everyone seems to have forgotten that with three airplane tickets purchased by phone and charged to his own credit card in a complex and synchronized operation that could have been taken from a James Bond movie, it was the one and only Charlie Fishman who managed to get the trio on a westbound TWA plane, and that's the plain truth!

I had not seen my parents since 1968 to 1970, when they went into exile in the United States, taking my sister Rosarito, who was still a child. In 1977 I had the opportunity to travel to Montreal with Irakere as part of a musical show, and I hoped to be able to meet up with them on Canadian soil.

Since we were paranoid about the possibility that our telephone lines would be tapped, I asked my brother Enrique to go to my aunt Josefa's home to try to call my parents in New Jersey to arrange a secret meeting in Montreal.

"Mamá, this is Enrique. . . . Yes, we're OK. . . . Look, I'm calling to tell you that on such-and-such-a date someone that you love very much is going to Canada. Do you understand?" my brother tried to explain. But my mother got so nervous that she hung up the telephone without asking what city of the immense northern country the beloved person would be traveling to.

Well, to make a long story short, while walking one night through the streets of Montreal, a dancer who worked with Enrique at the Tropicana blurted out to me in excitement, "Paquito, run to see your mother! She's going crazy looking for you all over the city! Right now she's on that corner, behind the church!" And lowering her voice, she pointed to the hotel where we were lodged and added, "Watch out, those security pigs are around, and they could mess everything up, OK? So get going right now."

My son:

As I read your recollections of those remarkable days, I noticed that there's a little bit missing from your account of the adventures that led to our encounter.

You describe that when I found out that you would be going for the first time with your group to a free country in North America, I immediately decided to meet you there. (I would have gone to the most remote corner of the world to see you again!)

I traveled to Montreal, along with Rosarito, my cousin Panchú, and your papá, who kept grumbling, like a broken record:

"My God, this woman must be sick in the head! How does she plan to find our son in such a big city without an address or phone number?"

But I thought, Why shouldn't I find him, if God is with me?

We arrived in Montreal at approximately 3:00 P.M., and as soon as we entered our hotel room on the outskirts of the city, we were glued to the phone, calling all the hotels in Montreal, inquiring if a musical group called Irakere was staying on their premises.

By 7:00 P.M. I said, "No more telephone calls, let's go to the commercial center of the city. They must have gone to eat somewhere, to look at store windows, or something like that."

So we headed to downtown Montreal in the "elephant with the white trunk," the name we gave to our red 1964 Chevy Caprice Classic because its former owner had damaged the front of the car, and since he could not obtain a matching red replacement, he used a white one instead.

Right in the middle of St. Catherine Street, with Rosie at the wheel, I ordered her to stop and go into reverse because I thought that those black men we had just passed were Cubans.

"Now she's really gone crazy, but that's what I get for following her!" exclaimed Tito in the back seat, covering his head with his hands.

But I didn't pay any attention to him. My daughter obeyed my instructions immediately, maneuvering in the very center of that crowded street and then getting out of the car to address the first prospective Cuban that she found (in front of the glass window of a shoe store). She asked him in plain Cuban idiom:

"*Oigame señor, usted es cubano?*" (Listen, mister, are you Cuban?)

The man's face turned ashen and he in turn asked one of his companions:

"Listen, Daniel, are we Cuban?"

By then, Tito's head was sticking out of the car window, and the Holguín-born violinist-saxophonist Daniel Guzmán recognized him right away and told him, with a mixture of affection and surprise:

"Damn, it's Tito Rivera! What a pleasure to see you after so many years! Look, your son came with us. See that Pepsi-Cola billboard at the end of the street? That's where we left him a while ago."

All of us jumped out of the car, leaving its engine running in the middle of St. Catherine Street and its four doors wide open, like in a gangster movie.

The rest you already know.

Maura Rivera-Figueras

The reunion with my family after so many years was indescribably happy and sad at the same time. My father, who was never able to adapt to the U.S. lifestyle, had aged considerably. He refused to play the sax anymore and smoked like a chimney.

My sister had become a woman, exactly as the afflicted old Tito had told me in a letter that he wrote from Spain when he was reunited with his little girl after not seeing her for over two years. Rosarito (who bears the name of our paternal grandmother) had inherited the good sense of humor of Ernesto, Josefa, and all the Figueras, in addition to artistic talent, but more oriented toward the visual arts.

My mother was the very same enchanting woman with a wide and lovely smile that made us believe, in the most difficult moments, that everything was going just fine. I can't even imagine what would have happened to us all if the eternal smile of that steely and silky lady had not always been there.

In Montreal, I befriended a very charming Guyanese guy by the name of DouDou Boicel, the owner of the Rising Sun Jazz Club. Since he knew that I had come from Cuba and had almost no pocket money, he let me in almost every night free of charge to check out Ron Carter's quartet, featuring Kenny Barron, Buster Williams, and Ben Riley.

That Guyanese gentleman, who wears only African tunics, is quite a picturesque character. He writes stories for children, composes poetry, paints, and lives with five or six women, with whom he has had several children. All of them live happily together in the same big house. He is an amusing fellow, don't you think?

Our visit to Montreal was full of surprises and remembrances. I don't even know how many suitcases we filled with things that my mother had prepared for the family in Cuba. The following year she went to Havana for a week to meet her little grandson Franco and to visit my aunts and uncles. By that time, the island's authorities had given permission to certain Cubans to visit their native country with special visas "generously" issued by the same emigration department that had made their lives so miserable before granting permission for them to leave Cuba.

It was back in the year 1977 when a boat carrying Dizzy Gillespie, Stan Getz, Earl Hines, and David Amram inexplicably made its appearance in Havana Bay. Suddenly, an afternoon jam session between the American and Cuban musicians was organized at Havana Libre Hotel's Cabaret Caribe, and in the evening, a joyful and surprising concert at the Mella Theater (formerly the Rodi) took place.

At the same time, a celebration was being held at the same hotel to honor some old men that had completed fifty years of service in the sugar industry. God only knows what sick mind came up with the idea of punishing hundreds of those old-timers by making them sit through that jazz concert, which lasted hours and hours, while so many musicians and jazz fans were stranded outside the theater. That sick mind must have belonged to the same bureaucrat who decided to purchase several snow plows in Czechoslovakia just because they were being offered at a very reasonable price! (This is a true story.)

The state security goons closed off two blocks around the theater where the Americans were scheduled to appear. You couldn't enter unless you were authorized or had an identification card showing that you were a fifty-year veteran of the sugarcane-cutting industry. (Magic realism, isn't it, Gabo?)

But for those of us who were lucky enough to participate, it was a wonderful experience. We alternated with musicians we had first known and admired through their recordings, such as Rudy Rutherford, Ron McClure, Billy Hart, Ray Mantilla, John Ore, Mickey Roker, Ben Brown, Joanne Brackeen, and Rodney Jones. With many of the visitors, including the journalist Arnold Jay Smith, I was able to establish very good friendships that have lasted all these years, and others —like Amram and Dizzy—became intimate friends of my family.

Representing the Cuban side, Los Papines and Irakere were featured, and at the end of the show, we all played a composition by David Amram entitled "In Memory of Chano Pozo."

Somehow or other, Dave was able to obtain a copy of the recording of that concert and released it in United States. That record was called *Havana–New York*, and I later used that name to baptize my own traveling group.

During Stan Getz's set, I went up to the balcony and sat next to one of the old sugarcane cutters who complained, "Oh, shit, when is this ever going to end?!" Next to him, someone else, with a palm-leaf hat over his face, was snoring, as if to accompany Ron McClure's contrabass solo. This was a Kafkaesque scene, ideal for a Buñuel or Fellini film—only in Cuba!

Upon their return to the United States, Stan Getz, Dizzy, and Arnold Jay Smith spoke to Bruce Lundvall, the president of CBS Records, about a "phenomenal Cuban group called Irakere." The result was a recording contract for the group, which made two albums for that label, as well as an offer from Lundvall regarding my own prospective recording as a soloist (an offer that didn't thrill the leading cultural commissars). CBS also produced the gigantic Havana Jam that was held from March 3 to March 5, 1979, at Miramar's Karl Marx Theater, where the gringos brought together a truly stellar constellation of jazz and pop artists, such as Hubert Laws, Dexter Gordon, Weather Report, Jaco Pastorious, Tony Williams, Jimmy and Percy Heath, Willie Bobo, Kris Kristoferson, Woody Shaw, Rita Coolidge, Bobby Hutcherson, Stephen Stills, and the Fania All Stars. The latter group featured prominent U.S. Latin musicians and singers such as Héctor Lavoe, Rubén Blades, and Roberto Roena.

Representing Cuban musicians, we had Tata Guines, Guillermo Barreto, Orquesta Aragón, Changuito, Irakere, and the political singer Sara González. (Nobody could understand what the hell she was doing at that festival, singing those odd songs to Ho Chi Minh.)

"If they send us bombs, we'll send them bombs; if they send us music, we'll give them music." That is how the musical extravaganza was inaugurated by the chronic drunkard Armando Hart, minister of "kulture," who was out of tune from the start.

A few minutes later, the huge curtain of the theater slowly opened, and out of a cloud of white smoke came the unmistakable sound of the great Jaco Pastorious as the group Weather Report presented its credentials. Behind them, an enormous screen simulated a blue and infinite universe with millions of shining stars—the perfect backdrop for music that sounded, to many of those in the audience, as if it were coming from another planet.

We were brought by CBS to New York, giving me the opportunity to meet more freely with my family members after our secret meeting in Montreal the year before. We performed without any publicity at the end of a concert featuring McCoy Tyner and Bill Evans in Carnegie Hall. That's where I encountered Mario Bauzá, whom I hadn't seen since 1960, and Bebo Valdés, who came to the concert with my parents.

At the end of the program, despite the significant opposition of our chaperone (whose function was to keep a close eye on us), we participated in a jam session with Dizzy, Maynard Ferguson, Stan Getz, and David Amram, who showed up to welcome us. Returning to the city of my dreams was a sublime experience. Since the Newport Jazz Festival was taking place at the same time (this was the first occasion it was held in New York), we obtained free tickets for some of the concerts, including the one with Chick Corea and Stan Kenton's orchestra in Carnegie Hall.

From New York, we went to Switzerland—with Stan Getz, Billy Cobham, John McLaughlin, and other CBS artists—to take part in the Montreaux Jazz Festival, which we had dreamed of attending for many years. A few days later, we returned to the Big Apple, where we had the opportunity, among other things, to dine for the first time at the legendary Victor's Café, when it was on Seventy-something Street in Manhattan.

The hardest part was our departure—to say good-bye to my parents, to my sister, and to that magical place where I had always wanted to live. But I had left my wife and my child Franco in Cuba, and I had to (and wished to) return to the island to be with them.

In Havana, we were involved in many activities, such as a concert that we organized and recorded live at the Karl Marx Theater (unfortunately, the quality of that recording was very poor) with the guitarist and composer extraordinaire Leo Brouwer, with whom we worked several times. In addition, my friend Emiliano Salvador asked me to collaborate with him on the orchestral direction of his first album, *Nueva Visión (New Vision)*, which later became a classic recording. For some reason, Emiliano—like his colleague Chucho—didn't like to play the role of conductor and preferred that I assume that position.

An underestimated and extraordinarily talented musician, Salvador died young in Cuba on October 22, 1992, of cardiac arrest. When I received the sad news, I wrote a commemorative article called "Nadie es profeta en su tierra" ("No One Is a Prophet in His Own Land") dedicated to his memory. It appeared in the *Miami Herald*, *Latin Beat*, and other U.S. publications.

Emiliano was destined to suffer from what Guillermo Barreto called geographic fatalism. His life was limited by being born in a country afflicted by malignant official influence combined with arrogance, vulgarity, and bad taste. That syndrome has made some talented youngsters believe that the only way to succeed inside and outside the country is based on showing off technically and indulging in other excesses. This is how Cuban music was turned into a pathetic martial-athletic phenomenon. Once, in Paris, I met Orlando Valle (alias Maraca), a very talented young Cuban musician who plays flute and piano and composes very well. After I had invited him to play a couple of numbers with my quintet, we had some beers in my dressing room at the New Morning Jazz Club, and I asked him why the music in Cuba sounded increasingly anxious and aggressive. The question caught him by surprise. He thought about it for a moment, then responded, "I believe that in Cuba there is such a general and tremendous state of anxiety that the music reflects it. Don't you agree?"

"What the hell do I know about that, Maraca?" I said in a half-joking way to the talented musician. "The only thing that makes me feel anxious is having to pay my taxes at the end of the year."

I should have agreed with him, taking into consideration the warlike titles, lyrics, and other vain macho terminology found in Cuban contemporary music: *Conmigo tiene que bailar . . . tírala por*

el balcón . . . los metales del terror . . . fulano apretó a mengano . . .
yo sí tengo el uno . . . dale con la punta'el palo. (She has to dance with
me . . . throw her out the balcony . . . the terrorizing brass section . . .
such-and-such squeezed so-and-so . . . I'm truly number one . . . hit
him with the sharp end of the stick.) This athletic braggadocio is
destroying the joyful and friendly nature of Cuban music. There are
many individuals around the world who admire Cuban musicians,
but they have begun to say that it is difficult for them to listen to
Cuban recordings from beginning to end because of the unrelenting
tension. The music doesn't have a single relaxed moment, not
even in the few romantic ballads that are recorded, which are even
more tense, excessively slow, and insincere, as if wanting to prove
something.

Buddy Rich, Oscar Peterson, Al Di Meola, Dave Weckl, Chick
Corea, Nino Bravo, Bill Watrous, Niels Pedersen, Michael Brecker,
Cleo Laine, John Patitucci, Maynard Ferguson, and other good musicians from abroad have been admired in our country basically as
a result of their technical capabilities. Otherwise, they would have
fallen into the "handless" musicians category or, at best, into the
category of those who "play cute."

I have heard pianists from my native land praise the maturity of
Ed Simon, their young Venezuelan colleague, and talk about how
Monk used time and space in his playing, and then immediately jump
on a motorcycle and travel at a thousand miles per hour on their
keyboards, as if the previously mentioned aesthetic rules didn't
apply to them.

I also have the misfortune of having a certain technical skillful-
ness, and I once had the same tendency to overplay, but just as I
stopped smoking years ago, I was able to break the habit of playing
too many notes. That ailment, which goes by the scientific name of
Galloping Notitis—or in the case of piano players, Typewriting
Keyborditis—is easily curable (like not being able to read music).

"More than a duet, it sounded like two madmen trying desperately to get to the exit door," said a Miami commentator about two of
today's finest and most influential cultivators of Latin jazz who are a

little too inclined to show off. Terms like *hot blood, Latin tempera-ment, passion, swing,* and *energy* are not necessarily related to (and are frequently confused with) speed, nervousness, and excessive volume in the same way that amnesia has nothing to do with magnesia. Like the Cuban son and the Argentinean tango, jazz is a very difficult musical genre, but it isn't a relay race, and you can't evaluate the quality of a musician by his speed or by the quantity of notes that he can squeeze into one bar.

Fortunately, not everyone in Cuba has fallen into this trap of playing "turbomusic," and the talented Emiliano Salvador was one of the few musicians who resisted this tendency. Today I listen nostalgically to the album *Nueva Visión* that we recorded together many years ago in Havana, and I realize once more that Salvador was one of the most illustrious figures on the Cuban contemporary music scene and among the few who understood the true meaning of the word *jazz.*

On the other hand, and taking all these "turbo-facts" into account, and any other defect that with good or bad intention might be brought to the surface by some critics, the truth is that while the rest of the jazz musicians of the world are satisfied to merely imitate the great maestros of the United States, Cubans of all generations, many times lacking in information and appropriate equipment, not to mention fighting against a frankly hostile regime, have been considerably more creative and original, and have contributed elements of their indigenous musical language to the jazz idiom. Outside the United States, where the genre originated, few countries (with perhaps the exception of Brazil) have developed their own distinct sound, but there is, without a doubt, a Cuban jazz movement, noted for its consistency as well as for the numerous performers and groups that cultivate and provide something innovative to the jazz style and its repertoire. We have to give credit where credit is due and honor people like Bebo, Chucho, Carlos Emilio, Enrique Plá, Omar Sosa, Changuito, Cachao, Irakere, and Rubalcaba, OK?

"But that's not jazz!" some puritan might object.

With her hands on her hips, the colorful comedienne and singer Juana Bacallao would respond, "*¡Y a mí qué!*" ("And what's that to me!").

Anyway, that's exactly what they told Charlie Parker, Cecil Taylor, and Astor Piazzolla about their own unique styles.

Around that time, in the seventies, the Angola war was the talk of the town. The Cuban government secretly sent thousands of youngsters, mostly black, to die for who knows what crap. Back then, our cultural leaders were also talking about an Irakere tour through many important American cities the following year. We took the risk and went to Angola to play for the Cuban troops whose existence had been so vehemently denied by Castro. We knew that if we refused to go, our tour of Yankeeland would be automatically canceled.

The Angola visit was supposed to last seven days, but we ended up staying there for more than three weeks, flying in Russian military transport planes, sometimes over the antiaircraft weapons of Jonas Savimbi and another ill-tempered guy who, as pointed out by the writer Roberto Luque Escalona, appeared to have his name written backward: General Holden Roberto.

When we had to travel by land, we were transported in automobiles—either Pandas or Golf VWs—moving at a high speed on highways that went across hostile territories. One time we got out of the car to urinate, armed with machine guns and stuff, in the middle of a dangerous highway. Chucho and El Niño were pissing next to a tree when from the distance I saw a black panther jump from it, just a few feet from where they stood. Struck with fear, they shouted so loud that the frightened feline took off in the opposite direction. No one could say who was more terrified: Chucho, El Niño, or the panther!

After going back and forth a zillion times, the contending sides in that horrible war finally reached an agreement in the midnineties, known as the Lusaka Protocol. There was a ceremony at the United

Nations in New York City attended by twelve Cuban generals. None of them was General Arnaldo Ochoa, the undisputable architect of the Angola war, who was executed during the notorious Ochoa affair.

An estimated two thousand young Cubans rest in graves (if they were lucky) lost in the large map of that strange and remote land. Ironically, when the nightmare was over, there was just one Cuban national invited to that agreement's celebration party, hosted by former enemies Jonas Savimbi and Edoardo Dos Santos, and that man was none other than Jorge Mas Canosa, president of the powerful Miami-based Cuban American National Foundation.

Miraculously, we managed to return in one piece from our

Angola, Africa (1978)

musical-military safari in Angola, and a little while later, we began preparations for our well-deserved U.S. tour, as opening act for Stephen Stills's rock band.

One afternoon, when Irakere was rehearsing at Vedados's José Ramón Rodríguez Polytechnic School, some security goons arrived, accompanied by people from the Ministry of Culture, who were escorting American impresarios in charge of the U.S. tour.

"Yes, we've done some touring in Bulgaria and the USSR recently," pointed out Enrique Plá, to which the American promoter Shelly Shultz immediately replied, "Maybe so, but let me tell you that touring the USSR has really very little to do with a tour in the United States, OK?" And of course he was right! After many years, I met up with Shelly again at the premiere of Fernando Trueba's movie *Calle 54* at Lincoln Center, and we had a good laugh remembering that afternoon as well as Irakere's happy tour with Stephen Stills.

At the end of our long tour through twenty-two cities on the East Coast, I had the chance once again to be reunited with my family and friends, and Irakere recorded its second and last album for CBS—*Irakere II*—in the company's studios, located on Fifty-second Street and Madison Avenue in Manhattan. For those two CBS recordings, we received a Grammy award and two nominations from the Recording Academy. The Grammy was very helpful in advancing our group in American show business. But with all due respect, I have to say to be called famous and influential is not always the same as being of high quality. You only have to think of the many mediocre and superficial artists who have become famous all over the world (and have remained so throughout the years). For example, the great composer Maurice Ravel never obtained the Grand Prix of Rome or the coveted orchestration award of the Paris Conservatory. On this side of the Atlantic, Carmen McRae never won any Grammys, and neither did Celia Cruz for her modern and very creative disk *Irrepetible*, marvelously produced and arranged by the multitalented Willy Chirino, who, by the way, didn't win either!

*   *   *

Like Celia, Machito and Dizzy Gillespie received their little golden phonographs very late in their careers, and not for their best recordings. I remember as if it were today when I called Machito to congratulate him for the award and he replied, "Come on, Paquito, don't give me that shit! That album I made in Finland isn't bad, mainly 'cause I always try to do my best, but tell me honestly, where were those guys when Bird, Flip Phillips, Chico O'Farrill, Cannonball, Diz, and all those heavyweight musicians recorded with my band, huh?"

Along with Slide Hampton, I worked as musical codirector of Dizzy Gillespie's United Nation Orchestra when we recorded *Live at London's Royal Festival Hall* in 1990. As God is our witness, we tried hard to teach certain members of that all-star band the meaning of the terms *good taste*, *teamwork*, and *modesty*. We were not successful—but we still got a Grammy! And consider that after several decades and the concerted efforts of Andy Garcia—a famous actor of Cuban origins in love with our culture—the legendary bassist-composer Israel "Cachao" López, one of the most influential figures in the history of contemporary Latin music, was finally able to get a recording contract. Now the venerable Cuban musician has so many awards that his wife Estela cannot find any more space on the walls of their Miami apartment to display them all. However, in my modest opinion, I think that many of those certificates, medals, and trophies should go to the true wizards of the award industry, the publicists who are capable of inflating the most insignificant performer into a worldwide star. On the other hand, we must recognize that Cachao, as well as Machito, Mario Bauzá, Dizzy, Bebo Valdés, Bird, O'Farrill, and (why not?) Irakere are the authentic living trophies that have awarded us with nothing more and nothing less than the best music for the last sixty years or so—haven't they?

In 1997, my CD entitled *Portraits of Cuba*, masterfully arranged and conducted by the Argentinean musician Carlos Franzetti, was released under the New York label Chesky Records. This project went on to win that year's Grammy Award under the category of Best Latin Jazz Performer. That same year, in diverse categories, people like Herbie Hancock, Wayne Shorter, John Corigliano,

Cassandra Wilson, and the rock group the Smashing Pumpkins were also honored.

I was later told by a friend that some of the award recipients were featured on a Cuban radio show named *Contacto* that was exclusively devoted to the Grammys. The absence of my name among the prizewinners couldn't have been more conspicuous.

My friend called the show when it was off the air. "Listen, comrade," my friend, a bit upset, addressed the hostess, "how is it possible that you talked about everybody on that program, and it didn't even occur to you to mention our compatriot who also received one of those awards. Could you please tell me why?"

To which the comrade answered (off the air of course), "Well, you figure it out, *m'ijito*. Don't play stupid with me, you know how it is here. Nobody wants to get burned, you know what I mean? . . . So knock that shit off, *asere*. Forget the tango and sing the bolero, 'cause I'm not going to stick my neck out for that Paquito or nobody. So now you know." Click!

This is just a single case in more than four decades of omissions. It reminds me of the stupidity of the Havana Film Festival organizers—both in Cuba and in New York—who did not accept on their official program Leon Ichaso's *Bitter Sugar* or Julian Schnabel's phenomenal film *Before Night Falls* about Reinaldo Arenas, one of the greatest Cuban writers of all times. In the same way, the cultural authorities never mentioned Guillermo Cabrera Infante's prestigious Cervantes Award from the Spanish Academy and have kept secret the successful careers of pianist Horacio Gutiérrez, violinist-conductor Luis Haza, guitarist Manuel Barrueco, and pianist-composer-conductor Tania León in the very competitive world of classical music. It's a well-known fact that neither those illustrious Cuban artists nor the vast works of high-caliber intellectuals such as Zoé Valdés, Antonio Benítez-Rojo, Levy Marrero, Nilo Cruz, Gastón Baquero, Carlos Alberto Montaner, and Daína Chaviano are studied at Cuban schools. This was pointed out by black prisoner of conscience Vladimiro Roca in his historic document "The Homeland Is Everyone's," so all I have to add to this shameful topic is that the national culture cannot be the exclusive patrimony of those who by mistake, fear, or convenience choose to represent the longest and most ridiculous dictatorship on the planet.

Among those who were awarded Grammys in 1997 was Enrique Iglesias, the son of Julio Iglesias, who competed with his first album.

Writer Reinaldo Arenas at a protest in front of the Cuban diplomatic mission in Manhattan

By giving him the award, the judges of the Recording Academy placed him above high-quality nominees like José Feliciano and Luis Miguel.

"And what can you tell us about the Grammy awarded to Julio Iglesias's baby, Maestro D'Rivera?" a reporter asked me from behind the barriers at Madison Square Garden, visibly upset that the young Spaniard had been honored. I wasn't expecting such a question, but I answered her with caution and tact, trying not to hurt anyone's sensibilities. "Please calm down," I said without showing any emotion. "Don't get yourself all worked up. Considering that O. J. Simpson was acquitted after such overwhelming evidence of the grave charge of murder, we shouldn't be surprised if one day in the not very distant future someone comes up with the idea of nominating the cannibal Jeffrey Dahmer for the Nobel Peace Prize, don't you agree?"

And speaking of prizes, on March 13, 2002, the National Association of Hispanic Publications gave me their annual prize for outstanding editorial column in a Spanish-language publication for the following article, which was published simultaneously in the pages of Chicago's *La Raza* and the *Miami Herald*, both in Spanish and in English. I want to share this column with you, since I think it's the first time someone has received an award for putting awards down.

A Nobel Prize for Cheetah

WEEHAWKEN, NJ. Throughout my long artistic career, I have received, and witnessed the presentation of, a vast number of diverse trophies, medals and diplomas . . . a practice as common in my medium as in almost all other fields of human endeavor. The manifestations of public recognition for the mere performance of one's duties or for personal satisfaction tend to multiply nowadays.

Although I'm sincerely grateful every time I'm the object of such a distinction, the frequent bypassing of many who are worthy of praise and the exaggerated tribute to others of questionable merit lead me to view the growing award-giving industry with mistrust and skepticism.

It's plain to see that the prestigious Nobel Prize is no exception.

"They should have given it to Borges," said Gabriel García Márquez when he received his . . . and I agree. But to go from that to the Norwegian parliamentarian Hallgeir Langeland nominating Fidel Castro for a Nobel seems to me as absurd as entering King Kong in the Miss Universe contest.

I wonder if Mr. Langeland doesn't think that the image of an anachronistic military goon surrounded by 100 scowling body-guards, wrapped in a suspicious and inexplicable olive-green coat in the midst of a Caribbean August, a pistol at his side, accepting no less than the Nobel Peace Prize is the closest thing to a tasteless joke that anyone could imagine.

It saddens me that such a lamentable decision came out of Nor-way, a country I love and admire, and Scandinavia, whose effective system of social welfare and ancient tradition of respect for human rights is so contrary to the arbitrary, dictatorial methods applied by Langeland's candidate in more than four decades of tyranny . . . the longest in world history.

Cuba is a small country, in fact, impoverished by the same sys-tem that smashed the economies of so many Eastern European countries. Cuba has managed to export not only physicians and en-gineers, Mr. Langeland, but also military advisers, drug traffickers, subversive elements, occupation troops, prostitutes, spies, war weapons, smugglers, saboteurs, experts in mass repression, gun-men, professional torturers, and other specialists in the manipula-tion of the personal freedoms that you and all other Scandinavians find so valuable. Add to that the almost two million Cuban exiles strewn in all directions, not to mention those who daily drown or are shot dead while trying to flee from their own homeland.

For all these reasons and many more, Mr. Langeland, I doubt that you or any of those who second you in this irrational nomina-tion would be capable of living three months in that Castro para-dise that you defend so warmly from a prudent distance. Yet I can't say that I'm surprised by your strange and—by your own admission—controversial proposal. Your irresponsible lack of compassion is nothing new, and your political myopia is not even an exotic disease because you certainly have remarkable company.

Let's remember that *Time* magazine in 1938 selected none other than Adolf Hitler as its Man of the Year. Moreover, with the passing of time, which wipes slates clean, Her Gracious Majesty the Queen of England decorated Mme. Ceaușescu for her contributions to the well-being of the world's children. That happened only a few months before the first lady and her blood-thirsty husband Nicolae were summarily executed by the Romanian people on the pauperized streets of Bucharest.

"The alleged crimes of Comrade Stalin are only lies created by imperialist propaganda," Paul Robeson once said from his plush mansion in Enfield, Connecticut. Imagine how those words, as spoken by the famous and disinformed singer, must have fallen on the ears of the relatives of the millions of victims of the irascible Georgian dictator.

It is both curious and frustrating to see how men of stature make themselves fools when they ignore the pain of other human groups, at times allying themselves to their torturers. Such was the case of Nelson Mandela, who visited China in 1990 to receive an honorary doctoral degree from Beijing University. "I wish to express my admiration for this great country, whose society has been a real inspiration to democracy, freedom of the press, and the free expression of mankind," said the former South African prisoner in his acceptance speech at the Chinese institution, leaving his stunned listeners in an embarrassed silence. Many of them had witnessed the horrible massacre of 1989 on Tiananmen Square, by personal order of Deng Xiaoping, when thousands of university students were shot dead in a single day during a peaceful demonstration that called for freedom and democracy.

Incredibly, shortly thereafter, then-President George Bush Sr. declared China a most-favored nation. Perhaps Li Hongzhi, another nominee, founder of the persecuted Falun Gong movement, can

With Armen Donelian, Billy Taylor, Keter Betts, Joe Williams, Charlie Byrd, and Valery Ponomarev at a tribute to Willis Conover

describe to you in detail, Mr. Langeland, that tragic incident, which Castro, of course, took pains to not condemn.

I would also very much like to ask former President Jimmy Carter, another worthy candidate for this year's Nobel Peace Prize, how he feels about sharing his nomination with a sly and deceitful old man who, in response to his goodwill gestures in 1980, flooded the coast of Florida with a number of raving lunatics, spies, and common criminals mixed with good people in search of freedom.

Believe me, Mr. Langeland, the only link between Alfred Nobel and Fidel Castro is the former's explosive invention and the latter's use and abuse of dynamite, training in our native land as many international terrorists as he can, sowing hatred, death, pain, and mourning throughout the planet.

If that deserves a prize, you might just as well nominate Cheetah the Chimp for the Nobel Prize for Literature next year, don't you think?

Cuba, alegre como su sol

Cuba, happy as her sun

—INIT (National Institute of the
Tourism Industry)

VARADERO–MARIEL

"Hello, this is the operator. How can I help you?"

"Yes, *compañera*, could you please connect me to 22-2749 in Havana?"

"Just a moment, comrade," answered the operator at the Varadero motel where I had been able to get a room for a few days.

"The connection has been made, comrade. You can speak now."

"Hello . . . what? . . . Speak a little louder, I can't hear anything."

"Listen, get Alberto on the phone—Alberto Romeu, the photographer. Tell him that Paquito is calling."

"Hold on—Alberto, that musician friend of yours is on the phone."

"Damn, my man, what cave have you been hiding in? We've been going crazy for days, looking for you everywhere. We were beginning to think that you had gone inside the embassy with Eneida and Franco."

"Embassy?" I asked, confused, "I have no idea what the f—— you're talking about, Alberto."

"Oh, haven't you heard about the extraordinary show going on in the Peruvian embassy?" the photographer almost shouted.

"Look, my brother," I tried to explain to him. "I've been exiled here for five days with my wife and kid because the atmosphere in the city was so unbearable. I took advantage of the fact that Monga [my wife's nickname] got a little job assignment from the INIT [National Institute of the Tourism Industry] and came here to kick back and relax on the beach. All of Irakere's instruments have been broken for over a month, so I could escape. You know, this is another world. Check this out—Manolo Valera, Felipe Dulzaides's sax player, told me that someone put a billboard at the entrance of Varadero, near the Oasis Hotel, that says WE STAND IN SOLIDARITY WITH CUBA. Ha-ha-ha!"

"Keep talking shit, you asshole, and then one of these days they'll tap my phone and I'll really have to go to the Peruvian embassy with Yoya, my dog Biyou, and even my Commie uncle Antonio."

"I don't know anything about anything, Alberto. Look, ever since I left Havana, I haven't picked up a newspaper. I don't want to know what's happening or not happening there. Understand?"

"No, no . . . the papers haven't published a single word about what's going on. It started with a bus that crashed into the embassy, and I heard that the son of your friend Sara was on that bus with his father. There was shooting and confusion, and in the last three days, over ten thousand people have taken refuge on that little piece of land. Among them were people on buses filled to capacity from Routes 100 and 86, high army officials, the trumpeter Juanito González [director of Tejedor's *conjunto*], heavy-duty big shots, cops that left their motorcycles behind and jumped the fence, party militants. . . . They're coming from every which way, holy shit! Even the village idiots are going in there! The Peruvian ambassador is pissed off. He came out, took one look, and went home."

"How could this be happening, Alberto?" I asked incredulously.

"Well, don't ask me how, but what I know is that there's a twenty-four-hour parade of people coming down from Seventieth Street. They're swarming here like ants from the interior of the country. A couple of hours ago, I was inspecting the scene and a tractor-trailer arrived loaded with people who came here from Santiago de Cuba faster than Speedy Gonzalez. Listen, that's over a thousand kilometers from here; that's pretty wild, right?"

Barbarito (the name has been changed for obvious reasons), a fellow member of Irakere, silently contemplated the depressing spectacle around the Peruvian embassy. He remained quiet for a long time, until he couldn't bear it anymore, and began to cry bitterly. "I shit on their mothers. To what extreme do these Communist punks want to drive these poor people?!" the exasperated musician thundered. "My God, what is this? . . . How long is this going to last?"

I waited until he calmed down a bit, and then I replied, "I don't know, and I don't care, Barbarito, how long these assholes are going to tighten the screws on the people, but I want you to know that I can't take this shitty system anymore. I'm going to get the hell out of here. I don't know how or when, but I can't put up with any more crap from these motherfuckers, you dig?"

It must have been about ten in the morning when the telephone rang at my house in Marianao, the same house built by my grandmother that still displays above the front door a pretty frosted white sign with her nickname: CUCA-1929. When my paternal grandmother died, we all moved to the Marianao house, and when my parents went into exile in New York in 1968, my brother Enrique and I continued to live there.

The person calling was Tony Henríquez, a professional overseer at the National Music Administration, who had been sent to that office several years earlier despite the fact that he knew nothing about music. "Hello, listen to me, Paquito," the opinionated and arrogant musical boss began to say. "The thing is, there's a Yankee journalist here from who-knows-what magazine, and she's going to write an article about the lifestyle of Cuban professionals."

"Listen, that woman came at a bad time with all this crap going on at the Peruvian embassy, right?" I told the bureaucrat, who continued to talk without paying the least attention to what I said.

"The bottom line is, we've chosen you because you have a pretty house in a good neighborhood, your wife is an architect, and there's that Lada automobile that we gave you. . . ."

"The car that you guys sold to me, Tony," I interrupted to clarify the matter. "Let's not get confused, OK?"

"Anyway, tomorrow afternoon at two o'clock, a comrade from the MININT [Ministry of the Interior] who's assigned to cultural matters will go to your place," he told me. "He's been instructed by a higher authority to take some provisions to your house. . . . You know, cheese, slices of ham, sodas, and things like that, just in case the gringa wants something to eat. So now you know what's up."

"Fuck it, Tony Henríquez." I couldn't hold back my anger. "That's some truly hypocritical shit. Why don't you take that damned gringa to Chucho Valdés's house, so that she can see him sleeping with his new wife in that small bed they set up at night in his mother Pilar's kitchen?"

CLICK! was the answer I got.

It's true I lived in a pretty house that had been kept standing against all odds thanks to goods obtained on the black market and graciously decorated with generous donations from the Cuban community abroad (also known as *gusanos*, or "worms," and traitors). The stereo was a gift from my family—exiled in New Jersey since the late sixties—and whenever we had electricity available I could enjoy my collection of more than three hundred jazz records (imperialist music), most of which had been sent from Helsinki, Finland, by my very dear friend, the musician Esko Linnavalli.

My elegant wife, along with her family and our charming son Franco, wore clothes and shoes and put on fragrances that had been sent by Grandma Maura, a designer of ladies' attire who had been working in New York since 1969. As far as the "Russomobile" was concerned, I was authorized to buy that car after suffering for almost twenty years on the chaotic system of public transportation. After I requested political asylum in Madrid in 1980, it was personally confiscated by Armando Hart. He said that he did it because it "came out of his *cojones*." That was the vulgar terminology used by that lisping and pitiful little fellow with a cardiac-sounding last name and ethylic breath whose position was none other than minister of culture.

Laura Berquist was the name of the friendly American journalist who came "unexpectedly" to our house, accompanied by a Cuban journalist whom she "casually" met in her hotel lobby.

"Good afternoon, *compañero* Rivera," said the agent disguised as journalist, or vice versa. "Long time no see, right?" (I had never seen the fuckin' guy in my entire life.) "Look, I want to introduce you to Laura Berquist, a visiting American journalist."

"*Comou estai ustei, senior?*" the pleasant lady asked in (broken) Spanish. She still remained attractive despite her sixty-something years of age.

"I met her accidentally at the hotel, and she expressed her interest in writing an article about the lifestyle of a Cuban professional. So, taking advantage of our old friendship [?!], I brought her with me, since you and your architect wife are, in my opinion, good examples of how our professionals live."

I thought, *Coño*, if this jerk was Pinocchio, his nose wouldn't fit in this entire living room. Nevertheless, I didn't have any other choice but to give her the most cordial reception. "Please excuse the mess, but we weren't expecting company," I lied to go along with the charade (the living room hadn't been so tidy since 1929).

After making introductions, my former wife, Eneida, apologized for not having anything better to offer and "improvisingly" came up with a platter of ham slices, olives, cheese, and small crackers, along with very cold beers, a bottle of aged Havana Club rum (marked for export), and, as a final touch of hospitality, some little cups of café Pilón—"Tasty to the Last Drop," as the slogan goes—that I had brought back from my mother's kitchen during our recent trip to New York with Irakere.

Five-year-old Franco engaged in his clownish behavior, and the family interview, discreetly monitored by my "old friend," the journalist Pinocchio, was conducted very smoothly.

At some point, there was a knock on the door. It turned out to be some people from the CDR (Committee for the Defense of the Revolution) who had come to ask if we were planning to attend the March of the Combating People convened by our commander-in-chief. They had come to deliver the signs that we were supposed to take to the event.

"But of course we're going. How could we miss it, comrade?" I had to respond to that repugnant fat woman married to Lieutenant Mayedo, the most hated guy in the neighborhood.

"We'll see you there," I said, with a forced smile that didn't convince her, since she had always doubted my revolutionary vocation. (I wonder why!)

The March of the Combating People was nothing more and nothing less that a gigantic, massive harangue organized by the Communists to ease their pain and vent their anger against the thousands at the Peruvian embassy who had publicly demonstrated their contempt toward the Cuban political system. In order to guarantee the success of the operation, all places of employment were closed, and party members went from door to door, convincing people that they had to "voluntarily" attend this important rally.

So I ended up at the march in front of the embassy with my wife and little son, carrying the signs delivered by the repulsive Miss Piggy–like woman and her equally repulsive husband. Along with this loathsome couple and the rest of the population, we manifested our total repudiation of the thousands of "antisocial elements" piled up at the embassy, who were "protected" by four lines of vigorously strong members of the Special Troops who wouldn't let anyone come close to the fence, not even Lenin, if he had showed up there. There was also, camera in hand, the gray-haired American journalist who had made the "surprise" visit to our home when the CDR members showed up. How much would I have loved to get a copy of the photo taken by Laura Berquist of those signs declaring THE HUMAN SCUM MUST GO AWAY and other similar expressions of stupidity.

Laura called me that same night to thank us for our hospitality, and I took advantage of the fact that my old friend Pinocchio, the cultural gendarme, was not around to ask her, upon her return to New York, to call my mother and tell her about our encounter. I can only imagine the look on her face when Mom told her that the exemplary socialist professional to be profiled in her article had just requested political asylum in Spain.

"And now the people will take action!" the television announcer Manolo Ortega exclaimed, almost with the same conviction with which he had repeated years earlier, "Clear, light, and delightful—Hatuey, the great beer from Cuba!"

This voluntary reaction (!?) of the people, voluntarily directed by the country's only political party, meant that the same people who until a little while earlier had taken clothes and food to their friends and relatives who had taken refuge in the Peruvian embassy had now suddenly and spontaneously become indignant and were throwing rocks, eggs, and excrement at the homes left behind by the "human scum." The government, aware of the international ridicule caused by the stand-off at the embassy, organized fierce mobs armed with chains, iron clubs, cans of paint, and golf clubs—a piece of sporting equipment that hadn't been seen since the "enemy" had left the island in 1959. The violent atmosphere throughout the city transformed Cabrera Infante's Havana into Dante's inferno.

The crisis at the Peruvian embassy culminated with the massive exodus from the seaport of Mariel, which brought more than 125,000 Cubans to the shores of Florida in a few weeks. The immense majority were good people in search of liberty, but there were also thousands of mentally ill individuals, criminals who had been released from prison, and spies that the dictatorship was able to infiltrate among them for the purpose of discrediting the enormous prestige accumulated by Cuban immigrants in the previous twenty-one years of exile in the United States, particularly in the Florida peninsula.

"These are false charges made up by the imperialists!" vociferated Castro, in a state of indignation. "We treat our beloved mentally ill citizens with too much care to send them to an uncertain destiny on the shores of the perverse and brutal northern country."

"Hey, señor," I said in surprise to a man with a very sad gaze whom I found late one night at the door of the Chateau Sevilla restaurant, located on the popular Calle Ocho (Eighth Street) in Miami. He was dressed as a *charro* (Mexican cowboy), with a toy gun and a guitar in his hands. "Forgive me, but . . . you look a lot like Charrasqueado!" That poor man was in fact Juan Charrasqueado, one of those Havana street characters with mental problems. For years he wandered in the streets of his native city, accompanied by an old guitar and wearing his *charro* outfit while singing *rancheras* (Mexican country songs), before he was ordered by dictatorial goons to get inside their paddy wagon to be shipped off to Miami.

"Look, I wasn't doing anything wrong. I don't know why they put me on that boat and sent me here, where I don't know nobody or nothing," the poor street musician said, confused and disconcerted.

For some reason that I can't explain Cuban immigrants have always been extremely hardworking and prosperous. My compatriots have been able to advance and prosper in every place where they have arrived, usually in sad and adverse conditions, since 1959.

This has also been true if we go further back in history. A typical case of progress despite adverse conditions was the community established by General Antonio Maceo in Costa Rica in the nineteenth century. After he refused to accept the Zanjón peace treaty that ended the Ten-Year War against Spain (1868 to 1878), and following the failure of the Baraguá Protest that he led, General Maceo went into exile. With the approval of the Costa Rican president José Joaquín Rodríguez, in 1890 he founded a Cuban community, which he later named La Mansión, by the Gulf of Nicoya on the west coast of the Central American republic, along with one hundred families headed by the brave soldiers who had fought under his command for their country's freedom. The famous military rebel signed an agreement with the Costa Rican authorities in which he promised to instruct any interested Costa Rican family in the cultivation of tobacco, cotton, and any other agricultural product.

According to the Costa Rican journalist Isidro Murillo Villareal, "Within three years, the Cuban exiles had turned La Mansión into one of the most prosperous towns in the entire country."

The Cubans planted sugarcane, coffee, bananas, cassavas, cocoa, and other agricultural products; constructed a wooden bridge over the treacherous Morote River; established a sugar mill; inaugurated schools and health centers; and, as if that weren't enough, built the Astillero Pier, one of the best piers of its time in the Gulf of Nicoya.

"These facts lead us to believe," concludes the Costa Rican commentator, "that if these settlers accomplished so much in three years, they would have been able to accomplish much more, if the industrious Cubans had stayed longer in our country." And I would respond to the Costa Rican journalist with one word: *Miami*. That is what they would have accomplished if they'd stayed longer, Mr. Murillo. Miami was an almost barren place when the penniless Cubans arrived in the beginning of the sixties; and if the industrious Israeli people have made gardens grow in the desert, then it is understandable why we have been called the Jews of the Caribbean.

Not surprisingly, such a prosperous and strong community must have its detractors, those people who wish to discredit the labor of its members, individually or collectively. This happens today with stories about the Miami mafia, just as in 1889, when José Martí had to put an end to the verbal diarrhea discharged by a certain asshole from Philadelphia who wanted to mess with the Cuban exiles of that era.

This individual vilified the exile community in the *Manufacturer* newspaper as follows: "The Cubans have an aversion for any effort. . . . They are worthless. . . . They are lazy!" And Martí replied from the pages of the *Evening Post:*

> These lazy and worthless immigrants came here almost twenty years ago empty-handed, with few exceptions. They struggled against the climate, learned the foreign language, earned a living with their honest labor, some achieving an economically comfortable position, a few in a state of wealth, but hardly any are in a state of misery. They enjoyed luxuries, and they worked to acquire them, but were not frequently seen in the dark paths of human existence. Independent and self-sufficient, they were not afraid to compete in any aptitude or activity. Thousands remain where they have succeeded despite the harshness of daily life, without the assistance of ethnic sympathy, religious community, or friendly idiom.

A handful of Cuban laborers built Key West. The Cubans have been known in Panamá for their merit as artisans, physicians, and contractors. A Cuban, Cisneros, has powerfully contributed to the progress of the railroads and the navigation in the rivers of Colombia. Like many of his compatriots, Márquez gained the respect of the Peruvian nation as an eminent merchant.

Everywhere, Cubans work as farmers, engineers, land surveyors, artisans, teachers, and journalists. Right here in Philadelphia, the *Manufacturer* has the daily opportunity to contemplate a hundred Cubans, some of heroic record and vigorous body, earning a living from their own labor in comfortable abundance. In New York, they are prominent bank presidents, prosperous merchants, physicians with a native clientele, electricians, owners of business establishments.

The poet of Niagara is a Cuban, our own Heredia, and a Cuban, Menocal, is the chief of engineers of the Nicaragua Canal. In Philadelphia itself, as in New York, the universities' highest awards have been given to Cubans on more than one occasion.

And the wives of these worthless and lazy Cubans, these enemies of all efforts, came here after a recent sumptuous existence, in the cruelest time of the winter; their husbands had been in the war, ruined, imprisoned, and killed. The ladies went to work, sat behind a counter, sang in the churches, hemmed hundreds of buttonholes, sewed by the day, curled feathers at hat shops, gave their hearts to their duties, wore away their bodies at work. . . . This is the morally deficient people described by the *Manufacturer!*

Changing some names here and some words there, we could well transport Martí's letter of protest to the present Cuban community that, despite all the defects that it might possess, offers even more to be proud of. For example:

According to the U.S. Census Bureau, Cuban-Americans have acquired an enormous amount of wealth and prosperity in an extremely short period of time. No other immigrant group has achieved this as quickly as the Cubans. Many immigrants have never achieved it at all, despite being in this country far longer than Cubans.

Second-generation Cuban-Americans were more educated than Anglo-Americans. More than 26.1 percent of second-generation Cuban-Americans had a bachelor's degree or better versus 20.6 percent of Anglos. Thus Cuban-Americans in 1997 were approximately 25 percent more likely to have a college degree than Anglos. Other Hispanic groups lag far behind. Only 18.1 percent of South Americans had a bachelor's degree or better.

In 1997, 55.1 percent of second-generation Cuban-Americans had an income greater than $30,000 versus 44.1 percent of Anglo-Americans. Thus Cuban-Americans are approximately 20 percent more likely to earn more than $30,000 than their Anglo-American counterparts. All other Hispanic groups lag far behind in average income.

In 1997, 36.9 percent of second-generation Cuban-Americans had an income greater than $50,000 versus 18.1 percent of Anglo-Americans. Cuban-Americans were twice as likely to earn more than $50,000. Also, approximately 11 percent of Cuban-Americans had incomes greater than $100,000 versus 9 percent of Anglo-Americans and fewer than 2 percent of other Hispanics.

Cubans constitute less than 4 percent of the U.S. Hispanic population; Mexicans, 65 percent; Puerto Ricans, 10 percent; Central and South Americans, 11 percent; and others, 10 percent. Yet of the top hundred richest Hispanics in the United States, more than 50 percent are of Cuban descent (ten times what it should be on the basis of population), and 38 percent are of Mexican descent. The rest are scattered among all other Hispanic groups.

I have no further comments!

In those days of horror and uncertainty in 1980, we received a phone call from none other than my cousin Muñeca, who had arrived by boat from New York and was at the seaport in Mariel, trying to get her sister Cusa off the island as well as my brother Enrique, who was desperate to "get the hell out of this fucking country, *coñoooo!*" as I heard him scream so many times when there was a blackout. "Get me out of here too, with my wife and child, for the love of Christ!" I implored my cousin. I didn't give a shit that someone could have been listening to my conversation. Such was our level of desperation.

"Listen, Monga, it's me, Marcos. Get Paco on the phone."

"Marcos, this is getting really fucked, brother. I can't endure this shit—" (He didn't let me finish.)

"Listen to me," he said authoritatively. "Don't move from there. Normita and I are coming over there right now."

Marcos Miranda, a phenomenal actor, writer, and director, is married to my longtime friend Norma Rojas, who has always been at my side during some of the harshest periods of this roller-coaster life of mine (as when I was bumped at the last minute as conductor at that Festival of Political Song).

The couple arrived at our home almost at midnight. Although he is known for his sweet character and his gentle and educated manners, Marcos came through our front door like a tornado, and aggressively and without prior greeting told me, "Don't ask me how I found out, but if you're still thinking about trying to leave through Mariel, forget it! Only a perfect imbecile like you could think of something like that, so now you just forget it! Did you hear what I said?"

"Well, but why?" I asked, a bit frightened.

"What do you mean why, asshole?" vociferated the actor incredulously. "You know that those cultural bloodhounds would love to fuck up your life after you have been fucking around for years, making fun of them with your jokes. If you screw up, you'll be serving them your ass on a silver platter. They're just waiting for the opportunity to bust your ass. The worse thing is that after they get through with you, they're not going to let you leave just like that because they don't want the bad publicity that you would generate from abroad.

Look what they did to Amaranto, that pianist who had an orchestra in Cárdenas."

"What happened to Amaranto?" I wanted to know, since Cárdenas is far from Havana, and the newspapers didn't publish anything about him.

"Nothing new happened to Amaranto," he continued in a less agitated tone. "You know that in this country, to be a dissident and black is a double sin, and the thing is that the poor guy had taken refuge in the embassy, and then he decided to accept one of those damned letters of safe conduct that the Commies invented to get those people out of the embassy until their immigration situation had been resolved. Well, when he went back to his town, one of those crowds was waiting for him. They broke his arms, placed a fifty-five-gallon garbage can over his head, and paraded him through the entire town, hitting the can and making fun of him. According to what I was told, the show lasted the whole day, and when they got tired of hitting him and humiliating him, they threw him on a pile of manure and left him there."

After a suitable pause, Marcos sadly added, "The poor black pianist died of a heart attack."

Miranda's arguments were irrefutable. The last straw came when we received a telephone call that night to inform us that the composer Mike Porcel had been planning to leave his family via Mariel and that somehow when Silvio Rodríguez, Sara González, Pablo Milanés, and other members of the *nueva trova* movement heard about it, they organized one of those horrible repudiation meetings against their fellow troubadour. Mike was unable to leave the island until several years later, and of course until then his career was totally blocked in Cuba.

"OK, Marcos, please relax. I understand what you're talking about. I don't know about you, but I can't put up with this anymore, so tell me what you think I should do." I tried to pronounce those words with all the tranquility that I could manage in the middle of the volcano of desperation that was erupting inside me while I listened patiently to what my friend had to say.

"I know that on May 6, Irakere has a trip scheduled to Spain. So it's very simple—you jump on the plane to Spain or anywhere else and request asylum there, and we'll talk afterward. Do you agree?"

"That's some crazy shit! . . . Things appear to be so easy for you, my mustachioed friend. Tell me, what do I do with my wife and the kid? Let's see."

The actor looked at me long and hard, making direct eye contact as if he were onstage interpreting a Shakespearean character.

"Your mother waited nine long years to be able to see you in Montreal, and she didn't die because of that separation. Others waited much longer, like Penelope!" he said joking. "Instead of the three of you getting fucked, it's better if at least one can be saved. We need less talking and more action, right?"

When we arrived at Paquito's house, chaos reigned in the streets of Havana. Paquito had placed an enormous piece of plywood behind the glass window facing the porch and was carrying a tribal knife in his hand that he had brought back from his trip to Africa, like a Cuban D'Artagnan brandishing his noble sword, while he barricaded his front door against a possible demonstration of repudiation against his brother, who was leaving the country via Mariel.

"If one of these sons of bitches tries to start a repudiation meeting against my brother, I'll strangle the motherfucker," said Paquito while we tried to calm him down. When we heard the screams of the crowd a block away, where they were holding a meeting for another unfortunate compatriot who was trying to leave Castro's inferno, we went out to the sidewalk.

"Listen to them. If they do that to Enriquito, I'll make them feel a quick, intense pain," repeated Paquito.

After he went back into the house and calmed down a bit, Paquito told me about his preposterous plan to leave in a boat from Mariel with his wife and son. I reminded him about what had happened to Carlos Molina, an excellent concert guitarist and person who had taught at the ISA (Advanced Institute of the Arts).

In order to leave the country, he had to request dismissal from his place of employment. He went to see his boss, the classical composer Carlos Fariñas, who calmed him down and asked him to sit and wait while he drafted the relevant paperwork. That document turned into a gang of government supporters who went after poor Molina in the street, putting him in the degrading position of running away, afraid for his life, from the place where he had spent so many years.

"What you need to do is travel with the group and ask for political asylum in Spain," I told him, convinced that it was the best option.

"Are you crazy? What about Monga and Franquito?"

"It's very easy. Enrique appears tomorrow with her and the boy. He tells them that he's the boy's father and that she's a lesbian. That way they'll be allowed to leave."

Monga resisted that plan and pointed out the problems faced by professionals like her when they attempted to get off the island.

"You have to outwit them and play your cards right, Monga. We'll fix your identification card. On the front, where it indicates your profession as *arquitecto* [architect], we'll add *D-I-B* [abbreviation for *dibujante,* or "designer"] and at the end, *n-i-c-o.* So it will identify you as *DIB arquitectonico* [architectural designer], not as *arquitecto.*"

"I'm too afraid to do that," she said. Paquito and Monga argued over what steps to take. Finally, I was able to convince Paquito, but not Eneida, who chickened out after giving it a lot of thought. The consequences were serious, as Monga had to spend several more years on the island, and a son was separated from his father for many years and many more tears. From that episode, I keep a photo of Paquito playing his instrument, with the following dedication: "For my great friends, Marcos (Marx) and Norma Luxemburg. Always headed for victory. *Salud y Belascoaín.*" (This last sentence is a wordplay frequently used by Paquito. *Salud* means "health," but *Salud and Belascoaín* is a famous intersection in Havana.)

—Marcos Miranda

There was no way that we could sleep that night. On the following day, at a very early hour, I went to the José Martí Airport in the small town of Rancho Boyeros. I got out of the car, and for the first time, I didn't say good-bye to my wife, nor did I kiss my adored child. Farewells are sad, and this was for me the saddest of all farewells. It was also the last morning that I spent with that woman, whom I loved so much. It would indeed take many years and more tears before I could be reunited with Franco. But I never had any regrets about taking this crucial step because someone wiser than I once said that when people migrate, it's because they have the wrong rulers.

"Eneida, they're calling Papi a worm," I told my mother after hearing the protesters rallying outside our house in Marianao, shortly after my father's defection. I was then five years old and a little confused about why all those people were standing in front of our house. I can't lie: at the time it was very amusing to see so many people in front of my house, holding cardboard signs and yelling things. It was also a little odd because, as far as I can remember and judge, they yelled very loudly, but they looked like they really would rather be doing something else. It was all very peculiar to me, not only because of the name-calling and meaningless phrases but also because they had even drawn on one of those placards a picture of my father as a saxophone-holding worm.

"Why are they calling him a worm? I don't get it," I asked blankly, because I couldn't make the association between this invertebrate and my two-legged and skeletally equipped father.

"Well, Franco," my mother began to explain, "worms are those people who are not in agreement with the system and aren't pleased with their present situation (whatever that situation may be) and choose to live someplace else."

"Oh . . . OK, I get it. So that makes me a little worm."

Almost nine years of turbulence, confusion, and a lot of waiting were ahead of me, as you can imagine. In the beginning, I spent most of my time waiting for Dad to come home. I was obviously in a state of denial mixed with a bit (or a lot) of innocence. I was always hopeful that someone would walk through the living room door (a master of ceremony or a magician of sorts) and say, "OK, OK, this game's over—you can have your dad back," and then my dad would jump out from behind the door, where he had been hiding all the time.

After this came the stage—I was getting older, after all—of accepting that he would not jump out from behind the door and that he would not be returning. I had to come to terms with the truth and accept that we were to go over there, to that forbidden land: violent, wild, uncontrollable, and brutal. Those colorfully innovative descriptions were commonly used to refer to La Yuma, or El Norte, or the United States in my country by the revolutionaries and some teachers, who in the same breath would whisper in my ear, "*Coño, Franco, no sea' hijoeputa,* and send over some blue jeans and deodorant as soon as you get there, OK?"

We were now the *pioneros,* or "pioneers," of God knows what! That was the term Castro stamped on kids of our generation and . . . also on the generations to come. We were the revolutionaries without a cause, the generation who neither followed nor understood but were just *pioneros por el comunismo.*

Then they wrapped some blue kerchief around my neck and told me to say loudly, "*¡Pioneros por el comunismo, serémos como el Che!*" ("We, pioneers of communism, will be like Che Guevara!") Shit! I didn't want to be asthmatic, and it was too late to be Argentinean, so what the hell were they talking about?! I'd much rather write music than carry a machine gun and run out of breath every five minutes, I thought.

So, wanting to be like Che meant wanting to look like the Mexican actor Cantinflas (without his magical charisma) and dying in Bolivia wearing a silly little hat, which wasn't exactly an ideal aspiration, so every time I yelled "*¡Serémos como el Che!*" it was with a hypocritical smile on my face.

As I said, we were to go there to be reunited. But it wasn't so cut and dried: to go we had to wait. And wait, and wait, and wait for a notorious yellow letter from the government that would give us authorization to leave the country. They teased us with letters that were canceled several times at the last minute at the sick whims of those in higher places. Needless to say, any form of correspondence that came through that slit under the door, yellow or not, was quickly seized.

At that young age I had no real understanding of how such complicated matters worked, only that they seemed to be more ridiculously complicated than necessary. As result of the frustration, my young mind began to rebel and started working on its own weird psychological plane. I would engage in ridiculous tasks to attain my goal of reunion since otherwise I was completely powerless against the situation. I would purposely, for example, for no reason other than self-sacrifice, go into terrible neighborhoods to pick fights with several kids at a time. Before starting to fight, I made the ridiculous heroic utterance "*¡Por mi papá!*" ("For my father!") and then got my ass kicked by two tough guys *del barrio* (from the neighborhood).

In another act of glorious self-sacrifice for the purpose of reunion, I climbed to the roof of the auditorium of the García Caturla Conservatory, and as I focused on a distant branch of a flamboyant tree, decided to leap and grab it, expecting that it would of course lower me slowly to the ground. I again dedicated this pointless Tarzanesque act *"¡Por mi papá!"* and jumped with unmatched enthusiasm. Suddenly, at an incredibly fast speed, I saw the ground of the school yard coming closer and closer toward me, which led to my first brain concussion. After ten or twelve minutes, I opened my eyes and I must truly tell you that I did feel like a worm: a flat, motionless worm on the ground. Lying there in a hallucinatory trance I transformed back to the night of the protesters' rally in front of our house: I began to think that what the protesters had been trying to communicate to us all that time was that my father (exactly like me) had just fallen from the roof of a theater.

One sunny afternoon, I, with a big purple bruise on my right cheek from another one of those clumsy days, was sitting in the living room, next to my dog Bruto, watching cartoons, when a yellow envelope was slipped under the door. My mother picked it up and opened it. She read it very quickly, and then read it another time slowly to make sure her eyes were not deceiving her. Half laughing and half crying, she sat down, and I thought to myself, Shit, now my dad's going to see me with my face all fucked up like this.

Several days later, on January 11, 1989, we took our long-awaited flight to reunion and freedom. We had waited nine years. Separating us all that time was a thirty-seven-minute flight to Florida.

We now live *felices como lombrices* (as happy as worms).

—Franco D'Rivera

Por la calle de Alcalá
Con la falda almidoná

Through the streets of Alcalá
With her starched skirt

—Spanish paso doble

MADRID-NEW YORK

None of my old Irakere mates, and much less our new delegation overseer, suspected that the suitcase I had checked in at the José Martí Airport was my farewell joke. It contained two bricks, a broomstick, a useless sugarcane-cutter boot, a vest, another old suitcase, and other pieces of junk. It was everything I needed for a one-way trip aboard a Cubana de Aviación Soviet IL-62 airplane that would soon take off for its seven-hour flight, bound for Madrid's Barajas International Airport. Seven hours of anxiety, forced jokes, and repressed tears.

My state of anxiety on that plane was so great you could actually see it. I think it was the trumpeter Varona who looked at me in surprise and asked me, "Hey, Slim, what happened to your hair?" Back then it was fashionable to have an Afro hairstyle, and when I looked in the mirror in the plane's small restroom, I discovered that my Afro was totally white, covered with dandruff. My nerves had provoked what I called a violent dandruff attack. . . . Yes, as dreadful as it sounds: DAN-DRUFF. . . . How horrible! Fortunately, I had a small palm-leaf hat to cover my dandruffy hair.

We finally landed. For some members of the band, myself included, it was our first time in Spain. All I had was my palm-leaf hat, my saxophone, a small carry-on bag, that suitcase filled with junk in the belly of the airplane, and my hidden dandruff attack.

There at Barajas we were to wait six hours for a flight bound for Sweden, or some other Nordic country, where Irakere's tour would begin. I knew that I could not, under any circumstances, board that plane. What I didn't know at the age of thirty-two was how to control twenty-one years of well-learned lessons in fear and not get on the next flight. To keep from boarding that flight, I had to make countless telephone calls to an office where no one answered (logically, as it was Sunday), drink half a bottle of very ordinary rum that I shared with the guitarist Carlos Emilio, make seventeen unproductive trips to the men's room and an additional trip to the ladies' room, from which I was expelled as soon as I pushed the door. . . . Well, you know how it is when your nerves are tense, right?

At last, when our last flight was called, I was involved in my last attempt to evacuate what couldn't be evacuated (mainly because there was nothing to evacuate), and when I came out of the restroom, I could only see, from far away, Chucho's back as he entered the airplane. I took off like a bullet, seized my inseparable companion (my saxophone, which seemed to be waiting for me under a small table in the reception area), and like a flaming meteor, I went down an up escalator that was ascending with two unfortunate female employees of Iberia Airlines, whom I nearly trampled in my stampede.

"Shit, this guy is a savage!" screamed one of the flight attendants, taken by surprise. I didn't have any time to apologize, so I continued my mad race until I arrived breathless at one of the information and customs booths situated at the lower level of the building. Then I gave the agent my passport, which had my airplane ticket inside.

"You'll have to go to the upper level to take flight 247 bound for Stockholm, sir," said the airport official, after examining my documents.

"But I'm not going there, I'm staying here. I have a three-day visa in Spain, right?" I tried to explain.

"My God, if you don't hurry, you're going to miss that flight for Sweden that cost a lot of money," he insisted. Already in a state of despair, I exclaimed, almost in tears:

Welcoming my son Franco at the Miami airport (1989)

"Listen, *compañero* [this must have been a linguistic flashback from Cuba], don't you understand, I'm being pursued by Communists!" I blurted out, truly believing what I was saying. "They're getting closer by the minute. Please, hurry up. You can see that I have a three-day visa stamped on my passport!" I begged.

The man observed me slowly, and very attentively, cautiously analyzing every part of my extravagant appearance—my small straw Cuban hat, the Afro hairstyle, and my strong Caribbean accent. Only then did he respond with a calm but firm voice, "Oh, now I see. . . . I should've realized it at the beginning."

The agent took another look at the cover of my red passport with golden letters, and around the national shield he could read the inscription "Official Passport, Republic of Cuba." After a pause that seemed to last an entire century, and while he loudly stamped an entry visa on my travel document, he added, completely convinced, "Now everything is very clear, of course. . . . You are Polish. . . . Welcome to Spain!"

Without daring to look back, and feeling my imaginary persecutors breathing down my neck, I didn't stop running until I opened the front door of the first taxi in a long row of cabs and squeezed myself next the driver.

"Take me to this address now, please. I don't want any problems, please," I told the driver, stuttering and placing with difficulty my saxophone and carry-on bag on my lap and extending to him a little piece of paper on which my friend Gloria in Havana had written the address of her daughter, Dr. Gloria del Carmen Agüero, who had been living in exile in Spain for several years.

"I'll be damned—Móstoles!? That place is farther away than hell!" said the driver without taking from his mouth a black cigarette butt that threatened to burn his lips. "And why are you in such a rush, like someone's chasing you?" he added, shaking off the ashes that were falling on the bosom of his dirty shirt.

I was too afraid to open my mouth, but when he said the words "chasing you," I felt drops of cold sweat escape from between the little hat, my hair, and the dandruff.

"Well, let's go. The sooner the better, right?" he said and looked at me while starting the engine of the Seat that smelled and looked like an ashmobile.

I had been able to hide in my bag about one hundred U.S. dollars that were given to me by my brother Enrique and an old friend of the family named Mercy Oliva, who had asked me to buy her some perfume. I was ashamed to take her money because I knew I would use it for a different purpose. Some years later, Mercy came as a visitor to New Jersey, and in the midst of our laughter, I reminded her of the incident and then presented her with a gift of perfume as well as the small sum of money that she had given me. In that way I was able to return many favors she extended to me in the difficult years after my parents went into exile.

"Where are you from, pal?" the taxi driver asked me in a gravelly voice. The foul-smelling driver hadn't shaved for days and resembled the villainous hog in the old Porky Pig cartoons.

"I'm Cuban, comr—err—mister," I answered, still feeling nervous.

"Cuban! Goddamn! You guys really have what this country needs!" cried out the human hog, frightening me when he almost lost control of the wheel. He began to squeal, "That Fidel of yours is a hell of a man! . . . I A-DORE HIM!"

"I think this is the building right here, comrade. Here are your rubles." That was my reply to his passionate harangue while I got out, quickly and with difficulty, from the filthy car with my sax, the bag, the hat, and my anger.

When I was already out of the taxi, I told him as a form of farewell, "If you like that bearded asshole so much, why don't you move to Cuba, *gallego de mierda* [shitty Galician]." The guy could not believe what he had heard with his own ears.

"How dare you call me Galician, you miserable Yankee worm, if I'm Catalonian? Your father is the one from Galicia, miserable bastard!"

But I was already too busy trying to find the apartment of my friend Gloria's daughter, so I couldn't stop to explain to the furious driver that not my father but one of my great-grandfathers was a real *gallego* from Galicia (and not a shitty *gallego* like him).

For some obscure reason, in Latin America, a Spaniard could be originally from Algeciras, Pamplona, Lanzarote, or Alcañiz-Teruel, but is always called *gallego* (Galician), as if all Spaniards were from the northwest part of Spain. Spanish immigrants to Cuba were victimized upon the arrival of the bearded character in 1959, when he seized everything they had acquired, leaving them down and out and penniless. But since man is the only animal that stumbles on the same stone twice, some years after that, the descendants of those who had everything stripped from them in 1959 were the first ones to engage in the stupid behavior of investing their cash in Cuba at the request of the dictator. By the way, that bearded character is also a descendent of *gallegos* (in his case, truly from the Galician region).

Those descendants have built fabulous hotels for tourists only, where Cubans of Spanish, African, Chinese, or Jewish origin, irrespective of race, sex, or religion, cannot enter unless they carry the enemy's currency, the Yankee dollar.

Due to their arrogance, certain Spaniards (not all of them) have again earned the dislike of our people. Someone told me that on a certain morning, a sign appeared near the tomb of General Antonio Maceo in El Cacahual with the following message: WAKE THE GENERAL UP, THE SPANIARDS HAVE RETURNED.

I had in my bag for Gloria an old bracelet that her mother had given her as a child and that I would use to identify myself. When I gave her that family jewel, the gynecologist almost began to cry. There aren't enough words to thank her for the tremendous generosity and tenderness that she bestowed upon me at such a difficult moment without even knowing me.

Dr. Gloria del Carmen Agüero, a Cuban gynecologist who left Cuba after being forced to work for a long time in the agricultural sector, revalidated her degree and established a private practice in Madrid. With uncommon generosity, she welcomed me in her Móstoles apartment. After reassuring me that I was safe and that no one could harm me there, she offered me shelter and accompanied me as I took the first steps toward applying for political asylum at the police headquarters located near the Puerta del Sol, in the very center of the beautiful city of Madrid.

A bit overwhelmed by the news of my drastic decision, my mother almost immediately traveled to be reunited with me in the Spanish capital, with the determined support of Evelyn Lynd, general manager of the Movie Star Company, where my mother worked for many years as department supervisor. Miss Lynd kept my mother's position open until she returned from her rescue expedition a month later.

Maura's arrival in Madrid was like a soothing tonic in the midst of the roaring volcano that my brain had become in those days. After finding a place to stay at the Hostal Rivadavia, near the center of the city, the first thing we did was call Cuba from the main office of the telephone company to talk to my wife and my young son Franco, whom I missed tremendously.

That same day we met some Cubans who were lining up behind some Vietnamese exiles to make free calls from one of those tampered phones at the Plaza de España, and there we learned how Uncle Ho Chi Minh's compatriots were also escaping from Marx and Lenin's Asian branch. After so many years of propaganda telling us about the achievements of communism in Vietnam, I found it very difficult to believe that those poor children of a humble and rural country, after a war that ended with Communist victory, would flee their homeland on fragile rafts, where many died of hunger and thirst, were gunned down, drowned, or were lost in the vast China Sea. Those standing on line were among the raft people who for humanitarian reasons were offered political asylum by the Spanish authorities.

Countless books, articles, songs, plays, and films have been made about this infernal conflict, which had as its stage the distant Vietnam, and from all those nightmarish images, the one that remained forever in our memories was the picture taken by the Pulitzer-Prize-winning photographer Nick Ut in 1972 in a village named Trang

Bang, close to Saigon. The picture showed a girl engulfed in napalm, running naked on the road, screaming from pain. The child, whose name was Kim Phuc, was only nine years old. Her image went around the world, a horrid testament of that war and any other war for that matter. It became above all the perfect symbol for anti-American propagandists.

After spending some time in Moscow, and as compensation for her wounds, the young woman was sent to the University of Havana for her studies. There she got married, and on the flight back to Havana from her honeymoon in the USSR, the plane made a stop in Gander, Newfoundland, where the newlyweds decided to say good-bye to Fidel Castro's paradise. After her silent escape from Cuba, Kim Phuc, with her husband and son, lived quietly in Toronto until later moving to the United States.

"I had no freedom. My life was totally controlled and I couldn't take it," the fragile, diminutive woman said. As described by the journalist Gina Montaner, she was the "victim par excellence of the atrocities committed by yesterday's enemies, and a victim once again of the manipulation and repression of today's enemy, whom some still try to justify."

Many of Kim's compatriots keep arriving at American airports to be reunited with their American fathers, soldiers who participated in that long and bloody war. They are desperate to leave their land and come to live in a country that one would imagine would inspire nothing but hatred. Are those the achievements of socialism that Stalin, Fidel, and Ho Chi Minh spoke of interminably?

The tampered phones in Madrid were a phenomenon that I will describe. In 1980 Spain's public phones functioned, according to a knowledgeable friend at the time, like a car's electrical distribution system. When a solution of vinegar and salt was applied to the mechanism by way of the coin slot, it created a crystalline bridge that allowed free communication with almost the entire world for a relatively extended period of time.

Thanks to this illegal system, many exiles from Cuba, Vietnam, and other nations were able to make free calls to their relatives around the world, creating a host of problems, of course, for the Spanish telephone company (and also making some public phone booths in Spain smell like a lettuce and tomato salad).

Around that time, a Cuban girl named Indira Novo came to visit us at the inn, and I established a very special relationship with her. She was married to a Cuban violinist, whom she had tried unsuccessfully to get out of Cuba. (The main reason for failure was that the man could never make up his mind about taking such a drastic step.) With much sacrifice, however, she was able to get her younger sister out, as well as her sick father.

For some reason, ever since I was young, I have related food with love, and Indira cooked very well. Also she was a very pretty brunette, and whenever she took her clothes off, she made me forget and remember at the same time the woman that I had left behind in Cuba, who had become sort of an obsession for me in my first stages of exile. That obsession with my wife and son in Cuba kept me from establishing a serious relationship with Indira.

When my mother went back to New York, I moved within a few days to a pension on San Marcos Street, where some Cubans whom I had met at a tampered phone were also staying, and they helped ease my sadness. There I set up a work desk with an attached lamp and began to write some arrangements commissioned by my friend Esko Linnavalli for the Finnish television orchestra and other Finnish groups. The best form of charity is to offer work, and Linnavalli put that wise concept into practice.

Madrid is a special place of unexpected encounters. There at a Chinese restaurant I met by accident a Uruguayan drummer named Carlos Carli, who knew about me from the Irakere recordings. He introduced me to a group of fellow musical *sudacas* (a deprecatory term used by Spaniards to refer to Latin Americans, probably derived from the word *Sudamérica* [South America]).

After my mother left and Indira received her U.S. visa, my loneliness was killing me, and the Uruguayan drummer took me to live in his small apartment. Along with his fellow *sudaca* band members, he found work for me at the Dallas Club, at 34 Orense Street, where they played regularly. Thanks to Carli and his friends, I could earn some money and learn something about Brazilian music, which I had always loved.

The group's repertoire was quite varied and full of South American musical elements, so I can say that this job was really my first professional gig as a Latin jazz musician. Between the money that I earned there, and the arrangements commissioned from Finland, I was able to support myself for some months without having to ask my poor mother to send dollars from New York while I waited for my entry visa to the United States. The fact that I didn't have to pay rent at Carli's place was also very helpful, and years later, I found out that

Bandoneonist *by Franco D'Rivera*

In a sauna with Esko Linnavalli, Dizzy Gillespie, and friends in Helsinki, Finland, in the early eighties

those South American musicians, at Carlos's urging, decided generously to donate part of their earnings to pay my salary at the Dallas Club, when I was down and out in Spain.

Carlos Carli is not the only Uruguayan who has been helpful to me. Besides my yearly jazz festival in Punta del Este and my musical and personal friendships with bandoneonist Raúl Jaurena and composer-journalist Elbio Barilari, another Uruguayan musician who has made significant contributions to my artistic achievements is the pianist-conductor Pablo Zinger (not to be mistaken with Argentinean pianist-composer Pablo Ziegler), the man responsible for my decision to resume my career as a classical clarinet player. Pablo also gave me the opportunity of recording with Astor Piazzolla. With Pablo's invaluable help and remarkable professional skills, we organized dozens of chamber music recitals and symphonic concerts across the United States and abroad.

▲▲▲

I met Paquito in New York City in 1983. His girlfriend—and later, his wife—Brenda had auditioned me for the title role in De Falla's opera *La vida breve* at the now defunct TOMI [Theater Opera Music Institute] on the top floor of a building on Seventy-third Street near Central Park West. With her powerful voice and passionate delivery, Brenda was a splendid Salud. My own wife, actress Adriana Sananes, was dancing flamenco in the production. Paquito attended, and he was very generous with his praise after the show. I vaguely knew that Paquito was famous, even though in my ignorance of Latin jazz I really didn't know his music at that time. I suggested, partly out of politeness, that he come read some chamber music with me. I was surprised to have him accept my invitation and to discover how much of a "classical" musician he was—I use quotation marks to indicate that we all feel that the division between "classical" and "popular" is artificial and detrimental to music making.

At that time I had a group called Música Hispana, dedicated to promoting Spanish and Latin American concert music, and Brenda was part of a quartet of sopranos—with Thelma Ithier, Mónica Ramírez, and Elizabeth Acosta—that performed with me at the piano. Paquito would joke that I was his hero for being able to stand four sopranos at the same time.

The sopranos were followed by the Trío Música Hispana, with myself at the piano; my father-in-law, the Uruguayan-born violinist Israel Chorberg; and the Cuban cellist Alejandro Bacelar. Occasionally Israel was unavailable, and I enlisted Paquito to play his parts. He soon became a regular, and sometime later we did a series of concerts at Repertorio Español in New York City, where Paquito and I were joined by Brazilian cellist Gustavo Tavares. That would be the beginning of Triángulo, a group that plays exclusively the music of Latin American composers such as Piazzolla, Paquito, and

Pixinguinha. Gustavo, Paquito, and I recorded two CDs very dear to me: *Chamber Music from the South,* recorded in Rio de Janeiro, in an apartment overlooking the Bay of Guanabara, and the Grammy-nominated *The Clarinetist, Vol. I,* recorded in Germany, in which we played my arrangement of Piazzolla's *bandoneón* concerto *Aconcagua.* Upon finishing *Chamber Music from the South,* Paquito left Gustavo and me in charge of supervising the editing. As we heard our takes of "Milonga del Angel," tears came to my eyes. Rumor has it that the Brazilian birthrate had a minor spike upward because of Brazilian couples making love to that tune. Many friends in the United States who listened to the CD had a similar reaction.

Triángulo continues to this day, with Venezuelan flutist Marco Granados brilliantly following in Paquito's footsteps, and Paquito's presence can be felt musically and personally in everything we do.

The Triángulo experience with Paquito was exhilarating and challenging for all of us. Paquito had to get his classical chops back and to work within the somewhat constraining limits of chamber music, while we had to contend with keeping up with a great improviser who would take off into the distance in Piazzolla's music and his own pieces. I think we all came out the richer. In April 1997 we did a concert in El Paso, Texas, one of many organized by the champion of culture in that city, the indefatigable and always gracious Alejandrina Drew. This one was at the Chamizal National Memorial, where years before we had started the zarzuela craze with Repertorio Español's doña Francisquita. This time we were playing the Trío de las Serranías, by Argentine composer Ángel Lasala. The clarinet part had been poorly copied in by me, and by the third movement Paquito's eyes were strained. He accidentally skipped one or two lines and found himself lost, so he started improvising! Gustavo Tavares and I were quite amused and continued with the regular accompaniment while Paquito bebopped happily along. After the concert, an old lady told us, "I particularly enjoyed that Lasala piece. I can see the influence of Gershwin in that last movement."

Another highlight of Paquito's Triángulo days was our tour of Brazil in November 1998. The three of us and producer Maria Cecília Nascimento Gonçalves—a tall blond that we soon baptized Xuxa—embarked on a tour of the great state of São Paulo, old style, doing one-nighters and traveling in a van.

At one of the stops we were playing in a large sports stadium alongside some of the most revered stars of Brazilian music (among them Paulo Moura and Leny Andrade, both of whom joined Triángulo in Pixinguinha's *Carinhoso*). Another luminary performing that night was the dean of Brazilian guitarists, Baden Powell (1937–2001). Mr. Powell, who was featured at the end of the concert, would precede each work with a quarter hour of reminiscences whispered softly into the mike. Then he would play—masterfully—a fifteen- to twenty-minute piece. This went on, and on, and on. . . . It was well past midnight and, little by little, the audience had started to leave when the producer called us all to the stage. We all came out, surrounded Baden Powell, and at the end of his piece paid tribute to him—and pushed him gently but firmly off the stage.

Another learning experience from that tour was about Brazilian punctuality: when we asked, "When are we starting the concert?" the people in charge would say, "Seven o'clock *em ponto* [sharp]." Seven o'clock and seven-thirty would go by, and we would ask again. This time the answer would be "Eight o'clock *em ponto.*" With luck the concert would start at nine o'clock, but it would be as enjoyable as could be, with the Brazilian public always ready to accept our unlikely mix of classical, jazz, and popular for what it was and is: good music.

Another aspect of my collaboration with Paquito was symphonic. At first I invited Paquito to appear with the Bronx Arts Ensemble, the orchestra with which I made my conducting debut in 1989. That was followed by appearances with the National Symphony of Costa Rica; the Simón Bolívar Symphony

Orchestra in Caracas, Venezuela; and the Maribor Philharmonic in Slovenia. The repertoire ranged from Gershwin to Carlos Franzetti, Chico O'Farrill, Jeff Beal, Mozart, von Weber, Villa-Lobos, and Piazzolla. Additional treats were the participation of the wonderful musicians in Paquito's quintet and Brenda's singing. The orchestral musicians always had nothing but admiration for Paquito's musicianship.

As for me, Paquito and Brenda are two of my very best friends, and I love them dearly.

—Pablo Zinger

▼▼▼

Back in Madrid in 1980, one afternoon I received a call from a Barcelona-based Argentinean trumpeter named Américo Bellotto, an exceptional master who trained Thad Jones so that he could play again after his lips were ruined by a punch he received while in the former Yugoslavia.

I was at the Zagreb Jazz Festival when that unfortunate incident took place. I was told that Thad had grabbed a woman's ass and that the man accompanying her didn't appreciate such effusiveness. He followed Thad to his car and, through the open window of the vehicle, punched him in the mouth, resulting in the trumpeter's inability to play his instrument for a long time.

Américo found out that I was in Madrid and asked me to go to Barcelona for a couple of days to play with the great Catalonian pianist Tete Montoliu at the jazz club called La Cova del Drac. I greatly admired Tete, so I took off for Barcelona right away, without even asking how much I was going to get paid. (As musicians, we often commit such foolish actions.) The rest of the band was composed of a Uruguayan drummer named Aldo Caviglias, the North American tenor player Bobby Stern, bassist Javier Colina, Américo, and me.

The reaction I felt when I listened to that great pianist for that first time was similar to the one I had previously felt one afternoon when, as an amazed thirteen-year-old kid, I heard Chucho Valdés at the Havana 1900 nightclub. Coincidentally, Chucho was the one who first told me about the formidable Tete Montoliu, a blind man who seemed to have an eye on each finger. Tete was one of the artists with whom we became acquainted through Willis Conover's Voice of America broadcasts.

In the early nineties, while touring with the Catalonian pianist, I arrived in the dressing room in a pissed-off mood because of some stupid remark a journalist had written about us in a daily newspaper. In order to appease me, the pianist asked me, "Listen, you grouchy *cubanito*, have you ever been to the Balearic Islands?"

I answered no, since at that time I hadn't been able to visit those beautiful and small Spanish islands in the Mediterranean.

"Well, let me tell you that on a certain occasion, an all-star big band was organized for a tour of Spain, with a bunch of American musicians who were brought from New York. The thing is that after we played in Palma de Mallorca, Ibiza, or Menorca—I don't remember exactly which island—a son of a bitch critic wrote in the daily paper's morning edition that our concert was a true disaster and that the only worthwhile thing about that entire orchestra was the extremely stellar performance of vibraphonist Bobby Hutcherson."

After a pause, and as if searching through his thoughts to find the best way to tell the end of the story, Tete said finally, "The small plane that flies to those islands (I believe that it was made in Germany) is a Fokker, a name that the Americans find quite amusing. It is a very small plane, and on that occasion, there was not enough room for Bobby's vibraphone, so the instrument never arrived at the theater where we played that night, and where—according to that journalist asshole—the only good things about the concert were Bobby Hutcherson's vibraphone solos." The Catalonian musician ended his narration with loud laughter.

Near the end of 1997, we received the sad news of the premature death of Tete, a victim of lung cancer. Although he'd recently stopped smoking, the nicotine he had consumed for so many years, plus the nicotine that is involuntarily forced on us by hard-core smokers in hermetically sealed planes, nightclubs, and other public and private places, ended the life of the exquisite pianist. That's why I hate that stinking habit so much. To honor the memory of the beloved artist, a concert was organized in the new and beautiful Alfredo Kraus Auditorium in Las Palmas, in the Canary Islands. The participants were Cedar Walton, Billy Higgins, Johnny Griffin, yours truly, and the vibraphonist Bobby Hutcherson, who was certainly one of the main attractions of the night.

And speaking of good pianists, at Barcelona's Celeste Club I saw Bill Evans playing for the last time, along with Marty Morell and Marc Johnson. I had previously seen him playing with McCoy Tyner at Carnegie Hall, during that little-publicized concert with Irakere in New York. Evans died a short time after his appearance in Catalonia.

That night, after all the musicians left the Celeste Club, as soon as I stepped out on the sidewalk, I realized that I had forgotten something valuable on my table. When I turned around and went back, my head struck the automatic glass door with such intensity that the door shattered. Hundreds of thousands of minuscule bits of glass fell on top of me, and for a moment everyone was petrified, perhaps expecting that I would disintegrate into small pieces, as in a *Tom and Jerry* cartoon. However, apart from the sudden terror I experienced, I came out miraculously unharmed and without a scratch.

I remember that for a project in the early nineties, our Valencia-born producer Julio Martí came up with the great idea of organizing a group composed of David Finck, Claudio Roditi, Akira Tana, Sammy Figueroa, Tete Montoliu, and me for a tour of several Spanish cities, and we had a wonderful time together, both musically and personally.

Sammy Figueroa is a phenomenal New York–born percussionist, half Puerto Rican and half Cuban, and entirely and impetuously demented. The first thing he did when I introduced him to the blind pianist was to ask him, in front of his wife Carmina (who took him everywhere), if it was true that he was the president of the Sexually Perverted Jazz Pianists Society of Spain. Tete, who couldn't believe what he had heard, almost fell on the floor laughing, along with

Carmina and the rest of us. We could never predict what the hell Figueroa was going to come up with.

Something similar happened when I introduced him to my former manager, Helen Keane, at a New York recording studio. Mrs. Keane (who was also the manager of Bill Evans, Art Farmer, Jeffrey Holder, Kenny Burrell, and other famed artists) was not exactly known for her jovial character or good sense of humor. But Sammy passed her baptism of fire with flying colors, making the serious American producer burst into loud laughter when he told her, in a well-articulated East Indian accent, that he was neither Cuban nor Puerto Rican but a native of Calcutta and that he (as well as the other male inhabitants of that land) didn't eat cows because they are regarded as sacred animals, but that he did enjoy screwing them, a delightful activity that didn't cause any harm to the venerated bovines.

In Málaga, the witty and mischievous percussionist hooked up with one of those Andalusian women who have such a deliciously raunchy way of talking. Sammy said that the girl told him in the middle of their romantic adventure, in a murmuring tone of voice, "Wait right here, sweetheart. I'm going to the bathroom to wash my bush."

Since that tour, Tete became a true fan of Sammy's, who is also one of the most versatile and subtle percussionists around—at a time when there are too many people making noise, playing in only two musical dynamics: forte and fortissimo.

I dislike percussionists who are convinced that energy and swing are direct products of an exaggerated volume, even though there are clear examples who prove just the opposite, such as Louis Nash, Grady Tate, Mel Lewis, Dennis Mackrel, and Portinho.

One of the musicians who plays the rhythm from south of the border with the most energy and swing is the Chicago-born drummer Mark Walker, who many times uses only a pair of brushes (an ancient percussive accessory used by good percussionists to enable the other musicians to be heard as well). The truth, by the way, is that this volume problem has become a plague in our business.

* * *

There is a publicity slogan to promote visits to this magical land that states "Spain is different." It is something that you cannot truly appreciate until you go there.

You might confuse Norwegians with Danes, Belgians with Frenchmen, Ethiopians with Somali, or even meet a South American Indian playing his harp or *quena* on the corner of Fifty-seventh and Broadway in New York and not be certain if he is Paraguayan or Bolivian. But believe me, wherever you find a Spaniard, with his peculiar form of pronouncing the last letter of the alphabet, his hemp-made sandals, his beret, and his bagpipe attached to his cross belt, not even José Feliciano would mistake him for a Hungarian or a Guatemalan.

In addition, Spain happens to be, at least for Spanish-speaking visitors, one of the most fun-filled places on the planet, whether you have money or not. What I'm referring to is that in my case, for example, while waiting for my visa, I stayed in Madrid for almost six months, living in very modest economic conditions, but I had a damned good time there, simply because to have a great time in Madrid all you need to do is step out of your domicile, go to any of the four or five bars found on each block, and start a conversation with the first person you find at the counter. Within half an hour, it will seem that you've known each other all your lives. Between beers and appetizers of olives, anchovies, and small chorizos, you'll spend hours conversing with the *galifardo* (another Cubanism for *Spaniard*) about soccer or about the horrible situation created by the current government (whatever government is in power), and before long you'll be clapping your hands to the sound of flamenco and toasting his family in Cádiz and your relatives in West Palm Beach.

Spaniards are the most hospitable and sociable people in Europe. However, they are as unique as they are divided.

"Hey, *gallego*, play a paso doble for us!" I shouted to Tete Montoliu, disguising my voice, on a night I happened to find the great pianist from Catalonia at a jazz festival in Canada.

"Aha! . . . That must be Paquito or some other Cuban son of a bitch!" he answered immediately from his piano, and he later added while I embraced him, "I don't mind being called Galician, but don't call me Spaniard because I'll punch your lights out! Do you hear me?"

Machiavelli said, "Divide and conquer," but I might add that self-division is even worse. The Iberian people, with their small islands included, have a marvelous country where good music, fine arts, exquisite food, and beautiful women can be found from La Coruña and Málaga to La Gómera, Santander, and Ibiza. But they want to break their country into small pieces. The problem of separatism doesn't affect Spaniards only. We did the same thing on this side of the Atlantic Ocean when we disregarded the celebrated dream of Simon Bolívar to establish a single, great fatherland from the Rio Grande to Patagonia, and once again when Martí and his Puerto Rican friend Sotero Figueroa had the brilliant and practical idea of establishing a Caribbean federation that would unite under one government the nations of Cuba, Puerto Rico, and the Dominican Republic.

Instead, nowadays in Latin America we have many small countries (and large ones, too) that are independent and sovereign, in which we collectively exhibit—in an independent and sovereign manner—our chronic administrative inefficiency; a vast population of beggars, illiterates, and malnourished children; and, above all, a wide range of dictators, from the most extreme right-wingers to the most fervent Stalinists, who always assert their "sacred" independence and sovereignty against foreign interference (including that of the United Nations) while spending all their time blaming the gringos for the economic and social ruin that those same dictators have created though centuries of theft and arbitrariness.

"Ladies and gentleman," declared a Brazilian congressman during a governmental meeting, "I suggest that we tighten our belts and steal less, because soon there will be nothing left in this country to steal."

Someone told me a funny story about a head of state in Ecuador whose presidential term was beset by complaints about his poor administrative abilities. He responded in his farewell speech, "My fellow compatriots, I have been unfairly criticized for many things, but I only wish to tell you that during my mandate, the country has neither advanced nor declined, but just the opposite!"

Latin American politicians frequently use and abuse the names of the great men in history. The Cuban bearded tyrant has dared to declare that José Martí is not only his accomplice but also the intellectual author of his failed experiment to create a new *sociedad* (which means "society" in Spanish, although in this case it should be called *suciedad*, or "filthiness"). In reality, the illustrious writer had a social and political vision diametrically opposed to the one inflicted on the Cuban people by the oldest dictator on the planet.

"These paragraphs written by Martí have an amazing relevance to our current times," wrote Dr. Carlos Márquez Sterling in his biography of the Cuban patriot:

> "The man who wants the State to care for him," said Martí, "so that he does not have to care for his own self, would have to work then in the measure, time, and labor that the State decides to assign to him, since all of the duties would be given to the State, as well as all of the powers necessary, of course, to obtain the means to comply with said obligations.
>
> "Instead of serving himself, man would become a servant of the State. From being a slave of the capitalists, he would then become a slave of the government functionaries. A slave is anyone who works for another man that has control over him, and in this socialist system, the community would dominate the man, who would supply his labor to the community.
>
> "And since functionaries are human beings, they are, therefore, abusive, arrogant, and ambitious; and would have great power in that system, supported by all those who profit or expect such abuse and by those sordid powers that are always bought by terror, prestige, or the ability of the rulers; this system of distribution of

common work would soon suffer from the weakness, violence, theft, and distortion that the spirit of individuality, ostentation, and zealous disposition, combined with the slyness of moral corruption, creates promptly and fatally in every human organization."

"Martí's struggle was not against Spain or the Spaniards, but against Spanish domination," I once commented to my Madrid-born friend Javier Estrella. We were having breakfast at the St. Moritz Hotel, which is located across from the impressive statue of the apostle of Cuban independence at the main entrance of New York's Central Park.

I know a drummer in Miami who inherited a certain antipathy toward Spaniards from his grandfather, no doubt based on the numerous abuses committed by the colonial authorities on our island during the times of Iberian domination, particularly during the wars of independence.

"Check this shit out, man," my friend Eloy told me. "There isn't a single country colonized by these *gallegos* that isn't still in a state of underdevelopment, and the worst thing is that they're going to the island now, along with the Mexicans and the Italians and the Canadians, to do business with Fidel, another son of a Galician bastard!"

He related how one morning he found a Dominican who lives downstairs from Eloy's apartment in Hialeah giving a tremendous beating to a Spaniard from Mallorca who resides in the same building.

"Mario, have you gone mad? Let him go! Why are you beating the Spaniard?"

"Look, Eloy, what happened is that these assholes stole all the gold from my country, killed all the Indians, and committed all these abuses against our people."

"*Pero coño*, Mario, that happened over five hundred years ago. Don't be so spiteful."

"Well, the thing is that I didn't find out until this morning!"

I happen to believe that our preference for one country over another is something like our preferences for cars: it's a matter of personal taste. For example, the saxophonist Oscar Feldman states that the old French Citroën model that looks like a horrible crab was known in Argentina as the fart because only the owner can stand it.

As to my own preferences in cars, I share with my brother Enrique and thousands of other automotive masochists around the world a passion for the Volkswagen model known as the beetle, *el cepillo* (brush) in the Dominican Republic, *fusca* in Brazil, *cucaracha* (cockroach) in Cuba, the Volky, the bug, the VW, "that uncomfortable piece of shit," a suppository on wheels, Kaffer in Germany ("And you call that contraption a car?" as our friend Tino Mateu would say), and so forth.

Speaking of different strokes for different folks, this book would not be complete unless I mentioned my fairly large collection of all types of objects related to that small German car: cigarette lighters, miniatures, cushions, Christmas bulbs, key chains, remote-control models, self-winding models, battery-operated models, candy bottles, perfume flasks, a child's urinal, ties, socks, T-shirts with drawings of human VWs making love in different positions, photo frames, watches, magnets, paperweights, a Walkman, pencils, staplers, posters, history books, magazines, a large photo of the automotive engineer Ferdinand Porsche, and the like. Knowing my weakness for this vehicle, a mechanic who owns an auto body and paint shop in New Jersey reconstructed for me a green 1972 model that ended up looking like a Volks-Royce.

"Come by to pick up your Rolls-Wagen," the mechanic called to tell me with pride. Indeed, the car was a true jewel.

I went straight from my Brazilian friend's shop to show it to my mother. To my surprise, however, she asked me in a sad voice, "Oh, my son, don't you have enough money to buy a nice car?"

"Mama, this is regarded as one of the best automobiles in the world," I said with conviction to Maura.

To which she responded, reminding me of the clever remarks of her older sister, my aunt Josefa, "The best what? This is nothing but an old coffeepot, and I wouldn't ride in that useless thing even if you paid me!"

Getting back to my life in Madrid in 1980, I must be honest and admit that my stay of almost six months in the beautiful Spanish capital was certainly much better than if I had had to wait for my U.S. visa in Bosnia, Greenland, or Kampuchea. For a musician, things can't be all that bad in a nation that placed the face of Manuel de Falla on its hundred-peseta bill. The Spaniards love and respect their most distinguished artists, which gave me a great feeling of relief after living in a country where the Charles Chaplin Theater, from one day to the next and without prior notice, became the Karl Marx Theater. Hell, if at least they had renamed it after Harpo Marx!

Miles Davis always spoke admiringly of the French precisely because of the high esteem with which they regard their artists. The same is true of the Brazilians, who have streets named after Vinicius de Moraes and Hector Villa-Lobos. They even declared several days of national mourning when Antonio Carlos Jobim died and later named the Rio de Janeiro national airport after him. Throughout the world, you can see dozens of statues, streets, buildings, and public squares that pay eternal tribute to Carlos Gardel, Agustín Lara, Gillespie, Piazzolla, Jean Sibelius, Chabuca Granda, Paul Hindemith, Celia Cruz, Diego Rivera, Teresa Carreño, Louis Armstrong, Olga Guillot, Béla Bartók, Claudio Arrau, Max Roach, Cantinflas, and Rafael Hernández.

While the French twenty-franc bill showed the figure of Claude Debussy, the useless bills of my poor and very musical country (with the exception of those honoring Martí, Maceo, and Máximo Gómez) exhibit guerrilla adventurers or gunmen armed to their teeth, if not the omnipresent figure of the egocentric autocrat with his anachronistic olive-green uniform.

In the city of Havana (whatever was left of it) in May 1980, at the time I took my music someplace else after twenty-one years of revolution (or should I say involution?), there was not a single monument to any of our innumerable and valuable artists who are famous

all over the world. By contrast, there are various squares, monu-
ments, and streets in Spain honoring the very illustrious memory of
Ernesto Lecuona. This fact alone puts Spain, with its many defects
and virtues, "forever in my heart," as Lecuona himself sang in his
immortal melody.

In Cuba, after so many years of repression against foreign music,
and specifically against Beatles fans, a few years ago, a statue of
John Lennon was placed in a park in Havana, and Leo Brouwer even
conducted a Beatlemania concert at the Amadeo Roldán Theater
with the National Symphony Orchestra, to which Brian Epstein, the
legendary manager of the famous British group, was invited. Shortly
after the monument was inaugurated, someone stole Lennon's bronze
eyeglasses. Also, Paul McCartney has announced his desire to play
in Cuba, the land where his music was once banned and declared
subversive.

"Listen, *chico*, don't forget that today is October 23 of 1980, and
tomorrow you'll be flying to '*Nueva Yor*,'" said Carlos Carli, making
fun of my Cuban accent, when I arrived at his home. "Your friend Luis
just called to tell you that he was hanging out with Roberto and that
there's a tampered phone by the Opera exit of the Madrid metro."

"Oh, if it's by the Opera, I'll certainly find Plácido Domingo,
Victoria de los Angeles, or José Carreras standing on line, trying to
contact Havana's Galician Center to get a gig with Natilla 'Custard'
Jiménez's orchestra at the National Cabaret located in that building's
underground cellar," I joked with the Uruguayan drummer.

I had met Roberto late one night at a tampered phone around the
Plaza de Toros de Las Ventas. He was one of the numerous former
Cuban merchant marines who had abandoned ship upon their arrival
in Spanish ports. He showed up one afternoon at the inn on San
Marcos Street to let me know that my friend Luis, who, according

to Roberto, played none other than the *guitarrón mexicano* (large Mexican guitar) with the orchestra Los Van Van, had requested asylum in Madrid and was going crazy looking for me all over the city. The sailor knew where that mysterious friend (who supposedly played the *guitarrón* with a *charanga* formation!) was staying, and he took me upstairs from a Chinese restaurant near the Plaza de Santa Ana to meet him. I was pleasantly surprised to find Luis Marsillí, a cellist with the orchestra led by Juan Formell. Luis had voted with his feet a few days earlier, during one of the frequent Spanish tours conducted by that popular group. Marsillí's arrival comforted my soul because that bohemian and good-humored native of Santiago de Cuba was the most pleasant Cuban company that I could have found far from our native soil.

You can take a Cuban out of Cuba, but you certainly can't take Cuba out of the heart of a Cuban, and from the very first days of our exile, we discovered our beloved island reflected in the calm waters of the small lake at Madrid's El Retiro Park or in the tears of every Cuban who wanders through the world, like the new Jews of the Caribbean Sea, asking ourselves, "Why did it have to happen to us?"

Because of people like Luis Marsillí, I consider myself a fortunate man when it comes to having good and long-lasting friendships. I also value above all else the radiant friendship that I've kept over the years with the flutist Félix Durán and his family.

I met El Pato (Duck), as we affectionately called the flutist, in the general staff band of the army, when we were called to perform our compulsory military service at Major Forneiro's Concentration Camp, which is how he named the unit occupied by the military band. We had some good times there but also some bad ones, mainly when, as a parting gesture, the army sent us to sugarcane fields to "cut our discharge." This meant that every recruit, before being discharged at the end of three years of mandatory service, was forced to work for several months cutting sugarcane in Camagüey

Province, the birthplace and battleground of Major General Ignacio
Agramonte. After freeing his own slaves in 1868, this remarkable
man fought and died for the abolition of slavery and the complete
freedom of all Cubans. Significantly, many of Agramonte's former
slaves voluntarily joined his troops, while in contrast, the young
slaves—white, black, or yellow—sent by Castro one hundred years
later to work in Camagüey's sugarcane fields are now almost all in
Miami, in Cuban prisons, or standing in crowds in front of the Office
of U.S. Interests in Havana, not to demonstrate against Yankee racism but rather to apply for the visa lottery to enter the United States.
When the dramatic events of Havana's Peruvian embassy took place,
I was told that after a black woman had jumped over the embassy's
fence with her two small sons, she was told by one of the guards assigned to maintain order there, "Comrade, I can't believe that you're
not aware that these little black kids aren't worth a cent in the brutal
and perverse north!" To which the lady replied, "Well, mister, I don't
know who could've told you that I'm taking these kids to sell them.
I'm taking them so that they can have something to eat!"

Félix Durán was one of the dear friends whom I wanted to see before
leaving on that Soviet plane of Cubana de Aviación that would take
me for the first (and perhaps the last) time from Havana to Madrid
on May 6, 1980. Since I didn't want to endanger him, I didn't tell him
my immediate intentions when I went to look for him at his work-
place in Havana's Teatro Musical. We spent a couple of hours in
conversation at a hotel bar on Prado Street, near the corner of
Neptuno, the celebrated Havana corner frequented by La Engaña-
dora (Deceiving Female), who became the title of Enrique Jorrín's
famous cha-cha.

"I wonder what's gotten into you today. Instead of getting together with your exuberant blond María Antonieta, as much as you
like to paint the town red with her, you take me here to drink beer in
this dark barroom. What's going on?" asked the intrigued musician, who
knew about my weakness for skirt-chasing. And with a mischievous

smile, he added, "Hell, don't tell me that you're coming out of the closet in your old age!"

"Don't worry, Duck," I answered, trying to tease him and conceal my deep sadness. "I won't rule out the gay issue, but let me tell you, you're not my type. While kissing me, you could poke my eye out with that big nose of yours."

That was the last time I saw Félix in Cuba. Many years later I found out through our common friend, the Canadian flutist Bonnie Lawrence, that this irreproachable man, who had never spoken a word in public about politics, lost many opportunities to travel abroad with artistic groups only because he refused to publicly repudiate our good friendship, which is evidently more valuable to him than all of the material goods in the world.

The existence of such honorable people allows me to love mankind a little more than my cat Mimi (but not much!). I think that if the rest of the Cubans who remain on the island (and out of prison) showed the moral and civic conduct displayed by this modest musician of humble origins, we would have another story to tell by now. As my son's grandfather, Tomás Pérez, wisely observed, "After they spent the whole day complaining and saying horrible things about the government, and praying to God and all the saints that the Americans would come to liberate us from this miserable green character, later they all go to Revolution Square to court him and clamor '*Cuba sí, Yankees no.*' . . . Look, the other day he crammed together seventeen thousand bicycles at the square, and one of them belonged to the guy who sells contraband meat on the black market. He's also the president of the CDR [Committee for the Defense of the Revolution] on my block."

> May God grant that something happens to suddenly erase you,
> A blinding light, an explosion of snow
> May God grant that at least it would lead to your death
> So that I don't have to see you so often, or see you always
> In all of my moments, in all of my songs
> —*Silvio Rodríguez*

El Pato implored me from the other end of the phone, "Paco, when you have a chance, send me a set of pads for my East German flute with someone who is going to be traveling here. Kiss Maura and Rosarito for me, and say hello to Tito and Enriquito. Make sure you take care of yourself in New York because you're too old to fool around, you hear me? . . . And rest assured that I'll visit Franco and Eneida once in a while to see if they need anything, so don't even worry about it. Do the right thing, *coño!*"

With a knot in my throat, I said, "OK, Pato . . . ciao." This was the only answer I could give to my faithful friend before hanging up the phone in the booth near the Opera metro station in Madrid in the early hours of October 24, 1980. It was my last dawn as a refugee in the Spanish capital.

ℬ

It was snowing a blizzard in New York, and the air was cold enough to freeze your bones. Fortunately, my brother Enrique drove me to the theater in his bright yellow convertible Volkswagen.

"Do you want me to put down the car top?" asked Enrique with his hand already grasping the device required to move it.

"Sure! We're going to look like a couple of Cuban penguins galloping on top of Big Bird," I answered, going along with his program.

I take after my father in my hatred of unpunctuality. We were already somewhat late, and when we arrived at the theater, I took off running through the lobby, where my sister Rosarito was setting up her exposition of paintings that night. The other artist involved in the evening exposition was Sergio Rivero, alias El Haitiano (Haitian), a versatile painter from Santiago de Cuba who had been working on an interesting cycle about rumba using only black, gray, and white, in marked contrast to my sister's wide-ranging palette.

"Hurry up, honey, you're already late, and you know how illtempered Benny is. This time you can't blame Brendita."

"Do you mind telling me why I can't blame the Rican?" I asked my sister without stopping.

"Well, I know that your wife and her mother have been in El Paso, Texas, for a couple of days doing the Cuban operetta *La Coyota* [*The People Smuggler*]."

"Ssshhh! . . . Remember that the walls have ears, you dig?" I told her, and continued my mad race to the stage.

"Listen, brother, do you think that this is a dance party with Beny Moré at the Tropicana or what? . . . I think you have the wrong Benny, you know?!" exclaimed the *timbalero* Orestes Vilató from the indigenous section (as the saxophonist Averhoff used to say), jokingly referring to the fact that the late Beny Moré was known for arriving late at his gigs.

"Don't worry, Paquito, we have time. Benny's sick, and he's not coming," Lionel Hampton told me.

"But this is a tribute to Benny Goodman. How are we going to do it without him, Lionel?"

"We'll see," the octogenarian former employee of the King of Swing said calmly. "Take out your weapons, and let's join Hank Jones and Milt Hinton, since they're already rehearsing 'Moonglow,' and then we'll deal with 'Seven Comes Eleven,' which is what Hank likes."

"Ha-ha-ha," the pianist Hilton Ruiz whispered in my ear, shaking with laughter. "Look at Bombillo ["Lightbulb," Claudio Roditi's nickname]. He's going insane trying to teach the samba pattern to Gene Krupa."

"Listen, buddy," said Mario Bauzá, grabbing my arm, "I want to introduce you to Vitín Paz, a great trumpeter."

"Yes, sir, my last name is Paz [peace], but they call me Víctor Guerra [war]; you'll find out why later," the prestigious and controversial Panamanian trumpeter said to introduce himself. He added, "You see? Things are different here compared with our countries. These black Americans are always talking about Africa; they want to be more African than Africans, but some of them have the worst sense of rhythm I've seen in my life. What do you think? . . . I'd like to know what the hell that bebop of theirs has to do with the Bantu, the Zulu, or anything from Africa. Bah!"

"Well, once Art Blakey was a little pissed off about that matter, and he spoke about it," I replied to the Panamanian musician. "The old Buhaina was making it very clear that in his opinion jazz is purely an American art form. 'No America, no jazz,' said Blakey, and I'd say similar things about the Cuban rumba, the Brazilian samba, or the Dominican merengue. Those rhythms were born on this side of the ocean, from an African mother and a Spanish, English, or Portuguese father. In other words, the fact that my grandmother was Asturian or Galician doesn't take away one inch of my Cuban identity."

"Yes, but there's bullshit all over the place in this business of ours, and you'll find that out sooner or later. It's just a matter of time," concluded Victor, and I didn't have time to ask him in detail what he meant, because Tito Puente and Mario Rivera began to shout at Cal Tjader and Carmen McRae, who arrived accompanied by Cachao and the conga-playing actor Andy Garcia.

"Hey, you two, what kind of arrival time is that?" said Tito in the direction of Carmen and Tjader. "Who are the Latinos here, anyway? I arrived on time, and even Mad Mario was here on time, *coño!*" clowned around the famous *timbalero*.

"What happens is that they acquired the contagious lateness virus by hanging out with all those crazy Latinos. You know that Willie Bobo is Carmen's pal," said the Chicano actor Edward James Olmos, butting in on the conversation.

"Bah, *a mí que no me jodan.* Don't bullshit me. I know a bunch of cats in Frankfurt who are always late, and almost none of them are from Maracaibo, Bucaramanga, or Pernambuco," said my dear friend Deddy Schneider in a perfect Cubanized Spanish. He's a German Latinophile who got the gig as disk jockey for the huge party we would have after the show.

"Oh, God! I don't know what's up with Fajardo and Herbie Mann. They haven't arrived yet, and we were supposed to rehearse the flute

". . . Oh, the Cuban sandwiches?! . . . I saved a couple of them inside my sax case under my desk in the Oval Office, Paquito. . . ."

trio chart that Hubert Laws wrote for us," interrupted Dave Valentin, somewhat worried.

"Phew! What's that? Fuck, it stinks! Whoever laid that fart must be rotten inside or had breakfast at the municipal trash dump! My God! . . . What a pig! He should take Naturalex or coal tablets. Lord, take him to the doctor urgently!" said Dizzy Gillespie, laughing boisterously and almost falling from a stage chair while the trombonist Al Grey fled from his side, running rapidly.

"Look who's talking, he's the one who farted. . . . I know that old son of a bitch very well," declared Mrs. McRae, covering her nose with a little white handkerchief.

As more and more musicians arrived, the disorderly noise created by the rehearsing musicians—preparing for the gigantic all-star concert that evening—became deafening.

"May I have your attention, please, ladies and gentlemen?" a sensual feminine voice with a distinctive Madrid accent interrupted this cacophony. In a matter of seconds, the musical instruments were silent and the animated conversation of friends was stilled.

"Within a few minutes, our Iberian flight number 1080 will land at John F. Kennedy Airport in the city of New York. Please fasten your seat belts, place your seats in an upright position, and don't smoke until you have left the airplane terminal."

I abruptly woke up and asked, in a daze, "Well, did Benny finally arrive, or what?" However, what I saw was the kind smile of the flight attendant whose sensual voice had woken me from my dream.

"Take it easy, *mi hermano*, everything is fine. . . . We're about to land in the jungle," El Haitiano affectionately said, who had traveled by my side for seven hours from Madrid. It was 7:30 P.M. on October 23, 1980.

"To your right, there's a beautiful panoramic view of the island of Manhattan, the city of the skyscrapers, the Big Apple," remarked the sweet voice through the speaker. "On behalf of the captain and the airplane crew, we wish to express to you our thanks for flying with us."

Immediately after her last words, and as a form of secret welcome especially for me, the cabin's sound system began to vibrate to the rhythm of "Let's Dance," the world-famous musical theme of Benny Goodman's orchestra.

New York, New York.
This city is so great that
you've got to say her name twice!

—Frank Sinatra

THE CALL OF
THE JUNGLE

In 2004, my first novel, *Oh, La Habana!*, was published in Spain, and that same year also marked my fiftieth anniversary as a performing artist. So the idea was to celebrate this once-in-a-lifetime occasion with concerts and book presentations in Uruguay, Argentina, Costa Rica, Spain, Puerto Rico, Germany, Mexico, and my dearest New York City, where I've spent almost half of my career as an instrumentalist, and where I've expanded my horizons as a professional composer and writer. After more than two decades in and around this fabulous jungle, it's inevitable to look back and recognize that to live here is to live in all parts at the same time. Here I met the woman that I love, who helps me as I cry daily over my separation from a country she has learned to love. Despite the many obstacles I found in my path, someone was always there who in the most frustrating moments extended a hand and encouraged me to continue.

In this country of immigrants, thousands and thousands of Cubans have made their careers, including my mother, my brothers, my son Franco, and his mother. Here, in the land of Langston Hughes and Leonard Bernstein, we buried my father and teacher. The same land took into its bosom the remains of Ernesto Lecuona, Cirilo Villaverde, Mario Bauzá, Heberto Padilla, Jorge Bolet, Reinaldo Arenas, Marco Rizo, Lydia Cabrera, Alberto Socarrás, René Touzet,

Mongo Santamaría, Chico O'Farrill, Miguelito Valdés, Machito, Enrique Labrador Ruiz, Osvaldo Farrés, Chano Pozo, Kid Gavilán, Desi Arnaz, Rolando Laserie, and many other illustrious Cubans who honored our country in a foreign land.

The twenty-first century arrived dressed in a shroud of terror and death. Nothing will be the same, not in New York, or in the rest of the world, after the tragic events of September 11, 2001. Later on war followed, first in Afghanistan and then in Iraq, preceded as usual by worldwide demonstrations against them, with almost no demonstrations condemning the tyrants who provoked those as well as almost every other war.

Sympathizers think that the extreme Left only makes mistakes but doesn't commit crimes. Human rights organizations generally look the other way when it comes to Hussein, Castro, and Company. I saw a demonstration against the war in New York in which the participants carried enormous banners with the image of the violent revolutionary Che Guevara. This is something like a feminist demonstration in San Francisco in which the participants wore shirts with the image of Mike Tyson!

In the meantime we've been waiting over forty years for the UN and the pacifists to help us get rid of Castro through diplomacy, since the gringos won't even throw a tomato at him. . . . But life continues its inevitable and turbulent course, and I have no other remedy than to go on with whatever enthusiasm I have left.

For myself the change of century has brought, as usual, roses as well as thorns. Sadly, on May 31, 2000, our beloved Tito Puente died in his native New York. It was an irreparable loss for music, and especially for those of us who were privileged to have worked with a person who exuded such joy. A few days before his death, I received a call from Puente asking if I could substitute for him at a concert his orchestra was giving at Christie's Auction House in New York. "Sure, Tito, should I take my timbales or use yours?" I tried to joke with the famed percussionist, sensing that something was wrong with his health.

When the concert at Christie's had ended, our mutual friend Bob

Sancho and I went to the hospital where Tito had just had surgery. When we arrived, we were informed that only close relatives were permitted to go up to his room. The following day I had an early flight to Puerto Rico to participate in the Heineken Jazz Festival. Upon arriving in San Juan we heard the sad news of the passing of El Rey del Timbal.

In 2003, the *Enciclopedia Latina* honored me by commissioning me to write a biographical note on my illustrious friend:

Tito Puente
Timbalero, vibraphonist, arranger, composer, bandleader
Ernest Anthony Puente Jr.
New York, April 20,1923–May 31, 2000

More than fifty years onstage, and over a hundred recordings to his credit, perhaps no other musician has made such a distinctive mark on Latin dance music as well as in the jazz field.

Born in El Barrio (Spanish Harlem) of Puerto Rican parents, his musical education started with piano lessons that cost twenty-five cents. Later on he studied drums and took some dance classes together with his sister Anna, and even sang in a local barbershop quartet.

Before joining the Army he studied at Juilliard, and when he was about nineteen, collaborated with José Curbelo, Anselmo Sacasas, Noro Morales, and his mentor, the singer and *maraquero* Frank "Machito" Grillo. Around 1948 he wrote his famous tune "Picadillo" and jocosely called his first group the Piccadilly Boys, helped by his lifelong friend, trumpeter Jimmy Frisaura.

Although he said that "I was not trying to be original or innovative, but only to follow the patterns," his merit is based precisely on becoming a very original artist without even intending to!

He was closely associated with Cubans from the beginning of his career, and his style is a clear combination of traditional Cuban music and jazz elements. He recorded many jazz tunes, such as "Take the A Train," "Lullaby of Birdland," "Take 5 (in 4)," and "Cuban

Fantasy," as well as music by outstanding Cuban composers such as Arturo "Chico" O'Farrill, Cachao, César Portillo, Gilberto Valdés, and Julio Gutiérrez.

A natural catalyst, the charismatic Rey del Timbal reunited in his different ensembles instrumentalists from diverse backgrounds, such as Doc Severinsen, Alberto Socarrás, Eddy Bert, Jorge Dalto, Johnny Pacheco, Claudio Roditi, Mario Rivera, and Kai Winding. The most renowned percussionists, including Mongo Santamaría, Manny Oquendo, Jerry Gonzalez, José Mangual, Ray Barretto, Willie Bobo, Cándido Camero, and Carlos "Patato" Valdés, passed through his rhythm sections, while such great vocalists as La Lupe, Santitos Colón, Vicentico Valdés, La India, Rolando Laserie, Miguelito Valdés, and Bobby Capó contributed to his many projects. His association with Celia Cruz, "La Guarachera de Cuba," and their extensive tours over five continents inseparably linked their names. Among his collaborations with mainstream jazz artists we should mention his work with Woody Herman, Billy Taylor, Buddy Morrow, Dizzy Gillespie, Clark Terry, Phil Woods, George Shearing, and Maynard Ferguson. His creations "Pa'los Rumberos" and "Oye Como Va" were big hits for rock guitarist Carlos Santana.

In 1996, Tito performed for the largest audience in history at the closing of the Olympic games in Atlanta. Besides his five Grammy awards and his star on the Hollywood Walk of Fame, Mr. Puente received a presidential decoration for his service in World War II, the Eubie Blake Award from the Recording Academy, the Medal of Honor from the Smithsonian Institution in Washington, as well as several honorary doctorates from prestigious universities. In the same year as his death, he was featured in Fernando Trueba's acclaimed film *Calle 54*. His last concert was his dream come true: he performed with the Puerto Rico Symphony at the Centro de Bellas Artes in San Juan just a few days before he passed away.

Well, despite it all, I'm an optimist. I keep believing that the roses far outnumber the thorns. For example, on the day of my fifty-second birthday, on June 4, 2001, after a full year of restoration, the car of my dreams was delivered to me: a sky blue 1957 Chevrolet Bel Air two-door hardtop. Similar to the one the miserable tyrant Rafael Leónidas Trujillo drove the day he was assassinated, the car had first dazzled me when my father took me to see it forty-odd years ago, in the vast showroom of the Ambar Motor Agency on the corner of Infanta and Calle 23. Impressed by its beauty, the great flutist Marina Piccinini (for whom my first concerto for flute and symphony orchestra was commissioned) suggested the subtitle of my Gran Danzón: *The Bel Air Concerto*.

Created in 1879 by Miguel Faílde, a cornet player from the city of Matanzas, the danzón is a direct descendant of the Cuban danzas and *contradanzas* that were played in ballrooms back during Cuba's colonial past. In those days the typical dance orchestra was composed of a cornet, two violins, two clarinets in C, an ophicleide or valve trombone (sometimes both!), a pair of timpani, and a *güiro* (gourd). Later on, at the beginning of the twentieth century, the *charanga* orchestras, also called *francesas* (French), consisting of one or several violins, a piano, double bass, Cuban timbales, *güiro*, and flute, appeared on the scene. Since then several generations of flutists—among them Antonio Arcaño, José Fajardo, Richard Egües, José Luis "El Tosco" Cortés, Pancho el Bravo, Johnny Pacheco, Joaquín Oliveros, Oriente López, Nestor Torres, and Eddy Zervigón—have contributed enormously to the stylistic development of this musical genre. At a certain point in my career I had lots of fun using what I had learned from them when I played the flute with some dance groups. The fresh and peculiar playing style of those artists was an inspiration for the flute concerto Marina Piccinini asked me to write. I immediately thought of basing the work on the Cuban flute, a wooden instrument of five keys and six holes that has played a major role in the typical orchestras of my country as well as in the development of its national dance, the danzón.

The central theme of the concerto is based on the rhythmic cell of the danzón, which is called the *cinquillo cubano*, and of course on *la clavé*, which is the foundation of almost all Cuban music. Other Cuban musical patterns and elements of African origin are found throughout the piece, as well as small phrases and quotations that remind us of old folkloric and popular themes.

After the solo flute, the second most important instrument in the concerto is the humble *güiro*, which forms, along with the Cuban timbales and the contrabass, the rhythm machine that moves the *charanga* as well as the feet of the dancers in the ballroom (and probably in the concert hall, too!). The title Gran Danzón was borrowed from Astor Piazzolla's Gran Tango.

Commissioned by the Rotterdam Philharmonic and the American National Symphony Orchestra, Gran Danzón (*The Bel Air Concerto*) was premiered on February 9, 2002, at the Kennedy Center in Washington, D.C., by flute virtuoso Marina Piccinini with the National Symphony Orchestra under Maestro Leonard Slatkin's baton. It was my humble tribute to the legendary *danzoneros* of the island Columbus called *la tierra más hermosa que ojos humanos vieran* (the most beautiful land that human eyes ever saw).

When the Gran Danzón had its debut performance, I was in the midst of a tour of Alaska with the Turtle Island String Quartet. Luckily, I had a free day on February 9, 2002, and I managed to find a flight that allowed me to attend the concert in Washington. I was touring with the Turtles to promote our new CD, coincidentally called *Danzón*, which contained a piece written for Mario Bauzá that he had baptized *Memories*. As part of their repertoire, this one-of-a kind quartet played a work I composed especially for them that had been commissioned by Chamber Music America. I called it *La Jicotea*, which is a small river and lake turtle in Cuba. "Almost all of them have swum to Miami," I joked as I presented the work in public for the first time.

The same institution commissioned me to write a piece for the Ying Quartet, a more classically oriented string group. That piece was inspired by an experience I had soon after I arrived in New York in 1980. As I walked through a street fair in Greenwich Village in the early summer, I was fascinated by the smell of the ethnic foods sold by dozens of vendors from all around the world, and especially by the variety of music played on the sidewalks by street musicians. Among them, in the middle of Washington Square Park, I found a string quartet formed by a black cellist, an Asian viola player, and a married couple who were magnificent violinists, the wife from Eastern Europe and the husband from Puerto Rico. The quartet's repertoire ranged from Bach and Beethoven to Gershwin and Piazzolla and included Cuban danzas, Brazilian *chorinhos*, Polish polkas, and Middle Eastern music. Even though I have used the string quartet format on a few occasions, *The Village Street Quartet*, written especially for the wonderful Ying Quartet, was my first serious approach to the format created by Joseph Haydn. In this work I wanted to recreate the multicultural atmosphere I felt for the first time so many years ago in that amazing New York neighborhood.

In 1996, the Aspen Woodwind Quintet asked me to write what became my most popular chamber piece, a suite in six movements I called *Aires Tropicales*. Impeccably recorded by the Numen Quintet in Buenos Aires and later on by the Imani Winds in New York, the work is constantly in demand by students as well as professional groups through International Opus, the company that publishes all my chamber catalog. Through my relationship with Lincoln Center and Chamber Music America, as artistic director for the New Jersey Chamber Music Society, and as artist-in-residence of the monumental New Jersey Performing Arts Center, I have received many commissions that have permitted me to expand my catalog as a classical composer. Also, the musical society known as the Commission Project asked me to produce a piece with my son Franco that we called *Quasi An Arabesque* to be recorded by the American Saxophone Quartet, with me on clarinet. We never mentioned which part of the work was written by whom, and now we don't even remember!

But the work that pleases me the most of all my compositions to date is the one that was commissioned by Jazz at Lincoln Center and premiered at Alice Tully Hall alongside another piece composed by the impressive trumpet player Nicolas Payton from New Orleans. Based on a lovely poem by the Cuban poet Annie Colina, with whom

I had collaborated in my suite *Rivers*, "Song for Peace," and other poetic-musical projects, *Panamericana* was perhaps the only piece that united in a jazz ensemble instruments as diverse as the *bandoneón*, *batá* drums, the marimba-vibraphone, a Venezuelan *cuatro*, and a soprano voice.

> Every day you made the Universe, sweet visitor
> Dressed in flowers and water,
> You are like a handful of stars with different colors
> You are one awesome mass of soil under one name.
> You are like nobody, since I love you
> And I remember you as you were then.
> Let me spread garlands of dreams from north to center
> Embrace your tiny islands in my heart,
> And ride with you the south among the stars.
> The heavens are your shelter,
> and the wind no longer cries in fear.
> Now your rivers sail a peaceful journey,
> Curled in your lovely arms so near.
>
> Your breasts are fully bloomed,
> And will remain forever so.
> You are my secret place,
> My garden of desires
> You my bride from heaven
> You and only you, America.
>
> You are like nobody since I love you.
> It's you and only you, America!

The instrumental version of this piece was chosen for the film *Calle 54* (*54th Street*), which featured Latin jazz musicians such as Bebo and Chucho Valdés, Cachao, Tito, Eliane Elias, Chico O'Farrill, Jerry Gonzalez and Fort Apache, Michel Camilo, Orlando "Puntilla" Ríos, Gato Barbieri, Patato, and the incredible Andalusian pianist Chano Domínguez.

With Bebo Valdés, Fernando Trueba, Brenda Feliciano, and Ricard Valdés at Avatar Studios in New York City (2002)

Chano, an exquisite artist who took his first musical steps as a flamenco guitarist, has created a perfect synthesis between jazz and his native music. In a natural and organic way he has transported a unique guitar-sounding style to the piano, a formidable achievement. After Trueba's movie came out in the fall of 2000, I went on several tours with Chano and the rest of the participating musicians. The success of the movie in Spain was such that a beautiful jazz club was opened in Madrid called *Calle 54*.

Although I have many wonderful friendships with Spaniards, that is to say Basques, Madrilenians, Andalusians, and Canarians as well, the truth is that from the very beginning Spain has on many (too many) occasions taken very regrettable positions regarding the inhabitants of the largest island in the Antilles. Cuba has suffered five centuries of abuses, from the evangelical annihilation of the Indians by Pánfilo de Narváez, the enslavement of Africans, and the excesses of the despotic nineteenth-century governor Valeriano Weyler to the present. Spanish visitors are the main clients for cheap sex in the streets of Havana, and near-slave wages are paid to employees in resort areas, which are off limits to Cubans, by the capitalist Spaniards who share the profits with the dictatorship on the island. (These are the so-called *empresas mixtas.*) And to top it off, even King Juan Carlos and his wife, doña Sofia, made an official visit to a government that in 1959 stripped all the property and personal belongings from thousands of Spanish immigrants in Cuba, who with great sacrifice had raised their families on our previously hospitable island.

But apart from that, I cannot deny that Spain has been a constant force in my life since I arrived there from Cuba in 1980. Based on a nomination by my friend, the orchestra conductor Luis Cobos, the prestigious and ancient University of Alcalá de Henares presented me with a degree honoris causa, alongside the guitarist Pepe Habichuela and the Italian movie star Claudia Cardinale.

In that happy and enthusiastic country, I have realized the most wide-ranging projects, among them bringing out a new CD by the fabulous Duo Hermanas Márquez, who had not set foot in a recording studio since the 1960s. The sessions with Trini and Nerza were indescribable because of the two women's freshness, Cubanness, musicality, and sense of humor. Those Holguineras (from the province of Holguín) who left Cuba in the 1940s are something spectacular.

Another project carried out in Spain was the presentation of Igor Stravinsky's *Soldier's Tale.* The original idea was proposed by the Basque actor Javier Gurruchaga and the producers Dania Dévora and José Luis Rupérez (who also produced the Hermanas Márquez). They assembled an impressive group of actors and musicians for the premiere in Alcalá de Henares, and later on at the Alfredo Kraus Auditorium in Las Palmas de Gran Canaria.

In the first part of the program we performed a suite of Cuban and Spanish pieces by Ernesto Lecuona, arranged by my extraordinary pianist, Alon Yavnai.

"Paquito, this Alon comes from heaven," the cellist Yo-Yo Ma once said to me with emotion. It was the day that the Chinese American cellist had come from Boston to play a trio and a sonata by Brahms, some Brazilian *chorinhos*, and a couple of tangos, and to eat some of those unforgettable black beans that Brenda cooks. It's true that among the good things that the twenty-first century has already given me is this young Israeli pianist, whose versatility and enthusiasm have no bounds.

Later on, we recorded in Madrid the first version in Spanish of that devilishly difficult Stravinsky work, with the famous Argentine actress Nacha Guevara as narrator. In 2003 that CD won the Latin Grammy for the best classical performance.

Alon helped a great deal by practicing with me the trio version of *Soldier* for clarinet, violin, and piano. Some say that the tremendous stress generated by that complicated and spectacular work produced the cardiac arrest that I suffered in April 2002. However, I think that the stress was also due to a disgraceful letter that certain Cuban intellectuals sent to Mexican president Vicente Fox, hypocritically defending the absolute freedom of expression and creativity that writers and artists supposedly enjoy on the Communist island. Among the signatories were Alicia Alonso, Leo Brouwer, Cintio Vitier, Marta Valdés, Miguel Barnet, and César Portillo. However, the signature that hurt most was that of my old friend Chucho Valdés. A short time later, the same writers and artists signed another, even more vile letter justifying the arbitrary jailings and executions in 2003. I am convinced, of course, that not only Chucho but also many of the other artists signed those letters against their will. Tired of such oppression and of listening to so many lies and half-truths, I fled Cuba more than twenty-three years ago, renouncing my marriage and my son's childhood in exchange for a freedom that Eneida and Franco wouldn't share until nine years later. Since then we live like Willy Chirino, Cachao, Bebo Valdés, and two million more Cubans: without a country but without a master.

At that time, I felt tremendously sad when the New York press published side-by-side photos of Chucho and myself, juxtaposing the one who supported the Cuban government's action with the one who condemned it. I didn't enjoy that newspaper publicity a bit, but it hasn't changed my dream of the day when Chucho and I can play a duo in the Teatro Auditorio of La Habana, without any letters to sign and with our photos in the arts section of the newspaper, not in the political section.

The majority of Cuban musicians who come on tour to the United States talk about the horrors of the system in private, but when a camera is put in front of them, they turn into the devil's advocates and serve as the most loyal and useful cultural representatives of the dictatorship. For this reason, when Los Van Van gave their first concert in Miami, the exile community reacted violently. What follows is the commentary of *New York Post* journalist Roger Hernandez about that show.

Cuban music is hot in the United States. The Ry Cooder–produced album *Buena Vista Social Club*, recorded in Havana, has become the largest-selling Spanish-language music record ever in the United States, and the accompanying documentary now playing in theaters has drawn crowds and praise from critics. There is also the current five-week tour by Los Van Van, a band based in Cuba that has played before enthusiastic sold-out crowds from coast to coast.

Not in Miami, though, where Cuban exiles oppose concerts by musicians based in Castro's Cuba.

The Van Van show there was almost canceled when local Cuban-American officials argued that allowing the band to perform violates the U.S. trade embargo. For a month they fought to stop it, until the ACLU threatened to sue. The show went on, but only 2,500 seats were filled at the Miami Arena this past weekend. Outside, twice that number of protesters chanted anti-Castro slogans. The whole town was in a frenzy.

"In my wildest imagination," said Los Van Van's promoter, Debbie Ohanian, "I never anticipated this." The band's leader, Juan Formell, said, "We are not on an official mission representing the government of the island. We simply make music and live in Cuba." But it is not that simple.

It is true that Los Van Van makes great Cuban dance music. The members of the band are first-rate Cuban pop musicians with formal conservatory training, a tradition that goes back at least to the 1930s. And their songs are not overtly political.

But the songs don't have to be overtly political, because the presence of Los Van Van in the United States already is.

The principle was well understood in the days of the struggle against apartheid.

In 1985, Bob Dylan, Bono, Ringo Starr, Jackson Browne, Gil Scott-Heron, Sting, and other pop luminaries banded together under Bruce Springsteen's guitarist Steve Van Zandt to record "Sun City," a rock anthem demanding that fellow musicians refuse to play in the South African gambling resort of Sun City as a protest against apartheid.

The video was widely played on MTV and had its desired effect. Most internationally known musicians stayed out of South Africa. Frank Sinatra played Sun City and was roundly criticized.

Of the younger generation, Paul Simon went to South Africa at the time and was threatened to be blacklisted by the United Nations Center against Apartheid, even though he played not in Sun City before racist whites but in Johannesburg with dissident black musicians from Soweto like Ladysmith Black Mambazo. "Sun City," of course, didn't on its own bring down the racist South African regime. But the song was in the spirit of the United Nations proclamation that called on member states to "take steps to prevent all cultural, academic, sporting, and other exchanges with South Africa."

That international campaign of isolation was the most potent weapon available to Nelson Mandela and the antiapartheid movement. It was the right thing to do. And it helped result in the end of apartheid.

Somehow, however, the same principle does not apply when it comes to Castro's Cuba. The United Nations wants the embargo lifted. Rock stars have not banded together to demand an end to the human rights abuses committed as a matter of policy by the Cuban government.

American music lovers think nothing of giving their enthusiastic approval to a band that (let me be as charitable as I can with Los Van

Van) in thirty years of existence has never had a bad thing to say about a government that since 1959 has crushed all free expression. And when Cuban Americans protest the presence of such a band in their midst, they are seen not as a people fighting for the freedom of their native land but as right-wing troglodytes bent on censorship.

I feel a great passion for the culture and music of Brazil, and it gives me pleasure to declare publicly that my heart is half Brazilian. This sentiment appears to be mutual, for I have been invited by many Brazilian artists to join them in performing their music, sometimes in their own territory. Also I was the artist of choice to represent Brazil in the documentary *Americanos*, produced by Chicano actor and filmmaker Edward James Olmos.

For the occasion I surrounded myself with three outstanding Brazilian musicians: guitarist Romero Lubambo, bassist-*cavaquinho* player Sergio Brandão, and the sparkling Portinho on drums and *pandeiro*. One of my happiest recording projects was the CD *Brazilian Dreams*, with the vocal quartet New York Voices. By the way, that CD also won a Grammy in 2003 for the best jazz CD. I'm very keen on vocal quartets, and with this venture I was able to kill two birds with one stone, as the old saying goes. They laughed a lot when I told them that in Cuba musicians listened to radio stations from Miami mostly for the jingles, sung by gringo vocal groups: "W-Q-A-MMM . . . Miami!"

The group backing the New York Voices, besides the trombone and guitar-playing brothers Jay and Marty Ashby (also the organizers of the recording in the Manchester Craftsmen's Guild), were Helio Alves, piano; Paulo Braga, drums; Oscar Stagnaro, bass; and Claudio Roditi, guest artist on trumpet.

In addition to my recordings *Tico! Tico!*, *Return to Ipanema*, and *La Habana–Rio Conexión*, another production of that kind in which I was invited to participate was *Obrigado Brazil*, with cellist Yo-Yo Ma. Under the direction of Jorge Calandrelli, the recording for

Sony Classical had a stellar cast in which figured Egberto Gismonti, Romero Lubambo, Rosa Passos, Cesar Camargo Mariano, the British pianist Kathryn Stott, and the fascinating guitarists Odair and Sergio Assad, two brothers from São Paulo. After the release of the CD, a small group of participants went on tour, playing works by Piazzolla, some of my pieces, and works from the Brazilian repertoire. We're even discussing a record with the Assad brothers, with whom we formed a great friendship, and another project, perhaps of Cuban (or Latin American) music, with Yo-Yo. It would be the Duo Rice and Beans, with yours truly and Yo-Yo, as Mary Pat Buerkle, a representative from ICM Artists Agency, joked.

"Your book has completely changed my views about communism in Cuba, Paquito," said the great cellist, after reading the manuscript of this book, which I gave him at the end of our first rehearsal with Alon Yavnai at my house. Born in France, far removed from the horrors of China's absurd political system, Yo-Yo doesn't seem too politicized to me, but I believe that after reading this book and seeing the common threads that unite the Chinese and the Cubans, our musical and personal relationship grew more solid roots. Whatever future projects may come out of our initial musical encounter, they will always be magical, because it is the nature of that very special artist to bring out the best in the artists and staff who surround him.

A few days before our 2003 tour to Amsterdam, Cologne, and London with Yo-Yo Ma, I was returning from Puerto Rico, where I had not been since the passing of Tito Puente in May 2000. This time the amphitheater where the Heineken Jazz Festival was held was renamed in honor of the legendary New York *timbalero*. The event was dedicated to Chick Corea, one of my favorite musicians, with whom I'd never had the pleasure of sharing a stage. By tradition, every edition of the festival is named in honor of a distinguished musician. Eddie Palmieri, Tito, Chucho, Eddie Gómez, Michel Camilo, Dave Valentin, and I have been among those honored. Among the artists that attended the 2003 Heineken Festival (impeccably organized by Luis Álvarez and Joey Sala) were Claudia Acuña, Flora and Airto, Makoto Ozone, Gary Burton, William Cepeda, the Dutch group

Nueva Manteca, and a magnificent big band of local musicians directed by the Boricua trumpet player Humberto Ramírez. All the soloists performed with Ramírez's orchestra, and at the end all played "Spain," by Chick. It was a memorable evening full of camaraderie and great emotion, when many friends got together who hadn't seen each other in a long, long time.

Unfortunately I believe that Latin America is a five-hundred-year-old experiment that backfired, a real disaster. However, I love going to Puerto Rico for many reasons, among them, because it's the only Latin American country where you can ride from the airport to the hotel and not see a long and dirty road full of misery, polluted water, and starving children begging for money. Anyone who takes a quick look into the recent history of that interesting country will realize just what I'm talking about.

I myself believe that everything that happens to me in Puerto Rico is good. In May 2003, I accepted an honorary doctorate from the Berklee College of Music, which is located in Boston but has an annual program in Puerto Rico. Among the delegation of Berklee professors who went to Puerto Rico that year was my dear friend, the bass player Oscar Stagnaro. At an emotional ceremony, the honorary degree was awarded in the middle of my performance with the sextet (the whole thing was very confusing!). On the stage with me were Michel Camilo, Gary Burton, and Chick Corea, all honored with the same distinction in years past, as well as the festival directors and Lee Berk, the president of the university. Other artists who have received this honor are Duke Ellington, Tito Puente, Paul Simon, Dizzy Gillespie, and Louis Armstrong. Although it is truly an honor to share such a high distinction with such illustrious colleagues, I was deeply saddened because I couldn't share the celebration with my countrymen in our own land. Also, with pride and deep respect, I remembered my old teacher Armando Romeu, who translated into Spanish Berklee courses in harmony and orchestration (and improved them in his translation), and then generously and freely shared them with dozens of students.

In the audience I could see the faces of the writers Cristóbal Díaz Ayala and Tina Casanova, as well as other friends and thousands of Boricuas who stood up and applauded me when I raised the tricolor Puerto Rican flag. With great emotion I shouted, "I'm proud to be a compatriot of José Martí, but if I weren't Cuban, I would like to be Puerto Rican."

A fresh breeze was blowing from the nearby sea, which helped alleviate the intense heat that I felt under the hot lights on the stage in that velvet academic gown I was wearing.

In the midst of all that nostalgia, I was happy to be on the sister island of Puerto Rico. The verses of the Puerto Rican poet Lola Rodríguez de Tió suddenly came to mind:

> *Cuba y Puerto Rico son*
> *De un pájaro las dos alas,*
> *Reciben flores y balas*
> *Sobre el mismo corazón . . .*
> *¡Qué mucho si en la ilusión*
> *Qué mil tintes arrebola,*
> *Sueña la musa de Lola*
> *Con ferviente fantasía,*
> *¡De esta tierra y la mía,*
> *Hacer una patria sola!*

> Cuba and Puerto Rico are
> The two wings of the same bird,
> They receive flowers and bullets
> In the same heart . . .
> So intense is this illusion
> That my cheeks are crimson red,
> The muse of Lola is dreaming
> An incredible vision—
> That this land and mine
> not be two islands, but one nation!

AZUUUCAAAA!!!!

—Celia Cruz

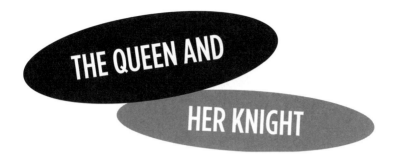

THE QUEEN AND HER KNIGHT

The phone woke me up in the middle of the night like a bad omen. I looked at the green light of the electric clock on my night table: it was 1:30 A.M. A cool, faint breeze blew in the tulle curtains, and the fragrance of the late night sneaked in through the partially open window of my hotel room in Dinslaken, near Dusseldorf, Germany. I looked around, trying to orient myself in the darkness. The phone kept ringing incessantly. When I picked up the receiver, the voice on the other side said, "Maestro, this is José Antonio Evora from the *Miami Herald*. I hate to bother you, but we need to know your reactions. . . ."

"La Negra died, right?" I interrupted him.

"Yes, maestro," he responded plainly, obviously moved. The journalist, anticipating my reaction, kept silent until I could recover from the initial shock. The news, although expected, was nevertheless devastating. I answered his questions with extreme difficulty and at the end of the interview I walked to the small balcony and out into the semidarkness. I breathed in the humid air of the night and waited for the dawn, quietly crying over the departure of that extraordinary being who spread so much happiness around this world. I closed my eyes and could hear again her jet black and gold voice jumping out of the small speaker on my grandma Pachita's radio in Marianao.

The Queen (Celia Cruz) and I, with Tito Puente and His Orchestra (Carnegie Hall, New York, 2000)

I went back in time to my father's tiny office in the very Habanera street of Virtudes near Prado, and again experienced the fragrant smell of newness that emerged from that beautiful leather and velvet case. I saw the enthusiasm on Pedrito Knight's face as he held for the first time the Martin trumpet that my old man had ordered for him directly from the manufacturer in Elkhart, Indiana. Oh, poor Pedro, I thought, the great and only love of La Guarachera. Back then she hadn't yet called him *mi cabecita de algodón* (my little cotton head), and they hadn't even married. She sang up front, slim and radiant in her sheer linen dresses adorned with white lace, and Pedrito, her gentle knight, blew his love from the trumpet section of the famous Sonora Matancera. Celia was his great pride and it wasn't baseless, for his girlfriend was already, although barely in her twenties, Cuba's most popular vocalist. He didn't know back then that his future wife would become the most beloved Cuban artist of all time. Poor Pedrito and poor us, who from now on would have to learn to live without her contagious joy and that smile of pearls and ebony.

I remembered that appearance—my first—at the Teatro Puerto Rico in New York City, alongside Lola Beltrán and Rolando Laserie, accompanied by the Puerto Rican trumpeter César Concepción and his big band. The theater was packed and La Sonora Matancera closed the show with Celia Cruz fronting the *conjunto*. It was 1960 and the whole ensemble decided not to return to Cuba. A short time later, the still young Castro dictatorship would make Celia's drastic decision to defect even more painful by denying her a permit to enter her own country to visit her mother on her deathbed. Despite all that happened, my father, along with many others who believed that mess would soon pass, decided that we would return home. That was against the will of my mother, who more prudently wanted the whole family to come to New York and wait out the developments in our convulsive land. The rest is a well-known story. So I didn't see La Guarachera again till New Year's Eve of 1980, after my arrival in the Big Apple, playing a gig as a sideman with Machito's orchestra in the Waldorf Astoria. Celia was the star of that show, and the first to arrive at the rehearsal was Pedro with a pile of sheet music under his arm. "Pedro, my old man says to stop by his little office in Virtudes, because he's got a brand-new Martin trumpet waiting for you," I whispered in his ear as he organized those sheets of music on the piano. The musician slowly raised his gaze, observed me very seriously for an instant, then displayed a big smile and shouted toward the back of the stage, "Celia, Tito's son escaped from Fidel." After that, there were many opportunities for me to share the stage in America and in Europe with those dearly beloved colleagues, with whom I only spent precious moments.

One cold January evening in 2003, we celebrated at our house the end of the recording sessions for the new CD by the Hermanas Márquez. Present was José Luis Rupérez, the Spanish producer who had organized a great show with Celia, Albita, Lucrecia, and me in Madrid and Lisbon the year before. Everything was relatively quiet until Celia and Pedrito arrived. Then it was as if a hurricane had come through the door. Upon seeing them, Alon began to play a *montuno* on the piano and soon all of us began to sing "Caramelo a Kilo," the swinging guaracha that she made famous. Dancing with the people who welcomed her, Celia went to the sofa, where she sat for the rest of the night. There she stayed quietly near Trini and Nerza Márquez, old girlfriends from the days the *soneras* emigrated westward to La Habana from their native province of Oriente. The charismatic Afro-Cuban singer-actor-dancer Alberto Morgan offered a delightful rendition of the immortal "Babalú" by Margarita Lecuona. Brenda, my wife, sang a duo with the tenor Mariano Vidal, and Celia had "the most delicious arroz con pollo that I've eaten in years, Maura!" as she graciously complimented my mother.

"I'm a happy person who loves to sing," the most Cuban of all singers would say. And that night she tried to improvise over our *montuno* chorus of her trademark *Bemba Colorá*, but sadly, a voice that once was like a *sinsonte* flying over the hills of Cuba stopped singing a few bars later and remained silent. Months later, terminally ill, she entered the hospital.

As I've mentioned before, José Martí defined music as the highest form of beauty, while Napoleon defined it as the least annoying of all noises. The diametrically opposed views of those men represent the abysmal difference between a tyrannical and musically deaf military despot, and a man of exceptional sensibility, whose modesty belied his extraordinary greatness. Cubans, who are by nature contradictory and extreme, have exhibited over the years in our colorful and varied human catalog more than one antimusical tyrant alongside talented, sensitive artists who fill us with pride.

Celia was one of those special artists, who even away from her homeland became, without realizing it, the person most representative of the Cuban national character, with all its virtues and none of its vices. She tore down all types of racial and generational barriers and transcended all musical, political, sexual, and religious prejudices. When I announced her passing during a performance of Brazilian music in a small German town, the public stood up to applaud her. A few weeks later, an audience of more than seventeen thousand at a performance I gave with Yo-Yo Ma in the Hollywood Bowl responded just as effusively. Her massive funerals in Miami as well as in her beloved New York were, for me, full of indescribable emotions. I've never seen so many people crying and at the same time singing, dancing, and laughing with the name and the songs of La Reina on their lips, nor have I ever seen so many famous people mixed with the general public in an uninterrupted line that went from the majestic St. Patrick's Cathedral, located in the heart of Manhattan, to Woodlawn Cemetery in the Bronx, many miles away from the city. I never could have imagined that so many men, women, and children of all nationalities would remain standing in torrential rain to watch the funeral cortege pass by hours after the Puerto Rican announcer Paco Navarro ended the service. "Celia is singing and the skies are crying," chanted the multitude upon the passing of the gorgeous horse-drawn carriage.

News of her death traveled quickly, occupying the front pages of the most important publications of the world. Probably the only sad exception was in our country, where the official Communist newspaper *Granma* dedicated two meager lines full of criticism and reproach.

From Paris, author Zoé Valdés called her Ceiba Cruz, evoking our national tree. A street photographer in Mexico City captured the moment in which a juggler, dancing barefoot under traffic lights, left on the statue of José Martí a photo of Celia torn from the newspaper. "The two icons clashed: the hero next to the *rumbera*, history and cabaret, sadness and happiness," wrote the Cuban Eliseo Alberto from Mexico.

From Havana, Chucho Valdés declared that the best guarachera of Cuba had died. Nevertheless, Eliseo continued, "The most Cuban of all Cubans had no rights in her natural kingdom, was listened to only in clandestine circles, reinvented by adoring fans at the altar of limitless admiration."

Silvio Rodríguez dared to poetize a tender and improbable scene between Compay Segundo (who also passed away around that time at age ninety-five) and the Queen of Salsa singing together on a cloud. But as the bolero says, "*Bájate de esa nube.*" ("Come down from that cloud.") Silvio, Celia neither alive nor dead would accept the idea of sharing a stage with any artist who represented the dictatorship. She rests now in Woodlawn Cemetery near Miles Davis, Duke Ellington, and Lionel Hampton. Can you imagine the face of La Negra when Compay tells her that his bones rest at the Armed Forces Mausoleum, alongside so many henchmen, jailers, and terrorists? She would fall from the cloud from shock! The truth is that Celia, as well as I and the vast majority of us who count more than seven or eight years in exile, had never heard of the old troubadour. Compay Segundo (whose real name is Francisco Repilado) remained in the shadows for more than eighty years, until he was launched into celebrity by the

At home with Celia, Pedrito Knight, and the Márquez Sisters

American rock guitarist Ry Cooder in 1997, after winning a Grammy with the now famous Buena Vista Social Club.

"Our mission is to defend the rights and highlight the dignity of the black man not only in the United States, but all over the world." They should have added "except in Cuba," because the NAACP (National Association for the Advancement of Colored People) failed to send its condolences to the family of a woman who was one of the greatest symbols of African American culture. Neither did Nelson Mandela, Harry Belafonte, or Danny Glover, nor did the singer Gilberto Gil, recently named minister of culture of Brazil by the socialist government of Lula da Silva. Frankly, it wasn't needed, since millions of people from all parts of the world who still cry over her departure will make sure that the immortal La Guarachera de Cuba lives in perpetuity, more so than any petty dictator.

Certainly Celia was a happy person who enjoyed singing and wished to be remembered with the same joyfulness that characterized her. And since the wishes of those who pass away should be respected, here is a charming anecdote:

They say that at the conclusion of one of her many outdoor concerts in Colombia, Celia Cruz was coming off the stage when from behind the police line that divided her from the public a fan, very drunk and sweaty, shouted, "Celia, Celia, please let me give you a kiss, my queen!" To which the singer responded with her eternal smile and with open arms, "Ay, *mi negrito*, you see I'm in a hurry, so please give that kiss to Pedro, who's right behind me!"

If I weren't Cuban, I'd pay to be one.

—Anonymous

CUBA ON THE BANKS

OF THE HUDSON

Around 1954 or 1955, when I was a very young child, my father brought home a Benny Goodman LP recorded live at Carnegie Hall, in the city of New York. It was the first concert by a jazz orchestra in that venue, which until then had been dedicated exclusively to classical music.

My old man (who wasn't old yet) took the LP from its colorful jacket and played it on the portable Silvertone record player he had recently purchased on credit at Sears in Marianao. He very carefully placed the needle on the black vinyl, and immediately we heard the happy and familiar notes of "Let's Dance," Benny's musical theme, the same tune that my father played on his old tenor saxophone while walking through the whole house when he was in a good mood.

Since then, the legendary Jewish clarinetist has become my idol, and it was his fascinating music that made a child's mind dream that one day he too would perform in that magical theater and become a jazz musician in the mythic city of skyscrapers.

But as the old refrain goes, "The drunkard thinks of one thing and the bar owner another," so one good (or bad) day, the Comandante arrived and put a stop to my New York dream. It was like an enormous fermata that levitated as a menacing gray cloud over a large resting bar. In a short time *jazz* became a four-letter word, referred to as "imperialist music" by the demented minds of the new high-ranking leaders of Cuban culture.

To make a long story short, we all had to go with our music to another place (*con nuestra música a otra parte*). *Yo vengo de todas partes, y hacia todas partes voy*, "I come from all places, and to all places I go": on an island inhabited by people of the most diverse origins, the prophetic words of José Martí were never more true and palpable.

On a cold winter night many years later, I was a guest artist in a spectacular tribute to the King of Swing at Carnegie Hall with the Wynton Marsalis Orchestra. At the end of the concert, a silent limousine waited outside to take me home on the other side of the Hudson.

As I cruised down Broadway to Times Square, the honking cars, the fast pace of the New Yorkers, the swarm of yellow taxis lined up on the reflective asphalt, and the snowflakes falling on the illuminated city made it look like a scene from a Hollywood movie. While riding through the Lincoln Tunnel, I turned on the light above the plush back seat of the car and entertained myself by reading a beautiful article written by Cuban American journalist Norma Niurka on the Cuban writer-folklorist Lydia Cabrera.

"I discovered Cuba on the banks of the River Seine," Cabrera wrote with emotion in the 1960s as a recent exile to the romantic city of Paris.

Who knows whether or not, in the midst of her sadness, the author of *El Monte* thought she saw Cuban palm trees reflected on the dark waters that travel through the City of Light? Or perhaps she heard the sound of the *batá* drums in the bells of Notre Dame. A similar feeling of nostalgia invaded my soul for an instant.

As we came out from the tunnel, I looked through the snowy window of the car and over the frozen river, and in between the lights of the night and the tall and brilliant skyscrapers of the Big

Apple, my thoughts flew toward my warm and remote land. In the distance I could once again see my father, blowing his old tenor sax alongside the record player with the music of Benny Goodman, the same beloved music that I had been playing just a short time earlier in the theater of my dreams. My eyes clouded up and a tear ran down my face, breaking my heart. I had discovered Cuba, on the banks of the Hudson.

CODA

March 21, 2003

Susan Betz
Editor in Chief
Northwestern University Press
Evanston, IL 60208

Dear Susan Betz:

Thank you for giving me the opportunity of rereading Paquito D'Rivera's *Mi vida saxual* (*My Sax Life*). It's a fabulous book whose publication in English I recommend in the strongest possible terms. I say this because Paquito's life story is not only written with edge, humor, and ingenuity, but goes beyond the boundaries of any autobiographical work that I know of.

What makes *Mi vida saxual* a unique kind of memoir is that it takes from the discourse of the postmodern novel both its nonlinear structure and the coexistence of different types of texts (puns, jokes, anecdotes, chronicles, citations, reflections, memories, travelogues, political opinions, biographical data, jazz history, and others). Moreover, without intending to do so, Paquito emerges as a Latino role model. His story is not only the successful story of a

With the great Benny Carter at the Smithsonian Institute in Washington, D.C. (1988)

gifted jazz musician—a virtuoso of both the clarinet and the sax—but the true narrative of a Cuban exile who, in spite of his skin color and Spanish accent, reaches for the moon.

Mi vida saxual will interest many readers: musicians, musicologists, music teachers and students, jazz fans, Cuban-Americans, Latino readers, and practically everybody.

Sincerely,
Antonio Benítez-Rojo
Thomas B. Walton Jr. Memorial Professor, Amherst College

FINAL CHORD

After returning home from our annual jazz festival in Punta del Este, Uruguay, on January 15, 2003, I took a short flight to Boston to appear on the multitalented Ilan Stavans's TV show. A resident of that beautiful city, my always enthusiastic bassist Oscar Stagnaro joined me and we played one of those charming Cuban danzas by Ernesto Lecuona that we had adapted for clarinet and bass from the original piano score. A writer, poet, educator, journalist, and brilliant scholar and lecturer, Ilan (whose name means "palm tree" in Hebrew) has been instrumental in the publication of the present book in its English version as well as in encouraging me to update it and keep writing more and more stuff. So taking that into account plus what my distinguished fellow countryman Professor Benítez-Rojo kindly says about this sax life of mine, I'll be thinking seriously about coming out of the closet and starting my bi-sax life pretty soon. Should I?! . . .

In January 2005, the National Endowment for the Arts presented Paquito D'Rivera with its prestigious NEA Jazz Masters Award, along with Artie Shaw, George Wein, Jimmy Smith, Kenny Burrell, and Shirley Horn. On the tenth of the same month, Paquito celebrated his fifty years in show business with a sold-out supershow at Carnegie Hall, hosted by comedian Bill Cosby and produced by Pat Philips and Ettore Stratta. The rather impressive group of his friends flew to New York from places as far away as Puerto Rico, Sweden, Brazil, Argentina, Japan, Spain, Costa Rica, Germany, and all over the United States just to attend the unique event.

FUJITSU JAZZ FESTIVAL

TRIBUTE TO

PAQUITO D'RIVERA

"50 Years & 10 Nights of Show Business!"

SPONSORED BY:

FUJITSU

Starring and Hosted by:

PAQUITO D'RIVERA

Special Guests:

BEBO VALDES
YO-YO MA • CACHAO •
MICHEL CAMILO
ROSA PASSOS
CANDIDO
ROMERO LUBAMBO
DAVE SAMUELS
CLAUDIO RODITI
NEW YORK VOICES
PABLO ZIEGLER
ANDY NARELL
LAS HERMANAS MARQUES
MANUEL AMARGO
YOUTH ORCHESTRA OF THE **AMERICAS**

Produced by: pat philips & ettore stratta

Conducted by: **PABLO ZINGER** & **TANIA LEON**

Soprano: **BRENDA FELICIANO**

Alon Yavnai ▶ Piano
Mark Walker ▶ Drums
Portinho ▶ Drums
Oscar Stagnaro ▶ Bassist
Sergio Brandao ▶ Bassist
Ralph Irizarry ▶ Timbales
Edmar Castanedo ▶ Harpist
Pernell Saturnino ▶ Percussion

CARNEGIE HALL

Mon • January 10th • 8pm

*ARTISTS SUBJECT TO CHANGE

INDEX

Paquito D'Rivera was born in 1948 in Havana, Cuba. A best-selling artist with more than thirty solo albums to his credit, D'Rivera has performed at famous venues including the White House and the Blue Note and with orchestras, jazz ensembles, and chamber groups around the world. He lives in New Jersey. For more information on Paquito D'Rivera, visit www.paquitodrivera.com

The great Mimi, my favorite pet of all time (1996)

LATINO VOICES/VIDAS

GENERAL EDITOR
Ilan Stavans

EDITORIAL BOARD
Francisco Goldman
Achy Obejas
Judith Ortíz-Cofer
Johnny Payne